Great Family Vacations

Northeast

"Stapen is a respected travel writer who has done some awfully good books on family travel. They're well researched, very well done."
—*USA Today*

"Stapen provides a reassuring and enthusiastic voice for families on the go."
—*Christine Loomis, Family Life* magazine

Also by Candyce H. Stapen

Great Family Vacations: South
Great Family Vacations: Midwest and Rocky Mountains
Great Family Vacations: West
Family Adventure Guide: Virginia
Cruise Vacations with Kids (Prima)
Ski Vacations with Kids (Prima)

Great Family Vacations

Northeast

Candyce H. Stapen

A Voyager Book

Old Saybrook, Connecticut

Cover photo background: © 1996 PhotoDisc, Inc.
Cover inset photographs: Lori Adamski Peek/©Tony Stone Images; Ken Fisher/©Tony Stone Images; Jess Stock/©Tony Stone Images
Cover design by Schwartzman Design

Library of Congress Cataloging-in-Publication Data is Available.
ISBN 0-7627-0056-4

Manufactured in the United States of America
First Edition/First Printing

As always,
to Alissa, Matt, and David,
my favorite traveling companions.

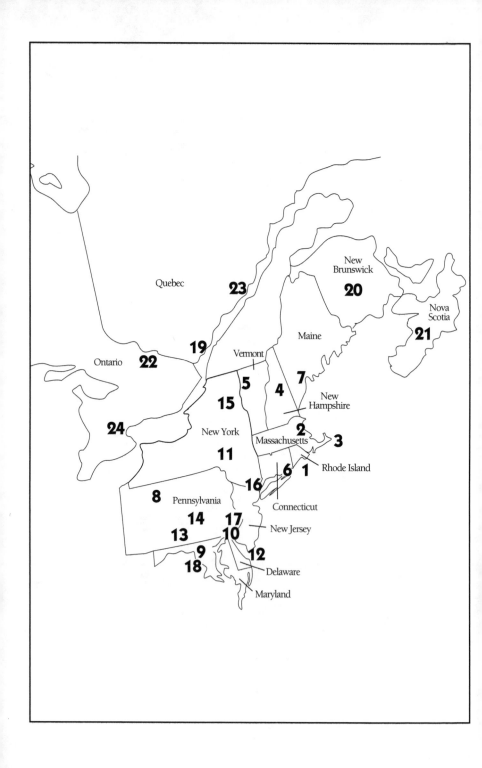

Contents

Acknowledgments

I want to thank my editors, Mace Lewis and Bruce Markot, for their patience and my agent, Carol Mann, for her support. Special thanks goes to Carol Eannarino, whose fine writing contributed much to this book. I appreciate the hard work of my editorial assistants, Valerie Bandura and Virginia Campbell, who worked carefully on this update.

Introduction

There is a Chinese proverb that says the wise parent gives a child roots and wings. By traveling with your children you can bestow many gifts upon them: a strong sense of family bonds, memories that last a lifetime, and a joyful vision of the world.

Traveling with your children offers many bonuses for you and your family. These days no parent or child has an excessive amount of free time. Whether you work in the home or outside of it, your days are filled with meetings, deadlines, household errands, and carpool commitments. Your child most likely keeps equally busy with scouts, soccer, music lessons, computer clinics, basketball, and/or ballet. When your family stays home, your time together is likely to be limited to sharing quick dinners and overseeing homework. If there's a teen in your house, an age known for endless hours spent with friends, your encounters often shrink to swapping phone messages and car keys.

But take your child on the road with you, and both of you have plenty of time to talk and be together. Traveling together gives your family the luxury of becoming as expansive as the scenery. Over doughnuts in an airport lounge or dinner in a new hotel, you suddenly hear about that special science project or how it really felt to come in third in the swim meet. By sharing a drive along a country road or a visit to a city museum, your children get the space to view you as a person and not just as a parent.

Additionally, both you and your kids gain new perspectives on life. Children who spend time in a different locale, whether it's a national forest or a city new to them, expand their awareness. For you as a parent, traveling with your kids brings the added bonus of enabling you to see again with a child's eye. When you show a six-year-old a reconstructed Colonial village or share the stars in a Vermont mountain night sky with a thirteen-year-old, you feel the world twinkle with as much possibility as when you first encountered these sites long ago.

Part of this excitement is a result of the exuberance kids bring, and part is from the instant friendships kids establish. Street vendors save their best deals for preschoolers, and, even on a crowded rush hour bus, a child by your side turns a fellow commuter from a stranger into a friend. Before your stop comes, you'll often be advised of the best toy shop in town and directed to a local cafe with a kid-pleasing menu at prices guaranteed to put a smile on your face.

New perspectives also come from the activities you participate in with your children. Most of these activities you would probably pass up when shuttling solo. Whether it's finding all the dogs in the paintings at the Metropolitan Museum of Art, going for a sleigh ride at a ski resort, or trying cross-country skiing in a park, you always learn more when you take your kids.

Surprisingly, traveling with your kids can also be cost-effective and practical. By combining or by extending a work-related trip into a vacation, you save money since your company picks up a good part of your expenses. Because tag-along tots on business trips are an increasing trend, several hotel chains have responded with a range of family-friendly amenities including children's programs, child-safe rooms, and milk and cookies at bedtime.

For all these reasons, traveling with your children presents many wonderful opportunities. It is a great adventure to be a parent, and it is made more wondrous when you travel with your children. You will not only take pleasure in each other's company, but you will return home with memories to savor for a lifetime.

Family Travel Tips

Great family vacations require careful planning and the cooperation of all family members. Before you go you need to think about such essentials as how to keep sibling fights to a minimum and how to be prepared for medical emergencies. While en route you want to be sure to make road trips and plane rides fun, even with a toddler. You want to be certain that the room that is awaiting your family is safe and that your family makes the most of being together. When visiting relatives, you want to eliminate friction by following the house rules. These tips, gathered from a host of families, go a long way toward making your trips good ones.

General Rules

1. Meet the needs of the youngest family member. Your raft trip won't be fun if you're constantly worried about your three-year-old being bumped overboard by the white water the tour operator failed to mention or if your first-grader gets bored with the day's itinerary of art museums.

2. Underplan. Your city adventure will dissolve in tears—yours and your toddler's—if you've scheduled too many sites and not enough time for the serendipitous. If your child delights in playing with the robots at the science museum, linger there and skip the afternoon's proposed visit to the history center.

3. Go for the green spaces. Seek out an area's parks. Pack a picnic lunch and take time to throw a Frisbee, play catch, or simply enjoy relaxing in the sun and people watching.

4. Enlist the cooperation of your kids by including them in the decision making. While family vacation voting is not quite a democracy, consider your kids' needs. Is there a way to combine your teen's desire to be near "the action" with your spouse's request for seclusion? Perhaps book a self-contained resort on a quiet beach that also features a nightspot.

5. Understand your rhythms of the road. Some families like traveling at night so that the kids sleep in the car or on the plane. Others avoid traveling during the evening cranky hours and prefer to leave early in the morning.

6. Plan to spend time alone with each of your children as well as with your spouse. Take a walk, write in a journal together, play ball, share ice cream in the snack shop, etc. Even the simplest of things done together create valuable family memories.

Don't Leave Home Without

1. *Emergency medical kit.* The first thing we always pack is the emergency medical kit, a bag I keep ready to go with all those things that suddenly become important at 3:00 A.M. This is no hour to be searching the streets for baby aspirin or Band-Aids. Make sure your kit includes items suitable for adults as well as children. Be sure to bring:
   - aspirin or an aspirin substitute
   - a thermometer
   - cough syrup
   - a decongestant
   - medication to relieve diarrhea
   - bandages and Band-Aids
   - gauze pads
   - antibiotic ointment

- a motion-sickness remedy
- sunscreen
- insect repellent
- ointments or spray to soothe sunburn, rashes, and poison ivy
- something to soothe insect stings
- any medications needed on a regular basis
- tweezers and a sterile needle to remove splinters
- antibiotic approved by your pediatrician for emergency use

Keep this kit with you in the car or on the plane.

2. *Snack food.* As soon as we land somewhere or pull up to a museum for a visit, my daughter wants food. Instead of arguing or wasting time and money on snacks, I carry granola bars with me. She munches on these reasonably nutritious snacks while we continue on schedule.

3. *Inflatable pillow and travel products.* Whether on the road or in a plane, these inflatable wonders help me and the kids sleep. For travel pillows plus an excellent variety of light yet durable travel products including hair dryers, luggage straps, alarms, adaptor plugs for electrical outlets, and clothing organizers, call Magellan's (800-962-4943). TravelSmith (800-950-1600) carries these items as well as clothing, mostly for teens and adults.

4. *Travel toys.* Kids don't have to be bored en route to your destination. Pack books, coloring games, and quiet toys. Some kids love story tapes on their personal cassette players. For innovative, custom-tailored travel kits full of magic pencil games, puzzles, and crafts for children three and a half or older, call Sealed With A Kiss (800-888-SWAK). The packages cost about $35. Surprise your kids with this once you are on the road. They'll be happy and so will you.

Flying with Tots

1. Book early for the seat you like. Whether you prefer the aisle, window, or bulkhead for extra legroom, reserve your seat well in advance of your departure date.

2. Call the airlines at least forty-eight hours ahead to order meals that you know your kids will eat: children's dinners, hamburger platters, salads, etc.

3. Bring food on board that you know your kids like even if you've ordered a special meal. If your kids won't eat what's served at meal

time, at least they won't be hungry if they munch on nutritious snacks.

4. Be sure to explain each step of the plane ride to little kids so that they will understand that the airplane's noises and shaking do not mean that a crash is imminent.

5. Stuff your carry-on with everything you might need (including medications, extra kids' clothes, diapers, baby food, formula, and bottles) to get you through a long flight and a delay of several hours . . . just in case.

6. Bring a child safety seat (a car seat) on board. Although presently the law allows children under two to fly free if they sit on a parent's lap, the Federal Aviation Administration and the Air Transport Association support legislation that would require all kids to be in child safety seats. In order to get a seat on board, the seat must have a visible label stating approval for air travel, and you must purchase a ticket for that seat. Without a ticket, you are not guaranteed a place to put this child safety seat in case the plane is full.

7. With a toddler or young child, wrap little surprises to give as "presents" throughout the flight. These work wonderfully well to keep a wee one's interest.

8. Before boarding, let your kids work off energy by walking around the airport lounge. Never let your child nap just before take-off—save the sleepy moments for the plane.

9. If you're traveling with a lot of luggage, check it curbside before parking your car. This eliminates the awkward trip from long-term parking loaded down with kids, luggage, car-seats, and strollers.

Road Rules

1. Use this time together to talk with your children. Tell them anecdotes about your childhood or create stories for the road together.

2. Put toys for each child in his or her own mesh bag. This way the toys are easily located and visible instead of being strewn all over the car.

3. Avoid long rides. Break the trip up by stopping every two or three hours for a snack or to find a rest room. This lets kids stretch their legs.

4. When driving for several days, plan to arrive at your destination each day by 4:00 or 5:00 P.M., so that the kids can enjoy a swim at the hotel/motel. This turns long hauls into easily realized goals that are fun.

At the Destination

1. When traveling with young children, do a safety check of the hotel room and the premises as soon as you arrive. Put matches, glasses, ashtrays, and small items out of reach. Note if stair and balcony railings are widely spaced or easily climbed by eager tots. Find out where the possible dangers are, and always keep track of your kids.
2. Schedule sightseeing for the morning, but plan to be back at the resort or hotel by early afternoon so that your child can enjoy the pool, the beach, miniature golf, or other kid-friendly facilities.
3. Plan to spend some time alone with each of your children every day. With pre-teens and teens, keep active by playing tennis or basketball, jogging, or doing something else to burn energy.
4. Establish an amount of money that your child can spend on souvenirs. Stick to this limit, but let your child decide what he or she wants to buy.

With Relatives

1. Find out the rules of your relatives' house before you arrive, and inform your kids of them. Let them know, for example, that food is allowed only in the kitchen or dining room so that they won't bring sandwiches into the guest bedroom or den.
2. Tell your relatives about your kids' eating preferences. Let the person doing the cooking know that fried chicken is fine, but that your kids won't touch liver even if it is prepared with the famous family recipe.
3. To lessen the extra work and expense for relatives and to help eliminate friction, bring along or offer to shop and pay for those special items that only your kids eat—a favorite brand of cereal, juice, frozen pizza, or microwave kids' meal.
4. Discuss meal hours. If you know, for example, that grandma and grandpa always dine at 7:00 P.M. but that your pre-schooler and first-grader can't wait that long, feed your kids earlier at their usual time, and enjoy an adult dinner with your relatives later.
5. Find something suitable for each generation that your kids and relatives will enjoy doing together. Look over old family albums, have teens tape record oral family histories, and have grade-schoolers take instant snapshots of the clan.

6. Find some way that your kids can help with the work of visiting. Even a nursery-school age child feels good about helping to clear a table or sweep the kitchen floor.

Family Travel Planners

These specialists can help you assess your family's needs and find the vacation that's best for you.

- **Family Travel Times.** This monthly newsletter (ten issues per year) offers the latest information on hotels, resorts, city attractions, cruises, airlines, tours, and destinations. For information call (212) 206-0688.

- **Rascals in Paradise.** Specializing in family and small-group tours to the Caribbean, Mexico, and the South Pacific, Rascals' tours usually include nannies for each family and an escort to organize activities for the kids. Call (800) U-RASCAL for more information.

- **Grandtravel.** This company offers a variety of trips for grandparents and grandchildren 7 through 17. Domestic trips include visits to New York, New England, and the Grand Canyon. Foreign destinations include safaris to Kenya. Call (800) 247-7651 for more information.

- **Grandvistas.** Grandvistas schedules a few trips each summer to western U.S. locations such as Custer State Park. Call (800) 647-0800 for more information.

- **Families Welcome!** This agency offers travel packages for families in London, Paris, New York, and other European cities. Its "Welcome Kit" includes tips on sightseeing, restaurants, and museums. Call (800) 326-0724 for more information.

The prices and rates listed in this guidebook were confirmed at press time. We recommend, however, that you call establishments before traveling to obtain current information.

About the Author

Candyce H. Stapen is an expert on family travel. She appears on many television, cable, and radio shows, including *Good Morning America*, CBS *This Morning, Our Home*, WUSA-TV, D.C., and National Public Radio. A member of the Society of American Travel Writers as well as the Travel Journalists Guild, she writes several family travel columns on a regular basis, including columns for *FamilyFun, Vacations,* and the *Washington Times*. She is also the consulting travel editor for Family. com.

Her articles about family travel appear in a variety of newspapers and magazines, including *Ladies' Home Journal, Family Circle, USA Weekend, Better Homes and Gardens, Family Travel Times,* the *New York Post,* the *Miami Herald, Caribbean Travel and Life, Florida Travel and Life,* and *Cruises and Tours.*

Other books by Stapen are *Great Family Vacations: South* (Globe Pequot); *Great Family Vacations: Midwest and Rocky Mountains* (Globe Pequot); *Great Family Vacations: West* (Globe Pequot); *Family Adventure Guide: Virginia* (Globe Pequot); and *Cruise Vacations with Kids* (Prima) and *Ski Vacations with Kids* (Prima).

Stapen lives in Washington, D.C., and travels whenever she can with her husband and two children.

1 ☼ Rhode Island

BLOCK ISLAND

Block Island, about 7 miles long and 3 miles wide, is for beach lovers. While not perfect—it can be crowded and noisy near the Old Harbor—the island still has all the ingredients necessary for an old-fashioned beach vacation. These include great stretches of sand, windswept dunes, and such picturesque touches as a lighthouse and 200-foot-high bluffs. Other bonuses include nature trails, birds, and white-tail deer. Many of the Victorian-era grand hotels, turreted homes, and cottages have been renovated and turned into bed and breakfast accommodations. Their silhouettes lend an old-world graciousness to the streets. Stroll or bike along the roads in-season, and you smell the honeysuckle, bayberries, and blackberries. Devotees swear Block Island is less expensive and less pretentious than other New England beach areas.

GETTING THERE

Block Island, located in Block Island Sound, about 9 miles south of the Rhode Island mainland, and 13 miles east of Montauk, New York, on Long Island, is most easily reached by ferry. If the waves are friendly, this is a fun trip and an exciting start, especially for young kids who may not have spent much time on a boat. Bring some bread to throw to the sea gulls who hover nearby. Then listen to your kids' giggles as these gulls dive for the treats.

Ferries run fairly frequently from mid-June to mid-September, and less frequently in the off-season. Only ferries from Galilee State Pier, Point Judith, Rhode Island, to the Old Harbor area, the quickest run, operate year-round. The first rule about ferries, though, is to make reservations well in advance, especially if you want to bring your car. Interstate Navigation (401-783-4613), which takes both cars and people, operates the run from Point Judith to Block Island.

Block Island at a Glance

- A small-island vacation

- Many outdoor activities including swimming, boating, beachcombing, and surfcasting

- Miles of nature trails and bike paths

- A variety of seafood restaurants

- Two summer-theater companies

- Block Island Chamber of Commerce, (401) 466-2982

Nellseco Navigation (203-442-7891) operates a summertime ferry from New London, Connecticut. The *Jigger III* (516-668-2214) totes people and bikes only for the two-hour ride from Montauk, New York, available mid-June to mid-September. Viking Ferry Lines (516-668-5700 or 800-MONTAUK) on Block Island provides the quickest ride (beachgoers and bikes only) from Montauk: one hour and fifteen minutes. In summer a ferry also makes the two-hour trip from Newport. For general ferry information, call (401) 789-3502 or (401) 421-4050.

Those with their own boats are welcome to dock at public harbors and private marinas. Since New Harbor has more public moorings than Old Harbor, it has become the place for private boats. Call the dockmaster at (401) 466-3235 for more information.

You also can arrive by plane, landing at Block Island State Airport; (401) 466-5511. Commercial airlines access the island via New England Airlines, Westerly State Airport, Westerly, Rhode Island; (401) 596-2460 or (800) 243-2460. Action Air, Groton/New London Airport (203-448-1646 or 800-243-8623), also provides air flights from Groton, Connecticut.

For a special treat try a personal aerial view of Rhode Island Sound by chartering an airplane. Capital Airlines, Waterbury/Oxford Airport, Connecticut (203-264-3727 or 800-255-3727), provides service from the Northeast and Canada.

GETTING AROUND

The best way to explore this 10-square-mile island is by bicycle or on foot. If your accommodations are near the harbor, you'll have no need for a car at all since the Old and New Harbors are less than a mile apart, and within walking distance to the beaches. While you might be tempted to book your car aboard the ferry, don't. Instead park in the long-term lots, and start your vacation free from automobile hassles and open to the slower holiday pace of strolling or pedaling.

If you must have a car, rentals are available from Block Island Bike & Car Rental (401-466-2297), Coastline Rental & Leasing (401-596-3441), and Old Harbor Bike Shop (401-466-2029).

You will probably want to rent bicycles, which come in all shapes and sizes for different island uses. Mountain bikes or beach cruisers with thick treads are best equipped to handle the dirt roads. The *Travel Planner* brochure available through the Block Island Chamber of Commerce (401-466-2982) has a full listing of several rental shops on the island. Mopeds are also available but are restricted to paved roads only. For bicycles, check ahead to be sure the shop has the right size equipment (as well as helmets) for your child. Ask if you can reserve bikes and mopeds ahead of time. Another shop you might call is the Moped Man (401-466-5011).

WHAT TO SEE AND DO

Since the island is so small, most locations are pinpointed by street names alone, not addresses.

Beaches

The island's best beaches are on the east side, running from Old Harbor up to Jerry's Point, in a strip called **Crescent Beach. State Beach** (401-466-2611) is a bustling place, equipped with public bathrooms, lifeguards, and refreshments. It's also one of the most crowded beaches. If you're looking to browse through the shops in town, but your older kids and teens can't get enough of the sand, drop them off at **Ballards Beach,** adjacent to Ballard's Inn at the Old Harbor. The beach has a lifeguard and is open to the public, even those not dining at Ballards.

Quieter choices include **Mansion Beach,** which is just north of the Great Salt Pond. You should bring a picnic (drinks included) and act as your own lifeguard. Your family will enjoy the waves, the sandy bottom, and searching for "points," small arrowheads left by the Manissean Indians. Another quiet choice is **Charleston Beach** near Harbor Neck.

Nature Exploration and Bicycle Trips

With 25 percent of Block Island's land designated as protected open space, getting off the beaten path is fun, and easy. One way to become acquainted with the island's wildlife is to book a ninety-minute hike with **The Nature Conservancy,** Ocean Avenue; (401) 466-2129. These guided nature walks are available mid-June through Labor Day. The *Block Island Times* lists some of the departures, but feel free to call and schedule your own tour, a special treat because guides are glad to tailor your walk and their commentary to any age group. Bring along binoculars to help you spot some of the hundreds of bird and insect species. In autumn some 150 species of migratory birds stop for their own island vacation on their way south.

After you are oriented, explore on your own. Bicycles come in handy here. Trip number one should be to the **Clayhead Nature Trail,** on the northeast side of the island off Corn Neck Road. Here you'll find 11 miles of grass trails winding through a 192-acre preserve. Start along the waterside cliffs and work your way north to **Settler's Rock** on the edge of Sachem Pond. This is where sixteen men from Boston, in search of religious freedom, landed in 1661. Read their names engraved on a plaque and try to imagine their first thoughts as they gazed out over Sachem Pond. Just off the Clayhead Trail, you'll find **Lapham's Bluestone** bird sanctuary, a.k.a. "The Maze." This puzzle of trails cuts through thick trees and brush and leads to unexpected ocean vistas.

Now continue on the dirt road to the **North Lighthouse,** on

The scenic Mohegan Bluffs area is just one of the beautiful places you can visit on Block Island. (Courtesy Rhode Island Tourism Division)

Sandy Point, the island's northernmost point. Check out the new **Maritime Museum,** and watch the sunset shimmering off the waves.

Visiting **Rodman's Hollow,** on the southwestern part of the island, offers another good bike trip. Once you've arrived you'll want to explore this ancient formation on foot. Created by a prehistoric glacier, the ravine is actually below sea level. A pond never formed here, however, since the sandy soil wouldn't hold water. One of the island's five wildlife refuges, the Hollow is a good place for bird watching.

After exploring here take one of the winding paths down to **Mohegan Bluffs** on the island's southern shore. The bluffs are named after fifty Mohegan Indians who invaded the island only to be tossed from these heights by the island's native Manissean tribe. From the bluffs, some of which are 200 feet high, it's a long fall to the rocks below! The view here of the ocean to the south and off the island's rocky southern shoreline is exceptional. On a clear day you can see all the way to Montauk Point in New York. **Southeast Lighthouse,** off South East Light Road (401-466-5009), is not far away. Constructed in 1875, this Gothic revival building with peaked gables has a beam that travels 35 miles out to sea. What's more impressive is that the lighthouse has recently been moved, piece by piece, from a dangerous perch just feet from the eroding cliff, to its current location.

Sports

Fishing is a favorite pastime here, and the Block Island Sound is known for striped bass, bluefish, cod, and flounder. Charter the *G. Willie Makit,* Old Harbor (401-466-5151), for a half- or full-day ocean adventure. Captain Bill Gould and his crew provide fishing equipment and instruction from April through October. More independent anglers can captain their own rowboat. **Twin Maples,** Beach Avenue by New Harbor (401-466-5547), rents rowboats, fishing equipment, and tackle and even sells bait. If you're a landlubber, walk to the end of Coast Guard Road and cast off the beach on the Great Salt Pond.

Little kids can ride the waves with a boogie board rented from **Island Sport Shop,** 995 Weldon's Way; (401) 466-5001. Surfboards and sailboards are also available here and at other sports shops.

The **Block Island Club,** Corn Neck Road (401-466-5939), a resort club that offers weekly memberships to island visitors, is a great idea for families too energetic to just sunbathe. Besides a life-guarded beach, the club, located on the island's Great Salt Pond, offers tennis, sailboarding, and sailing. Since the tide is gentle, the waves are manageable.

For horseback riding saddle up at **Rustic Rides,** West Side Road (401-466-5060), for a guided tour of the rocky west coast. Let your horse do the work as you ramble from trail-to-road to the west coast beach.

Performing Arts

Oceanwest Theater, Champlin's Marina, New Harbor (401-466-2971), presents first-run movies nightly as well as rainy-day matinees from late May to mid-September. If you've already seen the movie, check out the **Summerstock Theatre,** running Tuesday through Saturday nights, for fun family comedies. The **New Summer Theater,** at Champlins Resort (401-466-2641), also features first-run movies as well as live off-Broadway performances.

The **Historical Society,** Old Town Road, Old Harbor (401-466-2481), is a good rainy-day activity. Two permanent exhibitions focus on the Manisseans, the Native Americans who lived here for centuries, and the mounted birds of Elizabeth Dickens, an island legend.

Special Tours

For an overview of the island and the lowdown on its lore, legends, and local happenings, take a guided tour of the island from **O.J.'s Taxi,** (401) 782-5826 or (401) 466-2872. This is a particularly good trip if you have little tots too young to bike, or if you don't enjoy pedaling in the sun. A seasoned islander himself, O.J. gives you the inside scoop from the Indian skirmish at Mohegan Bluffs to the island's present-day fight against commercialization. He'll even tell you how Cow Cove got its name when white settlers made their cows swim ashore to test the depth of the water.

Other historic tours may be available through the Chamber of Commerce. Call them at (401) 466-2982 for more information.

More Local Family Fun

Playground fanatics will want to climb through the tunnels and ride the swings on the island grammar school's new wooden jungle gym on High Street. Or how about an island baseball game? Everyone is welcome to join in the evening youth games listed in the *Block Island Times.* If it's too windy to stay on the beach, and sailing is not your family forte, head over to the **Block Island Kite Company** on Corn Neck Road; (401) 466-2033. After a kite-flying demonstration, launch your own colors into the breeze.

SPECIAL EVENTS

Festivals

Listed below are festivals and special events for **Block Island** and **Newport.** For more information call the Block Island Chamber of Commerce (401-466-2982).

June: Annual "Taste of Block Island" Seafood Festival and Chowder Cook-off, with arts and crafts and kids' games. Block Island Race Week, sponsored by *Yachting* magazine.

July: July Fourth Celebration. Block Island Arts and Crafts Guild Fair. Annual Barbershop Quartet Concert. Newport Music Festival. Classical Music at the Mansions, Newport.

August: Block Island Triathlon. Annual Block Island House and Garden Tour. Nature Conservancy Annual Conservation Event. Ben & Jerry's Newport Folk Festival. Newport JVC Jazz Festival.

September: Annual Block Island Pasta Cook-off. Block Island Gardeners' "Edibles from the Fall Harvest."

October: National Audubon Birdwatching Weekend. Annual Harvest and Cider Festival.

November: Annual Block Island Christmas Shopping Stroll. Block Island Arts and Crafts Guild Fair.

WHERE TO STAY

Surf Hotel, Dodge Street (401–466–2241 or 401–466–2240), is one of the grand Victorian inns still standing on the island. Situated on the beach in the center of town, the Surf Hotel tempts with hearty breakfasts, grills for barbecuing on the porch, a playground and basketball hoop, and a parrot in the lobby! If you want to be where the action is, this is the place. But remember, it can be noisy, and most rooms have only a sink and no private bathroom. There's a six-night minimum stay in July and August.

The Atlantic Inn, High Street (401–466–5883), a short walk from the Old Harbor, offers twenty-one rooms, many with good views. Amenities include a croquet court, two tennis courts, and a playhouse replica of the inn just for kids. Children under twelve stay free. Three-night stay minimum during summer weekends.

The **New Shoreham House Inn,** Water Street (401–466–2651 or 800–272–2601), in the historic downtown district, overlooks the Old Harbor. This lodging offers special family packages in July and at various times during the late spring and fall and family fun suggestions all of the time. Kids under twelve stay free, and cots and cribs are available on request. If you can visit for a week, an apartment provides more flexibility.

The Bellevue House on High Street (401–466–5268 or 401–466–2912) has two-bedroom apartments and three-bedroom cottages for rent.

The Gothic Inn, Dodge Street (401–466–2918), perched on the beach, features two-bedroom efficiencies and a country cottage.

Most inns request a deposit. For a complete listing of accommodations, call the Block Island Chamber of Commerce at (401) 466–2982. Open-air camping is allowed for Boy Scouts and Girl Scouts only, at a designated campsite.

WHERE TO EAT

Seafood is Block Island's forte. Take a leisurely breakfast in the sun at **Ernies,** Old Harbor (401-466-2473), and watch the ferries pull in with new arrivals from the mainland. Later you can fill up on what some say is the best seafood on the island at **Dead Eye Dick's,** Payne's Dock, New Harbor (401-466-2654). Get goofy with the natives at singalongs with Jim Kelley at **Ballards Inn** (401-466-2231), a longtime island fish house.

If you're fished out, go to **Aldo's** (401-466-5871) for Italian food for the whole family and a video arcade for the kids. For pizza **Capizzano's,** Old Harbor (401-466-2829), has all kinds from pies to calzones to plain old pizza with almost any topping you want. If you want burgers, visit **The Beachhead,** Corn Neck Road (401-466-2249). Parents, older kids, and teens appreciate dining at **Manisses** on Spring Street (401-466-2421). Reserve ahead for the deck or a view from indoor tables, and enjoy the seafood and pasta specialties.

DAY TRIPS

On your way back from Block Island, take one of the ferries to **Newport, Rhode Island.** Tour the nineteenth-century European-style mansions cliffside along Bellevue Avenue; then stroll through Colonial Newport's brick-paved streets harborside. Music lovers should time their visit with the summertime classical, jazz, or folk festivals. (See Special Events for more information.)

Call the Newport County Convention and Visitors Bureau, 23 America's Cup Avenue, Newport (401-849-8098 or 800-326-6030), for a free travel planner with attraction, event, and accommodation information.

FOR MORE INFORMATION

Block Island Chamber of Commerce, Water Street, Old Harbor (401-466-2982), is a friendly and helpful source of tourist information. Their *Travel Planner* brochure is a comprehensive reference to the island's attractions and resources. Block Island Tourism Council (800-383-BIRI) has visitor brochures and tourist information on Block Island. Pick up a copy of the weekly *Block Island Times*, which has a map of the island and a list of community activities or the new CD-ROM at the harbor office.

Emergency Numbers
Ambulance, fire, and police: 911
Block Island Medical Center, PO. Box 919, Payne Road; (401) 466-2974
Block Island Pharmacy, P.O. Box 1179, High Street; (401) 466-5825
Block Island Police: (401) 466-3220
Coast Guard: (401) 789-0444
Poison Hotline: (401) 277-5727
Public Health Nurse, Mary Donnelly: (401) 466-2332

BOSTON

Ever since a group of Revolutionaries dumped tea in the Boston harbor, the city has held a special fascination. Despite the busy, big-city ambiance, Boston is eminently family friendly, offering an uncommon mix of history, museums, and fun. Don't miss the opportunity to visit here with your kids, whether you tour on a family getaway or take the kids with you as part of a business trip.

GETTING THERE

Most major domestic and international airlines, as well as several regional carriers, provide service to Logan International Airport, about 3 miles from downtown Boston.

Traffic in the morning and evening rush hours can significantly lengthen the time it takes to reach town from the airport, thus increasing taxi fares. For taxi information call MASSPORT at (617) 561-1769. One way to beat the traffic is to take the Airport Water Shuttle. The seven-minute trip—kids will love the ferry ride—departs from the airport to Rowes Wharf, downtown, and from downtown to the airport, every fifteen minutes Monday through Friday from 6:00 A.M. to 8:00 P.M. and Sundays every thirty minutes from noon to 8:00 P.M. No service is available on Saturdays and holidays. Call (800) 23-LOGAN for more information.

If you're traveling light, consider taking the subway. The MBTA (Massachusetts Bay Transit Authority) Blue Line stops at the airport. Call (800) 23-LOGAN for schedule information. This same number gives you information on bicycle access to the airport, parking, and schedules for airport shuttle buses to Braintree, Framingham, and other locations. This 800 line operates twenty-four hours, Monday to Friday from 9:00 A.M. to 5:00 P.M., and is staffed by information specialists (real people).

Boston at a Glance

- A historic city with a family-friendly mix of history, museums, and fun

- More than a dozen hands-on, kid-oriented museums

- History comes alive along the 3-mile Freedom Trail

- Theater for both adults and kids

- Three professional sports teams

- Greater Boston Convention and Visitors Bureau, (617) 536–4100 or (800) 888–5515

Amtrak trains (800–USA–RAIL) service Boston, arriving at South Station, on the Red "T" line, and Back Bay Station, on the Orange "T" line. Commuter trains link Boston with the suburbs. For information on the MBTA Commuter Rail, call (617) 722–3200.

Another airport note: When awaiting departures, be sure to stop by the airport's Kidport, a free play space for kids with climbing equipment for wee ones and several computer terminals for older kids.

GETTING AROUND

The only time your kids will be bored in Boston is when you're stuck in traffic. Take to the streets, not as the early Revolutionaries did to protest taxes, but to avoid the often clogged roads and to savor the city. Whenever possible, walk, or take the subway, known as the "T." Reasonably safe during the day—as in any city, be vigilant and use common sense—the "T" gets you around quickly and inexpensively. Divided into Red, Green, Orange, and Blue lines, the fares depend on the number of zones traveled. The Visitor Passport gives you unlimited travel within Boston for three days or seven days. Obtain these at the Visitor Information Centers (see For More Information), or call the T Customer Service Center at (617) 722-3200.

WHAT TO SEE AND DO

Museums

Forget about dry-as-dust exhibit halls with a look-but-don't-touch rigidity. Boston's museums offer lots of family fun. At **Children's Museum,** 300 Congress Street (617-426-8855), there's something for every family member from preschoolers to teens. Ask at the information desk for the booklet about exploring the museum with kids under five.

Toddlers dress up as circus performers in Backstage at the Big Top; in Playspace, kids four years and under climb in cars, build with blocks, and enjoy a variety of other activities. At Science Playground such simple acts as spinning tops and plates teach kids about scientific principles. This museum also engages preteens and teens. While Studio 10-15 is more a safe hangout for locals than an exhibit area, Teen Tokyo introduces American teens to their Japanese peers. Learn about the life of a Japanese student by stepping into a subway car and standing on the footprints that show you just how packed the place gets. You can push a mannequin of a sumo wrestler from his ring to learn about this sport, browse through *manga* (popular comic books), listen to Japanese rock 'n' roll, and compare fashions.

Computer Museum, 300 Congress Street; (617) 426-2800. Don't skip this place. The museum proves that computers aren't just for "nerds." The easy-to-follow programs let you and your kids enjoy such instant creativity as designing a sailboat, composing music, drawing a dinosaur, planning a car, and recording and editing your own television commercial. While kids love the place, parents, especially those from the precomputer generation, may have even more fun gaining familiarity with the programs and possibilities through play. Your children may have to tear you away from the terminals.

Nearby is the **Boston Tea Party Ship and Museum,** Congress Street Bridge, Boston; (617) 337-1773. For grade-school kids who have undoubtedly heard of the Boston Tea Party, boarding this replica of the ship involved in that famous incident is fun. Costumed guides retell the tale.

Museum of Science, Science Park; (617) 723-2500. Easily accessible via the "T," this museum gets mixed reviews. Skip the anemic rain forest and the deadly dioramas of marshes complete with mounted birds looking as bored as the viewers. Go directly to the must-see galleries. These include the egg hatchery, a giant incubator that allows you to watch chicks peck their way into the world, and the Discovery Space, which features three-dimensional puzzles of the human body that you piece together by placing the liver, lungs, ribs, and all the organs in the right spots. One of the liveliest spaces is Seeing the Unseen, which renders the world of fleas, termites, tadpoles, shrimp, and other tiny creatures visible through high-powered microscopes.

The Theater of Electricity will snap, crackle, and pop you into attention. Here the world's largest Van de Graaff generator produces bolts of lightning as the guide explains the phenomenon. Instructive with a flash of Frankenstein eeriness, the show is loud and flamboyant. Small children may be frightened, but older ones will be fascinated. Since the museum also features an Omni Theater plus a planetarium with both laser and sky shows, plan to spend several hours on-site.

The New England Aquarium, Central Wharf; (617) 973-5200. Fishy and fine, the New England Aquarium, while not large, opens a window on some watery wonders. You'll love watching the lazy sea turtles float, the sharks swim swiftly, and the schools of fish wriggle by in the big, central tank. Feeding time is especially interesting.

Be sure to visit the sea lions in the *Discovery,* the ship next door. Guthrie, a 650-pound performer, puts on quite an educational show as he swims, dives, "talks," and teaches kids about recycling.

Museum of Fine Arts, 465 Huntington Avenue; (617) 267-9300. This museum has noted collections of Asian art, American decorative arts, and nineteenth-century French works. Don't miss the Egyptian collection. Its mummies and hieroglyphics are kid favorites.

The Sports Museum of New England, CambridgeSide Galleria, 100 CambridgeSide Place, Cambridge; (617) 787-7678. This museum has three theaters that offer films and facts on great moments in New England sports history from high school through professional sports.

Markets, Historical Markers, Parks

From the aquarium it's an easy walk to **Faneuil Hall Marketplace.** The ranger talk about the historic liberty speeches delivered here isn't likely to rouse your children, but the rows upon rows of shops, stalls, and eateries in the nearby markets will. This place offers cheap eats for lunch and limitless possibilities for parting with some allowance money for souvenirs.

From Faneuil Hall follow the red path that details some of the best parts of the **Freedom Trail,** including Paul Revere's house and the Old North Church. There's something about Paul Revere's house that renders this famous personage real. Looking at the furnishings and rooms helps round out the life of this Revolutionary as father, provider, and silversmith. The 3-mile Freedom Trail, which passes by sixteen historic sites from the Colonial and Revolutionary eras, starts at the Boston Common.

Across from the Common is the **Public Garden,** a great take-a-break place. The ponds, swans, and brass ducklings, kept shiny by so many little bottoms saddling them, offer a pleasing city oasis. Plan to picnic or at least play awhile here.

Franklin Park Zoo, Franklin Park, off Blue Hill Avenue; (617) 442-2002. While not one of the great zoos, this seventy-two-acre facility, located in beautiful Franklin Park, offers some easy outdoor time. Preschoolers like the farm animals at the Petting Zoo, and everyone seems to enjoy the African Tropical Forest, a zoo highlight with leopards, antelope, and gorillas.

The Bull & Finch Pub, 84 Beacon Street; (617) 227-9600. Television history was made here. The outside of this pub served as the model for *Cheers.* While Norm and Sam are nowhere to be seen, parents can have a beer and buy their kids a T-shirt with the Cheers logo. Upstairs, there's a more formal restaurant. While kids are welcome, the prices may be high for some family budgets.

Special Tours

Whale Watching. From April through October get ready to yell "there she blows" when you spot one of these magnificent leviathans breaching the waves. Two places that book whale-watching tours in the city are A.C. Cruise Line, 28 Northern Avenue, Boston (617-426-8419 or 800-973-5281), and the New England Aquarium, Central Wharf (off Atlantic Avenue) (617-973-5277 or 800-973-5281).

Black History. Grab a Black Heritage Trail brochure for a self-guided tour of fourteen Beacon Hill historic sites including the memorial to the 54th Regiment. Guided tours are available by appointment (617-742-5415).

Walking Tours. Boston By Foot (617-367-2345) offers walking tours spring through fall. Boston By Little Feet has walking tours for children eight to twelve and their parents.

Performing Arts

In addition to the Boston Ballet, the Boston Symphony, the Boston Pops, and several theaters, check the schedule for the Boston Children's Theatre, the New England Hall, 225 Clarendon Street; (617) 277-3277. The engaging performances are by children for children.

More Useful Numbers

BOSTIX Ticket Booth, Faneuil Hall (617-423-4454), Fax (617-423-2131), offers tickets to entertainment and cultural events. Open Tuesday-Saturday 11:00 A.M. to 6:00 P.M., Sunday 11:00 A.M. to 4:00 P.M. BOSTIX also sells half-price tickets for same-day performances.

SPECIAL EVENTS

Boston is not only a town that loves its sports, but a place that knows how to celebrate. When phone numbers are not listed, for detailed information on festivals and celebrations, contact the Greater Boston Convention and Visitors Bureau at (617) 536-4100 or (800) 888-5515. Here are some happy highlights.

Sporting Events

The old Boston Garden has been replaced with the **Fleetcenter,** 150 Causeway Street; (617) 624-1000. Although the old building is still standing next door to the new, it is vacant and awaiting implosion. The center has expanded by nearly 5,000 seats and is much more family friendly. The food and rest rooms that were an embarrassment to the city in the old building are not a concern in the new. The Fleetcenter

A ride on the swan boats in Boston's Public Garden will delight every member of the family.
(Courtesy Greater Boston Convention and Visitors Bureau, Inc.)

continues to host the city's hockey team, the Bruins, from October through March, and the basketball team, the Celtics, from October through May. The Red Sox, the American League baseball team, play at Fenway Park, 4 Yawkey Way, April–October. For ticket information, call (617) 267-8661; to charge tickets (617) 267-1700. For TDD (617) 236-6644. Football fans wanting to root for the New England Patriots, Foxboro Stadium, Route 1, Foxboro, should call (800) 543-1776 or (800) 828-7080.

For three days during the World Cross-Country Championship Weekend in March, star athletes compete in track-and-field events. In April the world-famous 26-mile Boston Marathon takes joggers from Hopkinton to Copley Square, Boston. Grab some oranges and water, and enjoy cheering on the runners with your kids (617-236-1652). In October line the shores of the Charles River for the renowned rowing event, Head of the Charles Regatta (617-536-4100).

Festivals

February: At the Childrens Museum Chinese New Year celebration, have your name written in Chinese, make lanterns, and learn about Chinese customs. At the museum's Japan Day, try Kabuki face painting, origami lessons, and rice cakes. The Boston Festival, a citywide winter celebration, takes place on five consecutive weekends from Valentine's Day to St. Patrick's Day. Festivities include a laser light show, food festival, baked beans and Boston cream pie contests, and often ice dancers and dog-sled races. The Museum of Science Vacation Week helps kids combat the winter blues with special programming and events.

March: Bloom into spring with the New England Spring Flower Show.

April: Ducklings Day, honoring Robert McCloskey's classic children's tale *Make Way for Ducklings,* celebrates the city, children, and spring. Don't miss the parade of ducklings from the State House to the Public Garden.

Celebrate freedom's legends with the Reenactment of the Battle of Lexington and Concord and the Reenactment of Paul Revere's Ride.

May: Watch thousands of kites soar at the Annual Kite Festival, Franklin Park. Street Performers Festival, Faneuil Hall Marketplace, lightens the pace with mimes, jugglers, magicians.

June: Annual Teddy Bear Picnic and Sing-Along.

July: Celebrate America's independence with Boston Harborfest, more than one hundred waterside events, including the annual Boston Chowderfest, fireworks, special cruises, and also a Boston Pops annual Fourth of July concert.

August: Boston Seaport Festival, Charlestown Navy Yard, features boat tours and a regatta.

September: Boston Arts and Music Festival offers a variety of cultural events.

December: Holiday events include the lighting of a Christmas tree on the Boston Common and a reenactment of the Boston Tea Party, with a rally and a parade to the Tea Party Ship.

The city takes to the streets on New Year's Eve with First Night, a citywide celebration featuring music, mime, dance, theater, and film. Go with your kids, as the festival kicks off December 31st around 1:00 P.M. with a children's festival. The festival ends with a bang as fireworks light up the sky.

WHERE TO STAY

The easiest way to see the city with kids is to stay close-in at a well-located hotel near a "T" stop in a good walking neighborhood. Call the Boston CVB for accommodation brochures and information on the latest family packages available. Remember that hotels always have lower rates on weekends; ask for these. Several hotels offer kids' amenities. Some possibilities:

The Boston Marriott Long Wharf has a package that includes tickets to the Aquarium, Computer Museum, or Children's Museum; (800) 228-9290. **The Copley Plaza Hotel**'s Kids Love Boston package features free parking, a superior guest room, stuffed lion gift, and a roll-away bed. Call (800) 8-COPLEY. **The Copley Square Hotel** has a family suite package of two connecting rooms and a welcome gift for kids; (617) 536-9000. **The Four Seasons Boston** offers a Weekend with the Kids package that includes a free VCR, children's movies, and an executive suite with sitting area. Child-friendly amenities include kid-size bathrobes, turn-down service of milk and cookies, and box games and toys to borrow; (800) 332-3442. **Guest Quarters Suite Hotel** gives you a suite and breakfast; (617) 783-0090. **The Ritz-Carlton** can't be beat for sheer grandeur, although this comes at a cost.

The hotel's Children's Presidential Suite comes with books and toys, Nintendo, and children's play areas.

Boston has several **Bed and Breakfast** registries. Try the **Bed and Breakfast Agency of Boston** (617-720-3540 or 800-CITY-BNB for town houses, studios, and condominiums). **Host Homes of Boston** (617-244-1308) offers guest rooms in town homes and houses in Boston and its nearby suburbs. Make sure, however, that the property really is family friendly before booking.

WHERE TO EAT

It's not just baked beans, chowder, and Boston cream pies—though these can be very good here. Boston has lots of good restaurants. **Faneuil Hall Marketplace** offers many spots for quick and cheap eats. Nearby, **Ye Olde Union Oyster House,** 41 Union Street (617-227-2750), open since 1862, is well known for its seafood and pastas. The crowds at **No-Name Restaurant,** 15½ Fish Pier (617-338-7539), attest to the popularity of this inexpensive seafood place. **Boodle's,** 40 Dalton Street (617-266-3537), in the Back Bay area, has burgers, salads, and sandwiches. Adventurous kids might like **Casablanca,** 40 Brattle Street (617-876-0999), for its crab cakes, chili, and couscous. **Bnu,** 123 Stuart Street (617-367-8405), offers inexpensive pizza, pasta, and salads. For a wider Italian menu, try **Ristorante Lucia,** 415 Hanover Street (617-523-9148), in the North End.

The Official Guidebook of the Greater Boston Convention and Visitors Bureau lists many area restaurants.

DAY TRIPS

Boston can serve as the hub of a great family foray. **Lexington** and **Concord** offer more Revolutionary history, and in **Salem** the Salem Witch Museum and the Witch House will intrigue kids. Farther north try the beaches at **Parker River Refuge,** Newbury; **Plum Island; Newburytown;** and **Good Harbor Beach,** Gloucester.

FOR MORE INFORMATION

The Greater Boston Convention and Visitors Bureau offers many free maps, brochures, seasonal travel planners, and accommodation guides. The GBCVB also produces *Kids Love Boston*, $3.95, a big-type guide with pleasing illustrations aimed at elementary-school kids. Get one of these ahead of time so that your child can help plan your visit, a good way to ensure cooperation. For more information, including a guide to accommodations, call the bureau: (617) 536-4100 or (800) 888-5515.

Visitor information centers: Boston Common Information Center, 146 Tremont Street (617-536-4100), is open Monday–Saturday from 8:30 A.M. to 5:00 P.M. and Sunday from 9:00 A.M. to 5:00 P.M. Prudential Information Center, Prudential Plaza, 800 Boylston Street (617-536-4100), is open Monday–Saturday from 9:00 A.M. to 6:00 P.M. National Park Service, 15 State Street (617-242-5642), is open daily from 9:00 A.M. to 5:00 P.M. Cambridge Discovery, Harvard Square, Cambridge (627-497-1630), is open Monday–Saturday from 9:00 A.M. to 6:00 P.M. and Sunday from 1:00 to 5:00 P.M.

The Boston Parents Paper, P.O. Box 1777, Boston 02130; (617) 522-1515. This monthly publication lists special events and resources for families and children. Browse among the advertisers for kid-oriented shops and services.

Persons with disabilities can get referrals and information from **The Information Center for Individuals with Disabilities,** Fort Point Place, 27-43 Wormwood Street, Boston 02210; (617) 727-5540.

For Boston Parks & Recreation, call (617) 725-4505. You can reach the National Historical Park Visitor Center at (617) 242-5642.

Emergency Numbers

Ambulance, fire, and police: 911
Boston Police: (617) 247-4200
Children's Hospital Emergency Room: (617) 735-6611
Poison Hotline: (617) 232-2120
Twenty-four hour pharmacy: Phillips Drug Store, 155 Charles
Street, Boston; (617) 523-1028 or (617) 523-4372

CAPE COD

Cape Cod, a 70-mile stretch of land separated from the Massachusetts mainland by the Cape Cod Canal, is an idyllic seaside getaway. The Cape is divided into two diverse sections: the Upper Cape is closer to the mainland and highly developed; the Lower Cape, with Provincetown at its tip, is quieter and includes much of the Cape Cod National Seashore, established to protect the area from commercialism. Cape Cod consists of fifteen towns plus a number of villages. Those who want to be close to nature may consider a cottage or camping in the more isolated Wellfleet-Truro-Eastham area of the Lower Cape. Families who want nearby conveniences and attractions—and great beaches—however, prefer the Upper Cape. The West Yarmouth-West Dennis area, for instance, at the Cape's geographical center, has the best family beaches and is close to the shopping and conveniences of Hyannis. Heading west it's just one hour to the recreational area surrounding the Cape Cod Canal; on the east an hour's drive leads to the beautiful National Seashore.

GETTING THERE

Barnstable County Airport, near Hyannis (508-775-2020), is served by Delta Connection to Boston; and by Continental Airlines and the commuter line Colgan Air, from Newark.

Bonanza (800-556-3815) runs frequent buses from Boston and Logan Airport to Bourne, Falmouth, and Wood's Hole, plus daily service from New York, Danbury, Hartford, Albany, Springfield, and Providence to Hyannis and Wood's Hole. Plymouth & Brockton Company buses travel to and from Boston, Logan Airport, Plymouth, Provincetown, and towns in between. Call (508) 775-5524/(800) 328-9997 (Massachusetts) for schedules.

Amtrak (800-USA-RAIL) runs limited service between New York and Hyannis on summer weekends. Otherwise, you'll have to take a

train to Boston's South Station and link up with the nearby Bonanza Bus Line.

By car the Cape can be accessed from two main highways, I-495, which leads to the Bourne Bridge, or Route 3, to the Sagamore Bridge. It's about a two-hour drive (less if the traffic is light) from Boston to the bridges.

Bay State Cruises (617-723-7800) runs passenger vessels between Boston and Provincetown in the summer.

GETTING AROUND

Driving, sometimes a slow process, is the main form of transportation. There are three highways: Mid-Cape Highway (Route 6) is the fastest but has no water view; Route 28 goes along the south shore and is slow and highly trafficked; Route 6A provides scenic views of the north shore.

Public transportation: RTA (Regional Transit Authority) runs buses from the commuter parking lots at the Sagamore Bridge to Wood's Hole. Call (508) 385-8311 for schedules. Provincetown has a public shuttle bus (508-487-3353) that serves Provincetown and Herring Cove Beach from late June to early September.

Ferry service includes Hy-Line (508-778-2602) during summers to Martha's Vineyard and Nantucket from Hyannis. Steamship Authority (508-477-8600) operates year-round from Wood's Hole to Martha's Vineyard (the shortest route on the Cape, it takes 45 minutes) and from Hyannis to Nantucket. In the summer these ferries also run from the Vineyard to Nantucket, returning to Hyannis. Island Commuter (508-548-4800) heads to the Vineyard from Falmouth Harbor.

Cape Cod Canal's service roads are great for biking, walking, and jogging. You'll also find three bicycle trails within the Cape Cod National Seashore. See the Cape Cod visitor's guide for trail details and bike rental companies.

WHAT TO SEE AND DO

Museums and Attractions

While the Cape isn't teeming with museums with kid appeal, there are a number of kid-friendly attractions. The museums are generally low-key and best for rainy days or as part of a general sight-seeing tour.

Cape Cod at a Glance

- A diverse yet fun-packed seaside getaway

- Every town has saltwater beaches, a few offer sandy beaches on lakes and ponds

- Guided tours of the Cape Cod National Seashore

- Theater for both adults and kids

- Several small museums

- Many shops, galleries, and country stores

- Cape Cod Chamber of Commerce, (508) 362-3225; Massachusetts Office of Travel and Tourism, (617) 727-3201 or (800) 447-MASS

Bourne. **Trading Post Museum,** Aptucxet Road; (508) 759-9487. If you're near the Bourne Bridge, stop by the Pilgrim trading post, one of the first in North America. Its claim to fame: It was reconstructed in 1930 on the original site with original materials. President Grover Cleveland's private railroad is also on the premises, as are a windmill, herb gardens, and picnic area.

Brewster. Located mid-Cape on the bay side, Brewster has charming nineteenth-century homes built by sea captains, antiques shops, art galleries, a summer day camp for ages seven to seventeen (508-896-3451), and the following attractions:

Bassett Wild Animal Farm, Tubman Road; (508) 896-3224. Take the kids on hayrides and pony rides, and see a variety of birds and wildlife in natural surroundings. There's a picnic area, too.

Cape Cod Museum of Natural History, Route 6A; (508) 896-3867. While not huge, there are two floors of indoor exhibits, plus nature walks and family programs.

New England Fire and History Museum, Route 6A; (508) 896-5711. This large collection of antique fire-fighting equipment and

memorabilia includes eye-catching exhibits: a Victorian apothecary shop, blacksmith shop, and an interesting diorama of the Great Chicago Fire of 1871. The museum is open late May through Columbus Day. **Stoney Brook Mill,** Stoney Brook Road, grinds corn Thursday, Friday, and Saturday afternoons during July and August. Small kids will be intrigued, and they should like the small museum upstairs.

Falmouth. This picturesque town on Route 28 on the Cape's southwestern tip is the home of the **Cape Cod's Children's Museum,** which opened in temporary quarters in late 1992 with hands-on activities for ages one to ten. There are plans to move the year-round museum to a permanent space and to construct a Native American exhibit and a miniature Cape Cod village—including child-size houses, grocery, and fire station. Give them a call at (508) 457-4667 before you go.

Hyannis. Yes, it's congested and suburbanized, but it's also a transportation and shopping hub and boasts **Cape Cod Potato Chips,** Breed's Hill Road in Independence Park; (508) 775-7253. This probably will make a bigger impression on your kids than most museums. On weekdays, watch the hand-cooking process that results in these tasty tidbits. Then visit the gift store to sample some chips and, of course, buy a bag or two.

Provincetown. "P-town," the tip at the end of the Lower Cape, has beautiful beaches, sand dunes, shops, galleries, and also attracts a lively gay crowd. This colorful artistic colony also is the site of the first Pilgrim landing and boasts the Cape's most visited attraction: **Pilgrim Monument and Provincetown Museum,** off SR 6 on High Pole Hill; (508) 487-1310. If your kids are energetic, climb the stairs and ramps to the top of the 252-foot tower honoring the Mayflower Pilgrims, which provides splendid views of the town and harbor. You won't be disappointed by the museum, which contains lots of intriguing things: Mayflower memorabilia, ship models, items taken from nearby shipwrecks, old toys, scrimshaw, figureheads, and an old fire engine made by an apprentice of Paul Revere.

Sandwich. Located on the bay in the Upper Cape, charming Sandwich, the oldest town on the Cape, was the site of one of the country's largest glass factories during the nineteenth century. **The Sandwich Glass Museum** at 129 Main Street (508-888-0251) displays this beautiful vintage glass, but most kids will be ready to bolt in under five minutes. (Instead, they may prefer seeing the glassblowing demonstrations at **Pairpont Crystal** near the Sagamore Bridge; 508-888-2344/800-899-0953.)

One attraction that will appeal: **Heritage Plantation,** Grove and Pine streets (508-888-3300). Pack a lunch (there are picnic grounds, plus a windmill, outside) and plan to spend some time here. Take a ride on the restored carousel; then see the antique and classic cars in the Round Stone Barn. The antique miniatures at the military museum are appealing. There's also an art museum, although the large Currier & Ives exhibit will leave most kids bored. The seventy-six acres of trails and gardens offer a nice respite. If you came foodless, The Dan'l Webster Inn serves three meals.

Another Sandwich attraction: **Yesteryears Doll Museum,** at the corner of Main and River streets; (508) 888-1711. If there's a doll lover in the family, stop to see the lovely vintage dolls, dollhouses, and miniatures. In East Sandwich don't miss **Green Briar Nature Center,** 1 Discovery Road, (508) 888-6870. Besides the natural history exhibits inside, there are two reasons to stop at the center: the lovely fifty-seven-acre Briar Patch Conservation Area's nature trails and the Green Briar Jam Kitchen, where you can tour an old-fashioned kitchen to see jams, jellies, and preserves made in the traditional way. In the summer the demonstrators use an unusual sun-cooking method. Call for days when the kitchen is in operation.

West Yarmouth: **Aqua Circus of Cape Cod** on Route 28 (508-775-8883) has winning sea lion and dolphin shows. There is also a zoo with llamas, ponies, monkeys, and a petting zoo.

Beaches

Every town on the Cape has saltwater beaches; some also offer sandy beaches on lakes or ponds. Towns charge parking fees, and some require beach stickers. The visitor's guide from the Chamber of Commerce lists all public beaches and fees.

Some families with young children prefer the bay beaches because the lack of waves makes swimming and wading easier for little ones. On calm days, however, the ocean beaches are irresistible. Chances are you'll sample both during your stay. Particularly good ocean beaches for families include those in the West Yarmouth area, which have play-

The breaching of a whale off Cape Cod will thrill family members of all ages.
(Courtesy Cape Cod Chamber of Commerce)

grounds and frequently organize activities for kids. The West Dennis Beach has a huge parking lot close to the beach and attracts tons of kids —instant playmates for your youngsters. An outstanding bay beach? Try Sandy Neck, West Barnstable, off Route A on Sandy Neck Road.

Cape Cod National Seashore, a breathtaking natural wonder, encompasses a good deal of the Lower Cape from Chatham to Provincetown. It includes 30 miles of bay and ocean beaches, dunes, glacial cliffs, nature trails, and green forests that are protected by law from commercial development. Swimming is permitted on six beaches where there are lifeguards. If the crowds are too intense (arrive as early as possible), head to the warm waters of Gull freshwater pond in Wellfleet, which connects by channels to several others where you won't find a mob scene. The town is also home to Wellfleet Bay Wildlife Sanctuary, off U.S. 6; call (508) 349-2615. Daily organized programs, which might include a bird walk or canoe trip, often are suitable for youngsters. The sanctuary's mile-long Goose Pond Trail has plants and birds that kids can help identify, with the assistance of an inexpensive guide sold here.

The Seashore has a total of nine nature trails, all a mile long (except for the 8-mile Great Island trail in Wellfleet). The **Salt Pond Visitors Center,** off U.S. 6 in Eastham (508–255–3421), has information on the entire seashore, films, a free museum, plus a mile-long trail to the pond, where flocks of shorebirds congregate for "lunch." There's also a visitor's center some 25 miles away at Provincetown: **Province Lands Visitor's Center,** Race Point Road, off U.S. 6.

Special Tours

If your kids are seaworthy, take them on a fascinating whale-watching tour. (The trips often last several hours, so they're best with older kids. Just in case, check with your pediatrician ahead of time about possible seasickness preventatives and remedies.) A number of tours are listed in the Cape Cod Resort Directory from the Cape Cod Chamber of Commerce. Two examples: From Provincetown the *Portuguese Princess* has day and sunset trips, food, and guarantees sightings. Call (508) 487-2651/(800) 442-3188—Massachusetts, for information and reservations. The four-hour narrated **Hyannis Whale Watcher Cruise** departs from Millway Marina in Barnstable Harbor. Call (508) 362-6088/(800) 287-0374—Massachusetts.

The **Cape Cod Scenic Railroad,** consisting of first-class parlor cars and restored coaches, travels between Hyannis, Sandwich, and Sagamore. Ride past cranberry bogs, Cape Cod Bay, Cape Cod Canal, and other sights. Younger kids may get restless on the one-and-three-quarter-hour trip, but fortunately food is available. There are also three-hour dinner trips. Call (508) 771-3778 for information.

Shopping

You'll find antiques shops, galleries, and country stores throughout the Cape. If you need some basics, stop at Falmouth Mall, Route 28, open seven days. It has major stores, such as Bradlees, specialty shops, and a cinema. Bargain shop at Cape Cod Factory Outlet Mall, off exit 1, Route 6, Sagamore. Kids' stores include Toy Liquidators and Carter's Childrenswear.

Performing Arts

Melody Tent, 21 West Main Street, Hyannis, has nightly theater-in-the-round musical comedy concerts, with kids' shows on

Thursday mornings. Call (508) 775-5630 for schedules. Summer theater is also performed at **Falmouth Playhouse,** Theatre Drive, Hatchville; (508) 563-5922. Contact the Cape Cod Chamber of Commerce for other summer playhouses and for the date in mid-August when the Boston Pops plays its annual performance on the Village Green in Hyannis. Contact the Hyannis Area Chamber of Commerce at (508) 362-5230.

SPECIAL EVENTS

Check with the Cape Cod Chamber of Commerce for details on these annual fairs and festivals and obtain the calendar of events.

April: Brewster in Bloom, daffodil festival.

July: Barnstable County Fair, with rides, exhibits, and food.

September: Harwich Cranberry Festival, week-long event with food tastings, band concerts, parade, craft show and sale, and more.

Thanksgiving through New Year's Eve: Christmas in Cape Cod, series of events including choirs, orchestras, caroling on the green, town-green lightings, and more.

WHERE TO STAY

The Cape Cod Chamber of Commerce has a comprehensive resort directory that includes campgrounds. Don't be disappointed: Make reservations very early. If you re stuck, the information booths located throughout the Cape can also help with accommodations. The following, all on the Upper Cape, represent the variety of accommodations available for families.

The Breakers, 61 Chase Avenue, Dennisport, has newly renovated rooms, including minisuites and two-bedroom two-bath efficiencies. The heated pool faces the ocean, and there's a private beach. Lower rates midweek; (508) 398-6905.

Gull Wing Suites, 822 Main Street, South Yarmouth is an all-suite motor inn that offers refrigerators, two pools, and family and weekend packages. Call (508) 394-9300/(800) 541-3480.

Lighthouse Inn, West Dennis, has cottages on seven oceanfront acres, a restaurant, plus tennis, pool, miniature golf, a private beach, and supervised activities for ages two and up in July and August. Call (508) 398-2244.

New Seabury Resort and Conference Center, midway between Falmouth and Hyannis, features 160 villas spread out over 2,000 oceanfront acres, with pool, golf, and tennis. A summer program keeps ages four and up busy and there's a center for teens Call (508) 477-9111/(800) 752-9700/(800) 222-2044.

WHERE TO EAT

What would a visit to Cape Cod be without a lobster dinner? Consult *The Cape Cod Times,* the local daily paper, for restaurant listings. On the Lower Cape the self-service **Bayside Lobster Hutt,** Commercial Street, Wellfleet Center, is in an old oyster shack and offers inexpensive, fresh Cape seafood. Upper Cape locals love **Joe Mac's,** Taunton Avenue, Dennis. It's not fancy, but families feel at home (there's a game room for kids), and the menu includes everything from pizza to lobsters. **Hearth 'n Kettle Family Restaurant** chain serves affordable, traditional food at locations in Plymouth, Orleans South Yarmouth, Hyannis, and Falmouth. These restaurants are accessible for patrons in wheelchairs.

DAY TRIPS

American history comes alive in Plymouth, about halfway between the Cape and Boston. **Plimouth Plantation,** a 1627 village, is a fascinating place where costumed residents reenact daily life in New Plymouth. Adjoining the village is **Hobbamock's Homesite,** which features the Wampanoag Indians of southeastern New England and their culture. Step aboard *Mayflower II,* a reproduction of the ship that brought the Pilgrims to Plymouth in 1620. For more information call (508) 746-1622. Stop by to see **Plymouth Rock,** Water Street (which, with its portico protection is not very imposing). Another day, take a passenger ferry to explore the splendid beaches and picturesque towns of **Martha's Vineyard,** only forty-five minutes from Wood's Hole. (See Getting Around.)

FOR MORE INFORMATION

The main office of the Cape Cod Chamber of Commerce, exit 6 off Route 6, Hyannis 02601 (508-362-3225), has helpful brochures and guides, including a resort guide that lists which lodgings are wheelchair accessible. In addition to their main location, other offices are located at the Plymouth Information Center, Route 3, exit 5, at the approach to Bourne Bridge, Route 25.

For a complete Massachusetts vacation kit, which includes Cape Cod, call the Massachusetts Office of Travel and Tourism at (617) 727-3201/ (800) 447-MASS. Great Dates in the Bay State is a recorded list of statewide events, updated biweekly; call (800) 227-MASS (Northeast only).

Emergency Numbers

The Cape is tied into the 911 emergency system.

Hospitals: Cape Cod Hospital, 27 Park Street, Hyannis, well marked from all exits; (508) 771-1800. A smaller facility is Falmouth Hospital, 100 TerHeun Drive, Falmouth; (508) 457-3524. The twenty-four-hour emergency rooms at these two hospitals are jammed in the summer. If you have a smaller emergency, you may get faster service at one of the many walk-in clinics scattered throughout the Cape that are listed in the phone directory. Most keep standard office hours.

Poison Control: (800) 682-9211 from the Cape.

Most of the CVS pharmacies located on Cape Cod are open twenty-four hours daily in summer.

JACKSON AND THE MOUNT WASHINGTON VALLEY

Jackson and the Mount Washington Valley, in the heart of the White Mountains, offer a splendid array of outdoor family activities. In winter Jackson comes alive; it's a noted cross-country ski area. Gliding through a snowy forest is great fun, and the slow pace, perfect for admiring icicles and looking for deer tracks, allows for easy conversation with your kids, one of the prime reasons for going away together in the first place. From Jackson it's an easy drive to several downhill ski areas that feature quality children's programs. And in fall the woods fill with brilliant reds, oranges, and yellows.

In summer the mountains offer miles of trails for horseback riding and hiking, and clear streams for fishing and wading. One cautionary note: Avoid the region during black fly season. While the time period and the intensity of the infestation vary with the weather, generally these insects invade for three weeks from late May to mid-June. For anglers the black flies bring some of the season's best fishing, but most visitors will want to avoid the woods during this time. (Some seasoned campers swear that Avon's Skin So Soft, in addition to its other attributes, repels these pests.) So before booking in late May to mid-June, check with the locals first about conditions.

GETTING THERE

Portland Jetport (207-774-7301), about ninety minutes southwest of Jackson in Portland, Maine, is the closest major airport and is serviced by most major domestic airlines. Other airports include Manchester Airport in New Hampshire (603-624-6556), about 100 miles southeast of the region, Boston's Logan Airport (617-561-1800 or 800-23-LOGAN), 140 miles to the south; and the Eastern Slope Regional Airport in Fryeburg, Maine (207-935-2800), about twenty-five minutes from North Conway.

By bus, Concord Trailways (603-383-9041) runs a daily route from Boston, arriving in Jackson about 9:00 P.M.

For those traveling by car, Jackson and the surrounding towns are easy to locate off I-93. From Boston it's a three-hour drive into Jackson, taking 1-95 to Portsmouth, New Hampshire, then Spaulding Turnpike and Route 16 to North Conway, and into town. Avoid the North Conway traffic, which can be formidable, by taking West Side Road at the first light in Conway to River Road, and then taking Route 16 or Route 302.

GETTING AROUND

A car is an absolute necessity, although families should bring their bicycles as well. Car rentals are available at regional airports in Conway, which is just south of Jackson.

WHAT TO SEE AND DO

Since most area attractions use post office boxes and route numbers instead of numbered street addresses, route numbers are listed here. Call the attractions if you need more specific directions.

Mountains Magic: Summer Outdoor Recreation

Hiking. With more than 250 trails in the White Mountain National Forest's 750,000 acres, there's a great variety of paths for all ability levels. City kids especially appreciate the feathery green and cool woods.

Jackson and the
Mount Washington Valley at a Glance

- Year-round fun in the heart of New Hampshire's White Mountains

- Many cross-country and downhill ski areas open during the winter

- More than 250 hiking trails that wind through the mountains

- Canoeing, kayaking, and llama trekking available

- Ride a train up the highest peak in the continental U.S.

- Jackson Chamber of Commerce, (603) 383-9356; Mount Washington Valley Visitors Bureau, (603) 356-5701 or (800) 367-3364. Jackson Chamber of Commerce, (603) 383-9356; Mount Washington Valley Visitors Bureau, (603) 356-5701 or (800) 367-3364.

For some easy adventure with younger kids, try these under-one-hour round-trip trails. Wear your bathing suits on the ²/₅-mile hike to Gibbs Falls on the Crawford Path, which starts 13⁹/₁₀ miles west of Silver Springs Country Store and Campground, Bartlett. The road ascends slightly, and then there's a steep descent to the falls. Another easy hike, the Diana's Bath ²/₅-mile trail, takes you along a babbling brook to a series of small cascades and shallow pools.

Other popular hikes include the **Crystal Cascade/Tuckerman's Ravine,** Mount Washington. The ³/₄-mile round-trip hike starts from the AMC Pinkham Notch Camp, Route 16, north of Jackson, and leads to the waterfall. If you continue on to Tuckerman Ravine, 4⁴/₅ miles, three hours round trip, you'll see splendid views of Mount Washington. The trail to **Arethusa Falls,** Crawford Notch State Park, Bartlett (603–374–2272), begins from the parking lot on the west side of Route 302, Crawford Notch. Follow the north bank of Bemis Brook to the falls, the highest in the state, cascading from 200 feet. From the south side of Hurricane Mountain Road, North Conway, take the **Black Cap Mountain** trail for 1½ miles, one hour round trip. Rewards include an exceptional view of the valley.

For hiking that's a bit more challenging, good for hardy elementary school kids and teens, try this two-hour round-trip hike. **Winniweta Falls** is a 2¹⁄₁₀-mile relatively easy hike that begins 3¹⁄₁₀ miles north of Jackson's Covered Bridge. The trail crosses Ellis River, meadows blooming with wild flowers, and ascends for the last fifteen minutes as you near the 40-foot falls.

Obtain hiking information from the Mount Washington Valley Visitor Bureau and the Jackson Chamber of Commerce (see For More Information). The Silver Springs Country Store and Camp-ground, Route 302, Bartlett, New Hampshire 03812 (603- 374-2221), sells a tip sheet of "Twenty of the Most Rewarding Hikes in the White Mountains" for a nominal fee.

The Appalachian Mountain Club (AMC), another reliable source of information, has its main headquarters at Pinkham Notch, Mount Washington. Call (603) 466-2721 or (603) 466-2725 for trail information and (603) 466-2727 for workshop and family vacation package information. The AMC offers quality trail maps and advice, plus lectures and workshops for children and adults. Learn about flora and fauna, bushwhacking, bug and birding, and wild edibles. Many workshops include an overnight stay in one of the AMC area huts. Families new to hiking might consider a beginner backpacking and camping weekend workshop. If that's too long, try an AMC Family Discovery day hike for 4 miles of fun. AMC activities operate year-round. In fall follow a waterfall tour, in winter sample snowshoeing, and in early spring go maple sugaring.

For those who want to enjoy Mount Washington but only want a limited amount of walking, sign on for an AMC Alpine Garden Tour. Guides drive you to the top of Mount Washington then lead you on a hike through the Alpine Garden and back up to the summit for your van ride back down. Call (603) 466-2727.

Eastern Mountain Sports (EMS), Main Street, North Conway (603-356-5433), also organizes guided hikes on weekend mornings from June through September.

Llama Trekking and Dog Jorring in the White Mountains. Even a tenderfoot can see Maine's valleys and the purple ridges of New Hampshire's peaks from a scenic lookout high in the White Mountains. With a llama trek from Telemark Inn, Bethel, Maine, you get to these heights the easy way—the llamas carry all your equipment.

You and your kids (as young as four) enjoy the challenge of leading the llamas, intelligent and furry beasts of burden, to your backwoods camp. These trips appeal to families with young kids and to parents and grandparents who want to share the wilderness and the wildlife with their clan without the work or responsibility of setting up camp. The guides pitch the tents, cook dinner, and wake you up in the morning with hot towels, hot coffee, or hot chocolate.

In winter, owner Steve Crone offers dog jorring, which is dog sledding without the sled. You cross-country ski connected to a dog that pulls you along. Steve also offers a variety of other summer trips, including one-day llama treks, guided hikes, and canoe trips. For information contact the Telemark Inn Llama Treks. RFD 2, Box 800, Bethel, Maine 04217; (207) 836-2703.

Canoeing/Kayaking/White-water Rafting. Canoe outfitters Saco Bound, Route 302, Center Conway (603-447-3801), make it easy to enjoy a lazy paddle on the Saco River, combining sunning, swimming, and picnicking. Follow the current for 43 miles if you go the distance, or take a shorter trip. Saco Bound provides equipment and instructions. They even provide a guide for a day-long trip on Tuesdays and Thursdays in July and August. Call ahead. For a more exciting ride, try springtime white-water rafting. Most excursions include a steak barbecue lunch and time to swim and explore the river and surroundings.

The Appalachian Mountain Club (AMC) organizes a two-day canoe and camping trip to Lake Umbagog. Call (603) 466-2727 for more information.

Biking. For older children and adults, mountain biking offers a challenge along with some spectacular views. The North Conway Athletic Club (603-356-5774) organizes mountain bike outings and suggests good routes. Bike rentals are available at the Joe Jones Shop (603-356-9411) and the Sports Outlet (603-356-3133), both in North Conway.

If you want a guide, Off Road Cycling Adventures, North Conway (603-356-2080), operates one-to-five-day custom-tailored tours of the White Mountains that include a bike, helmet, and box lunch. Children must be eleven years or older.

Parks. **Echo Lake State Park,** Route 302, North Conway (603-356-2672), is a good family day trip as the park has a swimming area for children, picnic tables and grills for lunch or a barbecue, and a trail that circles the lake. You can even rent a boat. The park is open June through Labor Day.

Fishing. With forty-five lakes and ponds as well as 650 miles of streams in the region, Mount Washington Valley is an angler's delight. Good spots include the Wild and Saco rivers as well as Basin Reservoir and Russell Pond. A state license is required for nonresidents over twelve, and certain restrictions apply. Call the New Hampshire Fish and Game Department at (603) 271-3421 for more information.

Tennis. New England Tennis and Hiking Holidays, Mount Cranmore Recreation Center, North Conway (603-356-9696 or 800-869-0949), organizes hiking and tennis vacations, including meals and lodging at local inns or at condominiums. While not catering to families, their programs are suitable for parents and teens.

Golfing. Appreciate the beauty of the mountains from the valley golf courses. Duffers have their choice of three public eighteen-hole courses in the area: North Conway Country Club (603-356-9700), Hale's Location Country Club (603-356-6377), and the Wentworth Resort Golf Club (603-383-9641).

Additional Summer through Fall Attractions
Scenic Drives and Views

In summer and fall these mountain drives offer eye-popping vistas. The Mount Washington Auto Road, Route 16, Pinkham Notch, Gorham (603-466-3988), is famous. Take your car 8 winding miles to Mount Washington's summit; at 6,288 feet, it's the highest in the northeastern United States. The drive is worth the views, but only if you're comfortable with steep, winding roads as the grades average 12 percent. If the sky is clear, you can see six states; if not, you can still see the Sherman Adams Summit museum with its slide show, *Home of the World's Worst Weather.* The locals are not kidding either. Be sure to dress warmly, for this hour-long trip to the top of Mount Washington is known for its winds and quickly changing weather. To access the auto road take Route 16 about 8 miles south of Gorham to Glenn House, which is open mid-May to mid-October.

Another well-known scenic route is the **Kancamagus Highway,** Route 112, which runs 35 miles from Conway to Lincoln. Stop for a picnic at Lower Falls ($6^7/_{10}$ miles from Conway) and an easy hike through the Rocky Gorge $8^2/_5$ miles from Conway. The short walk from the parking lot at Sabbaday Falls, $14^9/_{10}$ miles from Conway, leads you by cascading falls. With any luck you'll spot some moose taking a splash at Lily Pond ($18^1/_{10}$ miles from Conway). Cool off at the Wilderness Trail, $28^4/_5$ miles from Conway. The trail from the parking area leads you along a suspension bridge to a spot with good river swimming.

But you can still enjoy the views even if you don't want to hike or drive. Children love the **Conway Scenic Railroad,** Main Street, North Conway; (603) 356-5251 or (800) 232-5251. This one-hour ride in an antique coach pulled by a steam- or diesel-powered engine departs from an 1874 railway station and chugs along through Bartlett and into Crawford Notch. In warm weather spend some time in the open-air car. Reserve in advance during the fall foliage season. The railroad is open from May through October.

For a more extensive and impressive train ride, climb Mount Washington on the second steepest railway track in the world. At the **Mount Washington Cog Railway,** Route 302, Bretton Woods (603-846-5404 or 800-922-8825, ext. 7), an 1869 steam-powered train takes you to the top on a three-hour trip over rough and rugged terrain. Early risers save money on a discounted 8:00 A.M. train ride. Reservations are recommended; it's open May through October.

The **Wildcat Mountain Gondola,** Route 16, Pinkham Notch (603-466-3326), provides yet another way to climb the White Mountains without hiking boots. This fifteen-minute ride brings you to the top of the 4,100-foot Wildcat Mountain for a sweeping view. Bring a bag lunch for a summit picnic, explore the surrounding trails, then ride back down. The gondola is open mid-May through mid-October. Call for scheduled hours.

Other Fall Attractions. In fall, bite your way into some of the area's edible wonders: crisp apples. Pick your own bushels at several area orchards, including Hatch Orchard in Center Conway; (603) 447-5687.

Additional Attractions. **Story Land,** Route 16, Glen; (603) 383-4293. This is a must-see if you have preschool children or young grade-schoolers. They will love the come-to-life Mother Goose settings complete with child-size buildings and recognizable characters. Humpty Dumpty—sitting on a wall, of course—greets you. Rest on a bench, and Little Miss Muffet's spider comes and sits beside you. Walk into Peter, Peter, Pumpkin Eater's house, and visit the Old Woman in the Shoe. Drift by the castle on a swan boat, get sprayed by a gentle raft ride, or sit in a Polar Coaster, where the seats resemble walruses. Story Land is great low-tech fun for little kids. Its open from June through October.

Next door, operated mid-May to mid-October by the same company, is **Heritage New Hampshire,** Route 16, Glen; (603) 383-9776. Explore local history here, beginning with a 1634 English village from which the ship *Reliance* sailed to Portland. Visitors "see" President George Washington, the effects of the Industrial Revolution in New Hampshire, and come back to the present on a simulated train ride through Crawford Notch at peak foliage.

Less educational but also fun, is the **Attitash Bear Peak Alpine Slide and Outdoor Amusements,** Route 302, Bartlett; (800) 223-SNOW. Choose the fast track or a slower one. The park also offers a scenic chairlift ride to the top of the mountain and plenty of space for a countryside picnic. It's open from May through October. Another play park, White River Amusements, Route 16, North Conway (603-356-6541), features minigolf and a water slide that twists and turns before dropping you into a pool.

Somewhat hokey, but also fun, especially for young kids, are Santa's Village and Six Gun City. **Santa's Village,** Route 2, Jefferson (603-586-4445), is Santa's summer home. Tots delight in their visit with Santa's helpers and with the big guy himself. Christmas-theme attractions include a kiddie roller coaster, a Yule Log water flume, animals to pet, and two shows—the Jingle Jamboree and the Live Tropical Bird Show. At **Six Gun City,** Route 2, Jefferson (603-586-4592), see the Wild West of the White Mountains complete with a frontier village, a bank robbery, and a sheriff and outlaw shoot-em-up. Kids may even earn a deputy's badge. At the Frontier Show, hear stories of this hard-knock life; at the Miniature Diamond B Ranch, pet miniature goats, burros, and horses. Amusements include a miniature golf course, water slide, and boat rides. It's open from mid-June to Labor Day.

Adventures abound in the majestic White Mountains. (Courtesy Mount Washington Valley Visitor Bureau)

Winter Fun

Horse Logic Hay and Sleigh Rides, Route 116, Jackson (603–383-9876), bundles you into its cozy carriage and takes you through Jackson's scenic winter wonderland.

Downhill Skiing. Mount Washington Valley is home to several family-friendly ski areas. It's a great place to learn how to ski (ask about Learn to Ski packages). **Attitash Bear Peak,** in Bartlett (603–374-0946), has something for all ages, beginning with an Attitots ski program for ages one to three and continuing up to an Attiteens racing program. Lift tickets for kids cost less with a pay-what-you-ride system and a Sunday kids-pay-their-age deal.

Waterville Valley, New Hampshire, offers comprehensive ski programs for kids, child care for wee ones, a family-friendly atmosphere, and a variety of packages. Often kids ski free midweek, so ask. Choose to stay in condos, bed and breakfasts, or lodges. In summer the ski area offers attractively priced family packages and lots of activities. For information call (800) 468-2553. (See Where to Stay.)

Consult the Mount Washington Valley Winter Fun brochure for a full description of ski area offerings.

Cross-Country Skiing. New Hampshire's White Mountains offer a classic ski getaway not only for downhill (Alpine) but for cross-country (Nordic) skiers as well. Besides 600 kilometers of groomed trails, the area frequently offers a special reduced-rate bed and breakfast ski package midweek. As you glide from inn to inn, the trails take you near covered bridges, over snowy fields, and along creeks. Several of the lodgings welcome children. For package information call Country Inns in the White Mountains, P.O. Box 2025, North Conway 03860; (800) 562-1300.

Jackson has been rated one of the four best places in the world to cross-country ski because of the abundance, quality, and variety of trails. The paths around the village through meadows and woods are particularly scenic. Ski up to a country inn for lunch or tea. The Jackson Ski Touring Foundation, Jackson (603-383-9355), makes sure that more than 90 miles of trails in the village of Jackson and throughout the White Mountain National Forest are groomed. Trails are marked by ability, and maps are available from the center. Ski rentals and lessons are available at the Jack Frost Nordic Shop. The Jackson area also makes snow for their teaching area and village loop.

Another big center is the **Mount Washington Valley (MWV) Ski Touring,** Intervale (603-356-9920), a similar organization that offers 65 kilometers of groomed trails. Special events include a Holiday Cookie Fest when skiers go from inn to inn tasting holiday cookies and, in late-February, a chocolate festival. The **Appalachian Mountain Club,** Route 16, Pinkham Notch (603-466-2727), offers its hiking trails for cross-country skiing.

Ice Skating. When you tire of the snow, take to the ice at public rinks in Jackson Village as well as in Conway and North Conway Villages. If you didn't bring your own skates, rent them at Joe Jones' Ski and Sports Shop, North Conway (603-356-9411).

Shopping. With more than 200 factory outlet stores and no sales tax in New Hampshire, shopping in North Conway is worthwhile despite the frequent crowds. Scores of people come here seasonally to outfit the whole clan. With Levis, Dexter Shoe, OshKosh B'Gosh, Benetton 012, Calvin Klein, Liz Claiborne, Donna Karan, Bugle Boy,

Danskin, London Fog, L.L. Bean, and lots more, families pack their cars with bargains. Check the Mount Washington Valley Visitor Guide, available at the visitor information centers, for a full listing of outlet stores.

Performing Arts. The **Eastern Slope Playhouse,** Main Street, North Conway (603–356–5776), offers Broadway-run musicals performed by the Mount Washington Valley Theater Company. Call in June for schedules and tickets. The **Arts Jubilee,** Settler's Green at Routes 16 and 302, North Conway (603–356–9393), is a music festival that features four concerts during summer.

SPECIAL EVENTS

For more information on events listed, call the Mount Washington Valley Visitor Bureau at (603) 356–3171/(800) 367–3364.

January: Jackson Skiing Legends, Black Mountain, features a vintage-attire ski race and a classic film festival.

February: Family Frolics Week at Mount Cranmore, North Conway. Wildcat Silly Slaloms and kid's special events week, Wildcat Mountain. Winter Carnival, King Pine Ski Area, with races, barbecues, and fireworks.

March: Canada Month in Mount Washington Valley, with special packages for the northern neighbors. Spring Carnival, Mount Cranmore, North Conway. March Madness at King Pine Ski Area, family fun for all ages.

April: Easter Bunny Express aboard Conway Scenic Railroad.

May: Wildquack River Race Festival, Jackson Village. Race your duck in the stream or join in the Quackers Parade.

June: Annual Mount Washington Valley Old Car Show, Grand Manor Antique Car Museum, Glen. Conway Village Festival, a weekend of fun featuring a parade, children's games, a pet show, and live entertainment. Mount Washington Auto Road Climb to the Clouds, road race and celebration. Heritage Days; ten days of cultural events.

July: New Hampshire State Parks Week features special family activities. Fourth of July Carnival, North Conway, has face painting, fried dough, and rides galore. Independence Day Parade, North Conway. Jackson Family Day in the Park has special children's July Fourth celebration.

July/August: Sunday night outdoor band concerts in North Conway.

August: Attitash Equine Festival, Attitash Mountain, Bartlett, is a world-class riding show that also includes a children's playground, pony rides, and food fest. Later in the month the Attitash Double R Rodeo comes to town with bronco riding, steer wrestling, and country music. Blueberry Festival, Attitash Mountain, Bartlett, has a kid's Blueberry Olympics.

September: Railfans' Day, Conway Scenic Railroad, celebrates old trains. White Mountain Jazz and Blues Festival, Fields of Attitash.

October: Fryeburg Fair, Fryeburg, Maine; more than a century-long tradition, this country fair is the real thing. Sandwich Fair, Sandwich, New Hampshire, bustles with farm animal activity, a parade, and kid's fun. Oktoberfest, a traditional Bavarian festival.

WHERE TO STAY

After a day full of mountain air and activity, come home to a cozy New England inn. Here are some that are family friendly and have hiking and cross-country skiing trails just out the back door. Be sure to ask about weekend or other family packages.

Attitash Bear Peak Mountain, Route 302 in Bartlett (800-862-1600), offers ski packages, family passes, and a variety of kids' programs for skiers and nonskiers alike. The Children's Center offers day care for infants and toddlers as well as a variety of full-day, learn-to-ski programs for Attitots, Attiteens, and Attitudes. Ask about weekend, midweek, and vacation lodging packages.

Attitash Mountain Village, across from the Attitash Bear Peak slopes, has one-, two-, and three-bedroom units, some of which have kitchenettes. For reservations call the **Attitash Travel and Lodging Bureau** (800-223-SNOW), which will provide you with information on bed and breakfasts, hotels, and inns. The service also arranges ski school lessons, rentals, lift tickets, and day care. Attitash Bear Peak also bought Cranmore Mountain in North Conway.

Ellis River House, P.O. Box 656, Jackson (603-383-9339 or 800-233-8309), is a turn-of-the-century farmhouse overlooking the Ellis River. The inn has family rooms and welcomes well-behaved kids.

Christmas Farm Inn, Route 16B above the village, Jackson (603-383-4313 or 800-HI-ELVES), pleases younger ones with its game room, sauna, an outdoor pool, and year-round Christmas decorations. A small sitting room off the main parlor features a child-size rocking chair, as well as puzzles, games, and a television.

The **Eagle Mountain Resort,** Carter Notch Road, Jackson (603-383-9111), has a nine-hole golf course that becomes a cross-country ski area in winter. Other features include a health club, an outdoor pool, and tennis courts. The **Wentworth Resort Hotel,** Route 16A at Carter Notch Road, Jackson (603-383-9700 or 800-637-0013), is right in the heart of Jackson and offers sixty-two rooms. The cross-country ski trails start nearby, and the property features an outdoor ice rink in winter and an outdoor pool in summer. In warm weather try your skill at the eighteen-hole golf course and on the tennis courts. At the **Sheraton White Mountain Inn,** Route 16 at Settler's Green, North Conway (603-356-9300 or 800-648-4397), kids under twelve stay and eat for free.

The **Mount Washington Hotel & Resort,** Bretton Woods, New Hampshire 03575 (603-278-1000 or 800-258-0300), is a grande dame hotel built in 1902 that keeps to its early century pace. The hotel features 177 rooms, wraparound porches, great views, and a golf course. The property also has the Bretton Woods Motor Inn and town homes complete with kitchens.

The **Nordic Village Vacation Resort,** Route 16, Jackson (603-383-9101 or 800-472-5207), offers one- and two-bedroom rental condominiums. The Mount Washington Valley offers a reservation service. Call (800) 367-3364 for more information.

For additional lodging suggestions contact the **Jackson Lodging Bureau;** (800) 866-3334.

In winter **Waterville Valley,** New Hampshire, has comprehensive ski programs and child care; in summer the area offers boating, tennis, horseback riding, a sports center, and a daily activity program for kids ages three to five, six to eight, and nine to twelve. Family activity packages get the gang going with daily tennis clinics, hikes, aerobic classes, as well as mountain biking, roller blading, and boating. Choose to stay at a variety of inns, lodges, or condominiums. For information call (800) 468-2553.

WHERE TO EAT

Try a smoked chicken and tortilla salad or a plain hearty New York sirloin at **The Christmas Farm Inn,** Black Mountain Road, Jackson (603-383-4313). Taste a Reuben Express or a Turkey Trolley at **Glen Junction,** Route 302 in Glen (603-383-9660), where a toy train chugs around the room on a track on the wall. For seafood **Snug Harbor,** Route 16, North Conway (603-356-3000), is the place with fried and baked regional fish and a little pirates kid's menu. **Elvio's,** Main Street, North Conway Village (603-356-3307), has the best pizza in town, featuring thin-crust, thick-crust, and/or white varieties. **I Cugini,** Route 302, Bartlett (603-374-1977), has particularly good soup, pasta entrees, and a menu tailored to children's appetites.

The **Appalachian Mountain Club,** Route 16, Pinkham Notch Gorham (603-466-2721), offers dinner get-togethers after a long day's hike. Dinner begins at 6:00 P.M., and don't be late. The menu changes daily. Call in advance for reservations.

After a trip on the Cog Railway, stop at **Fabyans Station,** next door, Route 302, Bretton Woods (603-846-2222), in the old railroad depot. They offer hearty burgers and sandwiches. For dessert out-of-towners will find a sweet surprise at **Ben & Jerry's Scoop Shop,** Norcross Place, North Conway (603-356-7720).

DAY TRIPS

There is no shortage of day trips from the Jackson area. **Portland, Maine,** is ninety minutes southeast, and **Boston** is two-and-a-half-hours south. (See the Boston and Portland chapters.)

Portsmouth offers **Strawberry Banke,** P.O. Box 300, Portsmouth, New Hampshire 03802; (603) 433-1100. This house museum includes more than forty houses that trace the development of the area from 1630 through the 1950s. Kids love the Colonial and Federal furniture and artifacts. The museum is open May through October and on weekends in December for a candlelight stroll. Portsmouth also features **The Children's Museum,** 280 Marcy Street, 03801 (603-436-3853), where there's hands-on fun for little ones.

FOR MORE INFORMATION

Jackson Chamber of Commerce, P.O. Box 304, Jackson (603-383-9356 from New Hampshire and Canada; 800-866-3334 from elsewhere), publishes a free visitor's travel guide and will book reservations for you. Mount Washington Valley Visitor Bureau, Box 2300, North Conway (603-356-5701/800-367-3364), publishes the *Mount Washington Valley Visitor Guide*. For information on recreational facilities, including biking and hiking trails, contact the White Mountain National Forest at P.O. Box 638, Laconia, New Hampshire 03247; (603) 528-8721. Also check with the Trails Bureau, New Hampshire Division of Parks and Recreation, P.O. Box 856, Concord, New Hampshire 03301; (603) 271-3556 (parks) or (603) 271-3627 (recreation services).

Tourist information booths are located in Jackson Village as well as North Conway and Conway villages. For specific locations call the visitor's numbers listed above.

Check out the local happenings with *The Mountain Ear* (603-447-6336), Mount Washington Valley's weekly newspaper. For twenty-four-hour weather-line call (603) 447-5252.

Emergency Numbers

Ambulance fire, and police in Conway and North Conway: 911
Ambulance and fire in all other towns: 1-539-6119
Health-Net information line: (800) 499-4171
Memorial Hospital emergency room, Route 16, North Conway; (603) 356-5461
Poison Control: (800) 562-8236
Police in Bartlett: 1-539-2234
Police in Jackson and Glen: (800) 552-8960
There is no twenty-four-hour pharmacy. A convenient pharmacy is CVS Pharmacy, Shaw's/North Way Plaza, Route 16, North Conway; (603) 356-6916.

5 ⛵ Vermont

LAKE CHAMPLAIN AND BURLINGTON

After the Great Lakes, Lake Champlain is the next largest inland lake in the United States. Extending southward from Canada, the 120-mile-long lake lies between New York State and Vermont, whose boundaries claim two-thirds of the lake. The sparkling blue water, beautiful bays, islands, and miles of Vermont shoreline are havens for swimming, sailing, boating, fishing, windsurfing, waterskiing—and just relaxing. (Keep an eye out for Champ, the sea monster who has allegedly been spotted several times over the years.) Burlington, Vermont's largest city, sits on the terraced eastern slopes of Lake Champlain and is the headquarters for navigation around the lake. It's also an important business and educational center, home to the University of Vermont. Burlington has a charming downtown, and some noteworthy attractions are nearby. Once you've explored the area, see what other pleasures the Champlain Valley holds.

GETTING THERE

Burlington International Airport (802-863-2874) is New England's third busiest. Car rentals are available at the airport.

Vermont Transit, 133 Saint Paul Street at Main; (802) 864-8611/(800) 642-3133—Vermont/(800) 451-3292—New England. Buses go to and from other Vermont towns as well as Boston, Albany, and Montreal, with connections made with Greyhound.

Amtrak is at 29 Railroad Avenue, Essex Junction (5 miles east of Burlington); (802) 879-7298/(800) USA-RAIL. Trains run to and from New York and Montreal. A bus leaves hourly for downtown Burlington.

Auto/passenger ferries link Vermont and New York at three northern crossings: Burlington to Port Kent, New York (one-hour trip): Charlotte, Vermont, to Essex, New York (eighteen minutes); and Grand Isle, Vermont, to Plattsburgh, New York (twelve minutes). All are operated by Lake Champlain Transportation Company, King Street Dock. (802) 864–9804.

Burlington is at the end of the scenic portion of highways I–89 and SR 116.

GETTING AROUND

Public CCTA (Chittendon County Transit Authority) buses operate Monday through Saturday throughout the city and to outlying areas, including Shelburne, from the CCTA hub on Cherry and Church streets.

WHAT TO SEE AND DO

Museums and Historical Sites

We're starting with the biggest and the best: **Shelburne Museum,** U.S. 7, Shelburne; (802) 985–3344. The heritage of New England is celebrated here with impressive eighteenth- and nineteenth-century folk art, artifacts, and architecture. But this collection of Americana—among the best in the country—isn't presented in a boring, dry-as-dust museum manner. Instead, the history and artifacts are incorporated into a small village of buildings, most transported from various places in Vermont: a covered bridge, 1800s homes and shops—even a private, furnished 1890 railroad car and a vintage railroad station. Discover the life and art of another era in a vital living-history setting.

Kids especially like the 1830 one-room schoolhouse; the 1890 jail, featuring cells, stocks, and pillory; and the old-time general store with barbershop, taproom, and post office. A big hit with all ages, the circus building houses carvings of a miniature circus parade, big-tent wonders, vintage carousel animals, and circus wagons.

Don't miss the *Ticonderoga,* the last vertical beam sidewheel steamboat intact in the United States, which was built in Shelburne Harbor in 1906. A film on board shows the ingenious way the ship was moved to the museum. The Toy Shop will delight with penny

Lake Champlain and Burlington at a Glance

- Swimming, sailing, boating, fishing, windsurfing, waterskiing—and just relaxing—on a 120-mile sparkling blue lake

- The nineteenth century lives on at the Shelburne Museum

- Grab a bite of the best—Ben & Jerry's Ice Cream— at the source

- Two full-service family resorts

- Beautiful fall foliage

- Lake Champlain Regional Chamber of Commerce, (802) 863-3489; Vermont Travel Division, (802) 828-3236

banks, mechanical toys, dolls, and animals; for more dolls, as well as dollhouses, see the Variety Unit. Also eye-catching: the big red round barn and the white lighthouse. Steer kids in the direction of paintings by masters such as Rembrandt, Degas, Manet, and Monet.

The Family Activity Center at Owl Cottage features a reading area, costume play, and art projects. From late October through late May, theme tours for children ages five and older (with adults along) are given twice on Saturdays. One theme might be searching the museum for "cats," and then picking a favorite for an art activity. (Reservations are required.) In July and August the museum offers a weekly series of children's workshops. These fill quickly; to register in advance, call the Educational Department at (802) 985-3346, ext. 395, weekdays.

Try to time your visit to coincide with one of the special-events weekends. In late May the museum celebrates the opening of its warm-weather season with Lilac Sunday, nineteenth-century entertainment and leisure activities that include a Victorian picnic, croquet, carriage rides, music—and lots of fun. July Fourth is celebrated with Old Time

You and your family can learn what life was like in another era at the Shelburne Museum, which features, among other things, an authentic print shop. (Courtesy Shelburne Museum)

Farm Day, featuring horse-drawn wagon rides, farm animals, traditional folk music, dances, games, crafts, and storytelling. There's all old-time baseball game, too, and the chance for your family to milk a cow, churn butter, make ice cream, and shell peas.

Plan on spending at least three hours, though you could easily spend much more; there's a "second day free" admission policy. A snack bar and cafeteria are on-site, and a jitney service helps with touring the museum's forty-five acres. Baby strollers and carriers aren't permitted in some of the buildings because of the narrow hallways or fragile exhibits. A physical accessibility guide and wheelchairs are available at the McClure Visitor Center.

Nearby is **Shelburne Farms,** 102 Harbor Road, Shelburne; (802) 985–8686. Designed as an "ideal" farm at the turn of the century, this property now features an inn, a barn and carriage tour and walking trails. Set on 1,000 acres with ample Lake Champlain frontage, the grounds are alluring. The barn tours are a bit boring despite the beauty of the facility. Two things are especially nice to do here: Obtain a walking trail map from the Visitors Center and meander through meadows and enjoy the splendid scenery. With little children visit the Children's Farmyard, with its goats, rabbits, and horses to pet. Check the schedule of special events.

Located on the grounds of the Basin Harbor Club, the **Lake Champlain Maritime Museum,** RR 3, Box 4092, Vergennes (802–475-2022), details the region's nautical history. Displayed watercraft include old sail craft, a Native American dugout canoe, and the museum's pride, the *Philadelphia II,* a replica of a 54-foot Revolutionary war gunboat.

If you have more time in the area, the following sites offer kid-pleasing diversions.

Discovery Museum, 51 Park Street, Route 2A, Essex Junction; (802) 878-8687. This small hands-on museum, located in a historic home, gears its exhibits and programs to kids up to age twelve. Attractions include a Science Center area with a 727 cockpit, fossil table, freshwater fish tank, rocks and minerals, and—everyone's favorite—bubble experiments. Call for information about weekly and monthly programs.

Ethan Allen Homestead, off Route 127; (802) 865-4556. School-age children may like a visit to this restored 1787 timber farmhouse that belonged to Revolutionist Allen, leader of the famous Green Mountain Boys. Guided tours are given, and there's a multimedia show on this local hero who helped establish the state of Vermont. When you're through, enjoy a respite at the 258-acre Winooski Valley Park, with hiking trails, that surrounds the homestead.

Factory Tours

The factories for two made-in-Vermont popular products are located in the Shelburne area, and each offers a factory tour. It's hard to resist the cute bears at the **Vermont Teddy Bear Company,** 2236 Shelburne Road (Route 7); (802) 985-3001/(800) 829-BEAR. The guides, who act more like vaudeville comedians than docents, enliven your factory-floor visit with bear facts and antics, almost making you believe the bears are real. At the end your children will certainly want a teddy of their own.

Ben & Jerry's, P.O. Box 240, Waterbury (802-244-TOUR). This ice cream factory created by two buddies started in Vermont. To please the crowds awaiting tours, various booths outside offer face painting, bubble play, and crafts. When the lines are long, skip the tour, which consists of a video about the company's beginnings and a not-too-interesting look at the factory floor; simply enjoy the outdoor activities and the ice cream.

Parks and Beaches

North Beach, reached by following North Avenue to Institute Road, is Burlington's most popular place to swim, bike, walk, rollerblade (rentals available), and picnic (grills are provided). This is also the site of seasonal festivals and special events.

Catamount Family Center (802-879-6001), near the airport, offers 500 acres for mountain biking (rentals and lessons available), orienteering, walking, and winter cross-country skiing.

Downtown you'll find a scenic oasis in **Battery Street Park,** the scene of an 1812 skirmish between American land batteries and British vessels on Lake Champlain. Sit back and enjoy the now peaceful view of the lake and, beyond, the Adirondack Mountains. In summer free concerts add to the appeal.

Shelburne Farms, off Route 7, Shelburne; (802) 985-8686. Enjoy the best of the countryside at this 1,000-acre historic site with spectacular lake/mountain views. There's a restored inn and restaurant on the property, cheesemaking and tasting, plus daily tours that feature the lovely formal gardens.

Vermont Wildflower Farm, U.S. 7, Charlotte, 5 miles south of the Shelburne Museum; (802) 425-3500. Even the youngest tot will be in heaven, strolling along pathways leading through open fields and forests with acres of wild flowers. Each flower is identified, and facts about its history and characteristics are provided. In July and August in an air-conditioned theater, there's a short but striking film. Seeds are for sale—and just try to leave without a gift. Kids will undoubtedly want the coloring book.

Special Tours

The *Spirit of Ethan Allen* excursion boat leaves Perkins Pier for shoreline cruises that include Captain's Dinner Cruises. Call (802) 826-9685. Tell the kids to keep their eyes peeled for Champ. In 1984 seventy passengers made the largest mass sighting of the elusive sea serpent, according to the cruise line. Numerous charters and boat rentals are available around the lake.

Performing Arts

Flynn Theatre for the Performing Arts, 153 Main Street, offers excellent dance, music, and theater performances. Call (802) 88-FLYNN for ticket information. **Saint Michael's College,** Route 15, Winooski Park, puts on professional summer theater performances from late June to mid-August. Call (802) 655-0122 for schedules. A number of cultural festivals are held annually (see Special Events).

Shopping

The traffic-free downtown **Church Street Marketplace** is a pleasant place to shop and eat, with street musicians and sidewalk cafes adding to the festive atmosphere. **The Vermont Teddy Bear Company,** 2031 Shelburne Road, Shelburne, invites visitors on a guided tour to see how these cuddly, handmade bears are created. This is a winner. Call (802) 985-3001/(800) 829-BEAR.

SPECIAL EVENTS

Culture—and fun—is the theme of many of Burlington's fairs and festivals. Contact the Lake Champlain Regional Chamber of Commerce for more information on the following events.

January: Teddy Bear Ski Weeks at the Mount Snow Resort at Wilmington has magic shows, teddy bear ice cream sundae parties, and more. Children under twelve are welcome free.

June: Discover Jazz Festival. Lake Champlain Balloon Festival, Champlain Valley Fairgrounds, Essex Junction, includes children's petting zoo and amusement rides, entertainment, exhibits, and more.

July: Champlain Shakespeare Festival.

July–early August: Vermont Mozart Festival.

August: A Taste of Stowe and For Art's Sake, Stowe.

September: Harvest Festival, Shelburne Farms, entertainment, crafts, and hayrides.

WHERE TO STAY

Families have a wide choice of accommodations in the area, but first decide if you want to stay in town, on the lake, or at one of the full-service, year-round resorts not far from Burlington. (Actually, you might want to do all three.) *Vermont Traveler's Guidebook* lists lodgings throughout the state. Here are a few with family appeal.

Burlington

Radisson Hotel Burlington, 60 Battery Street, has 25 rooms, many overlooking the lake and the Adirondack Mountains. Features you'll like: indoor heated swimming pool, restaurants (including a casual cafe), complimentary airport shuttle, and free covered parking. Adjacent is the Burlington Square Mall and Church Street Market-place. Call (802) 658-6500/(800) 333-3333.

Lake Champlain

Basin Harbor Club, Basin Road, Vergennes, 25 miles south of Burlington, is directly on Lake Champlain's eastern shore. Everything here is well manicured: the lovely grounds, the staff, and the guests. Boys and men are required to wear coats and ties in the public area after 6:00 P.M. The playground offers supervised activities for ages three to ten in summer from 9:00 A.M. to noon. Kids eat dinner together too. Afternoons bring craft activities suitable for all ages. Older children can avail themselves of the resort's superb recreation: golf, tennis, swimming, softball, and lots of water sports on the lake or poolside. If there are enough teens on the property, evening activities are planned. The resort is open from June through mid-October. Call (802) 475-2311/(800) 622-4000.

Tyler Place Inn and Cottages on Lake Champlain, Highgate Springs. If you're looking for less formality but lots of fun, this family favorite may be just the ticket. Located on a mile of private lakeshore, the casual resort offers twenty-seven fireplace cottages or family suites, all with separate parents' bedroom. Programs are held for toddlers to teens, with sports, activities, early dining, and mother's helpers for younger kids. Ask about special May, June, and September rates. Meals are included. Reserve early: This place is popular; (802) 868-4291/868-3301.

All-Season Resorts

Two popular family resorts near Lake Champlain are Bolton Valley and Smuggler's Notch.

Bolton Valley Resort, Bolton, 19 miles from Burlington offers hotel rooms (some with kitchens) or modern, trailside condominiums (all with kitchens) in a splendid mountain setting. The resort's nature center has daily summer activities, rotated during the week, that might include nature photography, a moose watch, or mountain biking classes, plus guided nature walks. Camp Bear Paw occupies the days of ages six to twelve, and there's a nursery for ages three months to six years. In winter the nursery is open, and there are pre-ski and child-care programs for ages four and five, plus full-day skiing sessions for ages five to fifteen (divided by ages). Call (802) 434-2131/(800 451-3220—hotel reservation/(800) 451-5025—condos.

Smuggler's Notch, Route 108, 30 miles northeast of Burlington International Airport, consistently ranks among the top family ski resorts in North America. Much has to do with what it does for kids and parents. Alice's Wonderland child-care for ages six weeks and older, with indoor and outdoor play, is open in summer and winter seasons. In winter the resort has ski camps for ages three to six and seven to twelve and a teen program that includes sports and evening dance parties. Ski Week packages feature family game nights and sledding parties. While the five-day FamilyFest includes camp and one free Parent's Night Out—selected supervised evenings for ages three to twelve. Summer brings day camps and programs for ages three to seventeen. When the kids aren't in camp, they head to the three water slides or two pools (there are toddler wading pools, too). Mountainside lodgings, from motel units to five-bedroom condos, are in the walkabout village, where you'll also find a miniature golf course, horseback riding stables and hayrides, restaurants, a convenience store, a deli, and indoor and outdoor tennis—even a post office. Call (802) 644-8851/(800) 451-8752—United States/(800) 356-8679—Canada.

WHERE TO EAT

Vermont Traveler's Guidebook lists area restaurants—or consult the Burlington *Free Press*. Here are some possibilities.

Get a tasty, inexpensive bite and hobnob with the locals at **Henry's Diner,** 155 Bank Street, which has been at this site for years. If your kids are adventurous eaters, don't miss the **Five Spice Cafe,** 175 Church Street with a variety of Asian dishes including Shanghai Noodles, Hunan Chicken with Leeks, Vietnamese Calamari, Thai Red Snapper, and dim sum on Sunday. At **Poppy's Prime Factor,** Main Street in Winooski, enjoy a river view and menu that includes prime ribs, chicken, and soup and salad bar. Kids can eat for a nickel times their weight. Out on Route 2A to Williston, **Espresso** serves fresh pasta, pizza, and homemade desserts; they offer a kid's menu.

DAY TRIPS

A popular winter ski resort, the Stowe area is more peaceful in the summer, when it offers a wealth of recreational possibilities. At the **Stowe Mountain Resort,** take a gondola ride on Mount Mansfield, the highest peak in Vermont, and enjoy spectacular vistas. There's also an alpine slide ride (adults can accompany younger kids). On Sunday evenings concerts are held at the Trapp Family Concert Meadow (yes, the *Sound of Music* family offspring operate a lodge in town). Biking, swimming, hiking, golfing, tennis, and loads of special events are all at your fingertips. Call (802) 253-3000/(800) 24-STOWE for information and central reservations.

FOR MORE INFORMATION

Summer and winter editions of the *Vermont Traveler's Guidebook,* including the Burlington area and other literature, can be obtained from **Vermont Travel Division,** 134 State Street, Montpelier 05602; (802) 828-3236. Contact **Lake Champlain Regional Chamber of Commerce** for their *Vermont Area Guide* to the region: P.O. Box 453, 209 Battery Street, Burlington 05402; (802) 863-3489. Or stop by the

Information Center at the Church Street Marketplace, corner of Church and Bank, mid-May through mid-October. Call (802) 828-3239 for fall foliage reports.

The **Vermont Chamber of Commerce** publishes a *Winter Travel Guide;* call (802) 223-3443.

Emergency Numbers

Ambulance, fire, and police: 911

Poison Control: (802) 658-3456

Twenty-four-hour care for minor or major emergencies: Medical Center Hospital of Vermont, 111 Colchester Avenue; (802) 656-2345

Twenty-four-hour pharmacy: Price Chopper, 555 Shelburne Road (U.S. 7, 2 miles south of downtown); (802) 864-8505

MYSTIC, GROTON, AND NEW LONDON

The area surrounding the old shipping and whaling port of Mystic offers enough family-pleasing diversions to warrant spending several days. The town of Mystic is divided by the Mystic River. On the east bank is the Mystic Marinelife Aquarium, the area's best-known attraction. Family-pleasing attractions can also be found in the neighboring towns of Groton and New London. Mystic is also superbly located on Connecticut's Long Island Sound, near the Rhode Island border, a scenic spot.

GETTING THERE

Major carriers fly into Bradley International Airport, Windsor Locks (860-627-3000), about 1-1½ hour's drive from Mystic. T.F. Green Airport, Warwick, Rhode Island (401-737-4000), about a 1-hour drive from Groton's New London Airport, is served by commuter lines.

Greyhound bus lines arrive and depart from New London. Call (860) 447-3841. Amtrak (800-USA-RAIL) serves Mystic daily on a limited schedule and nearby New London on a more regular basis.

Several ferries serve the area. The Block Island Ferry goes to New London (seasonally); call (860) 442-9553/442-7891. The Cross Sound Ferry serves New London-Orient Point, Long Island; (860) 443-5281. The Montauk Passenger Ferry provides New London-Montauk, Long Island service, May through October; (516) 668-5709/(800) MONTAUK.

To reach Mystic by car, take Connecticut Route 27 approximately 1 mile south of I-95, exit 90.

GETTING AROUND

SEAT (Southeastern Area Transit, 860–886–2631) has buses that serve Mystic on a limited basis.

Yellow Cab Company, 64 Brainard Street, New London (203–536–8888), provides twenty-four-hour service within Mystic as well as to Mystic and to the airport.

WHAT TO SEE AND DO

Museums

Mystic Seaport, 75 Greenmanville Avenue; (860) 572–0711. Your family will love this indoor/outdoor, nonprofit, educational maritime museum, which includes a nineteenth-century coastal village on seventeen waterfront acres. Visitors often help out during the frequent demonstrations throughout the village—so you and the kids may find yourselves setting type at the printing press or giving the barrelmaker a hand. The more than 130 programs and special events held throughout the year (including some wonderful Christmas programs) add another dimension to a visit here. Check the schedules at the visitor's center near the main entrance.

Many of the twenty-two historic buildings—including homes, trade shops, and workplaces—were brought from other New England locations while several remain on their original sites. Board the three major historic ships, and explore the shipyard, where old vessels are rehabilitated. Nineteenth-century sailors navigated by the stars. Learn about the skies at the daily planetarium shows.

If you're blessed by good weather, you'll find yourself spending most of the time outdoors. If not, you'll find much to see and do indoors, even in the off-season. Plan on spending the entire day. If you only have a few hours, though, head to **Chubb's Wharf** where you can board the seaport's prize: the *Charles W. Morgan,* the last of America's wooden whaling fleet. During its eighty years the ship was home to more than 1,000 whalers. At least five of the ship's twenty-one captains brought their wives and children along, a fact that never fails to impress the youngsters who step on board. Try to be here for the fascinating whaling demon-

Mystic, Groton, and New London at a Glance

- Family fun in a former shipping and whaling community

- Mystic Seaport, a re-created coastal village

- Cruise on the SS *Sabino,* the last coal-fired passenger steamer operating in the U.S.

- Theater for both adults and kids

- See 6,000 sea creatures at the Mystic Marinelife Aquarium

- Tour whaling captains' homes in New London

- Mystic Chamber of Commerce, (860) 572–9578; Southeastern Connecticut Tourism District, (800) 222–6783

stration. You'll also want to visit the 1921 *L.A. Dunton,* a Gloucester fishing schooner and the *Joseph Conrad,* an 1882 training ship.

Kids ages two to eight shouldn't miss the **Children's Museum,** located in the circa-1885 Edmondson House. The recently redesigned facility includes several activity spaces that show how sailors and their families lived on sea and shore. Kids play with replicas of nineteenth-century toys and games, read books, and try on replicas of nineteenth-century clothes. In winter, spring, and fall, a Morning Fun for Kids program (parents included) is held in the Children's Museum on Wednesdays. Call (860) 572–5322 for a schedule.

Older kids and adults marvel at the ship models, paintings, and scrimshaw in the **Stillmen Building,** the colorful figureheads and ship's carvings in the Wendell Building, and the beautifully restored small craft in the North Boat Shed.

During the summer when Mystic Seaport is open from 9:00 A.M. to

7:00 P.M., attend the free drop-in activities on the **Village Green.** These let kids duplicate what nineteenth-century children did for fun—before television and videos. Games might include a tug-of-war, stilt walking, or rolling hoops.

At the museum several "tours" are available for extra fees. These include a horse-and-carriage ride through the village, which leaves from Chubbs Wharf. Sail on the catboat *Breck Marshall,* which leaves from the Boathouse on Lighthouse Point. Take a daily river tour, downriver excursion, or, on Sunday, board the SS *Sabino,* the last coal-fired passenger steamer in operation in the United States, for a Dixieland cruise.

The Galley, near the Visitor's Services building, is an informal, self-service place for sandwiches or burgers. The Seamen's Inne, near the North Entrance, serves lunch and dinner, reservations are suggested (203–536–9649).

If your kids like it here (and they will), they may want to return some day for the six- and nine-day youth sailing programs for ages twelve to fifteen, and ages sixteen to nineteen. If you're staying in town for awhile, consider the Seaport's Summer Day Camp, which offers one-week sessions for ages seven and eight and two-week sessions for ages nine to eleven.

Mystic Marinelife Aquarium, 55 Coogan Boulevard, exit 90 off I-95; (860) 536–3323. More people visit here than any other admission-based attraction in Connecticut, according to the aquarium. With 6,000 marine creatures displayed in fifty exhibits, there's plenty to see. The outdoor Seal Island complex on two-and-a-half acres re-creates New England, Alaskan, and California habitats and features four species of seals and sea lions. School-age kids enjoy watching sharks swim in a 30,000-gallon tank behind a sixteen-window display, the largest fish exhibit at the aquarium. Even the tiniest tot will delight in the daily dolphin, whale, and sea lion demonstrations in the Aquarium's Marine Theater. And everybody loves the penguins; view their antics above and below water in their outdoor pavilion. *The Deep Frontier,* shown on a large screen in the Aquarium's main building, explores marine life 2,700 feet below the ocean's surface, using footage provided by scientists in a submersible.

Parks, Preserves, and Beaches

Denison Pequotsepos Nature Center, Pequotsepos Road, Mystic; (860) 536–1216. About 2 miles from Seaport is this 125-acre wooded

At the children's museum at the Mystic Seaport, kids can play with nineteenth-century toys and games. (Photo by Judy Beisler/courtesy Mystic Seaport)

wildlife sanctuary with 7 miles of hiking trails that traverse ponds and meadows. There's a small natural history museum, too. Bring a picnic lunch and stay awhile.

In downtown Norwich, about forty minutes from Mystic, **Chelsea Harbor Park and the Marina at American Wharf** is beautifully landscaped, with flower beds and green lawns. The marina has promenades and walkways, and there are outdoor grills, benches, and, in winter, an ice-skating rink. In summer bring your bathing suits, as you can swim in Mohegan Pond. Phone (860) 886–2381/889–6516—weekends. While you're in Norwich, see if there's a performance of the **Gazebo Summer Music Series** at Howard T. Brown Memorial Park. The series, which runs from May through July, includes everything from jazz to sea chanteys. Call (860) 886–2381.

For ocean swimming locals head to **Watch Hill,** Rhode Island, a good family beach about 13 miles east of Mystic. The sandy **Ocean Beach Park** on Ocean Avenue in New London has gentle surf and also offers a freshwater pool, water slide, miniature golf, game arcade, and picnic area. **Esker Point** in Noank, 3 miles southwest of Mystic, is a local beach on the Sound.

Special Tours

Whale Watch Sunbeam Fleet, Captain John's Sport Fishing Center, 15 First Street, Waterford (860-443-7259). Spend a day watching for whales with a naturalist and research teams from Mystic Marinelife Aquarium. From late June through Labor Day, the tours head out toward the waters of Montauk Point on Sunday and Thursday. For these tours the boat departs from Captain John's Dock, near Niantic River Bridge, Route 156, Waterford.

From February to early March, Sunday excursions look for bald eagles along the Connecticut River. The boat departs from the Dock and Dine Restaurant, Old Saybrook, about 15 miles west of Waterford. Other nature tours are also available. From mid-March to May there are three-hour Sunday excursions to Fisher's Island, south of Mystic, to visit harbor seals. This trip departs from the Waterford dock. Always call ahead for the latest information.

Voyager Cruises operates the *Argia,* Steamboat Wharf, Mystic (860-536-0416/(800-243-0882), a replica of a nineteenth-century schooner. The 81-foot-long ship offers half-day and full-day sailing trips.

Performing Arts

Garde Arts Center and Vangarde Gallery, 329 State Street, New London, is a professional performing arts center that features family theater, Broadway shows, and comedies. Call the box office at (860) 444-7373. **Summer Music at Harkness Park,** Route 213, Waterford, offers Saturday evening concerts ranging from jazz to classical; (860) 442-9199: Summer children's theater is held on Friday or Saturday at the **Ivoryton Playhouse,** 103 Main Street, Ivoryton, near Essex; (860) 767-8348.

Shopping

Olde Mistick Village, Route 27 at I-95, Mystic, is a colonial-style shopping center with more than sixty shops, restaurants, and a theater. There are free weekend concerts June through October. Call

(860) 536–4941. Across the way bargain shop for clothes, toys, crafts, and more at **Mystic Factory Outlets,** Coogan Boulevard; (860) 443–4788.

Mystic's nearby neighboring towns offer these attractions:

Groton

Groton is about 5 miles west of Mystic.

USS *Nautilus* Memorial/Submarine Force Library and Museum, U.S. Sub Base; (860) 449–3174/(800) 343–0079. The self-conducted tour aboard the world's first nuclear-powered ship is free. The *Nautilus* was built in Groton by General Dynamics and launched in 1954. You see the torpedo room, officers' and crews' living and dining areas, and the attack center. The museum has submarine memorabilia, including a model of Captain Nemo's *Nautilus* from Jules Verne's *20,000 Leagues Under the Sea*. There are also working periscopes and a fascinating display of submarines dating from the Revolutionary War and midget submarines from World War II. The library, however, is open only to researchers.

Project Oceanology, Avery Point; (860) 445–9007. Your family will learn a good deal during your two-and-one-half-hour trip aboard this 55-foot research vessel run by a nonprofit marine education association. Marine scientists teach you how to measure lobsters, identify fish, test seawater, and perform other seaworthy chores. The cruises depart daily at 10:00 A.M. and 1:00 P.M. during summer; reservations are recommended.

New London

New London is about 9 miles west of Mystic.

The whaling industry once thrived here, and you can relive some of the glory by strolling through the downtown historic district, which comprises **Whale Oil Row,** an area of Greek revival homes, and surrounding areas. **Nathan Hale Schoolhouse,** Union Plaza (860–443–8331), is where this Connecticut hero taught before he enlisted in Washington's Army.

Lyman Allyn Art Museum, 625 Williams Street; (860) 443–2545. The kids gravitate toward the extensive collection of dolls, dollhouses, and antique toys. There are regularly changing exhibits by contemporary artists as well as American, European, and Oriental fine and decorative arts. The museum is free, though a donation is requested.

Science Center, Gallows Lane; (860) 442-0391. This museum focuses on the land, life, and technology of eastern Connecticut. A marine touch-tank, beehive, salt-marsh diorama, slide show, plus changing exhibits and kids' programs make this an interesting stop for younger school-age kids. Free admission. Guided tours are available of the nearby nature trails, part of a lovely arboretum on the campus of Connecticut College. You and your family can explore the 434 acres on your own, too; open from dawn to dusk.

U.S. Coast Guard Academy, just off I-95 on SR 32, Mohegan Avenue; (860) 444-8270. If you're driving by, this is worth a stop, especially when the cadet corps pass in review (most Friday afternoons at 4:00 P.M. during the spring and fall). There's a visitor's pavilion on Tampa Street with a multimedia show on life at the academy. Board the training ship *Barque Eagle* when it's in port.

Scheduled to debut in 1998 is **OceanQuest,** OceanWorld Learning, Inc., 81 Pequot Avenue, New London; (860) 437-6585. This facility will include a museum of oceanographic and marine sciences and will offer five-day educational marine camps for children in grades five through twelve, as well as a hotel to house parents, families, and visitors.

Beaches

Ocean Beach Park, 1225 Ocean Avenue, New London; (860) 447-3031/(800) 510-SAND. This large public facility has ample parking, a boardwalk with an arcade, a wide sandy beach, plus an Olympic-size outdoor pool.

SPECIAL EVENTS

Ball Games, Fairs and Festivals

In addition to listing the many seasonal events held at Mystic Seaport, the *Mystic Discovery Guide* from the Mystic Chamber of Commerce has a complete calendar of events. Here are some annual festivities.

June: Mystic/Noank Library Fair includes a plant, food, and book sale.

July: Sailfest, New London, international food, music, arts and crafts. Blessing of the Fleet, Stonington Borough, includes Saturday-night lobster feast and band, and Sunday parade.

August: Mystic Outdoor Art Festival, downtown.

Columbus Day Weekend: The Annual Chowderfest is held in the Mystic Seaport boat shed, with seventeen acres of waterfront, folk musicians, and concerts of sea chanteys. New England favorite foods include apple fritters, apple cider, wine, and, of course, the many varieties of chowder. Children roam through the hands-on exhibits at the Museum of America in Mystic Seaport, open throughout Chowderfest. Nineteenth-century tall ships will be open for visitors' curiosity, and the 1908 steamboat *Sabino* cruises passengers down the Mystic River.

The Norwich Navigators, P.O. Box 6003, Yantic; (860) 887-7962/(800) 64-GATOR. This AA league team, affiliated with the New York Yankees, has an attractive stadium, the 7,500-seat Senator Thomas J. Dodd Memorial Stadium. Because of its comfortable size, baseball fans, especially little ones, feel more involved in the game.

WHERE TO STAY

You'll find a listing of lodgings in the Chamber's *Mystic Discovery Guide.* Be sure to reserve in advance. The area has a mixture of guest houses and motels; some of the inns have age restrictions. **Covered Bridge Bed and Breakfast Reservation Service** (203-542-5944) offers a wide range of selections in the area. **Nutmeg Bed and Breakfast Agency** (203-236-6698) has 170 listings throughout the state.

Large motels with outdoor pools include the **Comfort Inn** (800-228-5150 or 860-572-8531), and the **Days Inn** (800-325-2525 or 860-572-0574) in Mystic. Other possibilities for families include the following.

Randall's Ordinary, Route 2, Stonington. This country inn, a registered landmark, is on twenty-seven acres and is less than a mile from Mystic. Fifteen guest rooms and suites are furnished with four-poster canopied beds and other antiques. The rooms in the Jacob Terpenning Barn come with televisions. The farm setting appeals to families, and children are welcome. Call (860) 599-4540.

Sandy Shore Motel and Apartments, 149 Atlantic Avenue, Misquamicut, Rhode Island. Stay right on the ocean in rooms with refrigerators or one- and two-bedroom apartments with kitchens. There's a kids' amusement area nearby. Call (401) 596-5616.

Taber Inn and Townhouses, 29 Williams Avenue, Route 1, Mystic. Two-bedroom townhouses have Jacuzzis and water views. Modern motel rooms are available, too. Call (860) 536-4904.

WHERE TO EAT

The Chamber's *Mystic Discovery Guide* details a number of area restaurants. These are some good choices for families.

Kitchen Little, Route 27, Mystic (and Kitchen Little in the Village in Stonington) is the place to go if your family loves breakfast. You'll probably have to wait in line for the creative egg dishes and pancakes. Light lunches served, too; (860) 536-2122. Where to get locally caught lobster and other seafood specialties? Follow the crowds to **Abbot's Lobster in the Rough,** 117 Pearl Street, Noank (ten minutes south of Mystic). If it's nice, sit outside at picnic tables that overlook the Sound; (860) 536-7719. **Two Sisters Deli,** 4 Pearl Street, Mystic, serves tasty sandwiches with catchy names (such as Big Sister's Midnight Snack) and delicious desserts. (860) 536-1244. And, yes, there is such a place as **Mystic Pizza**—in fact, there are two: One is on West Main Street in Mystic (860-536-3700); the other is in North Stonington (860-599-3111).

DAY TRIPS

The town of **Essex,** northwest of Mystic, with sea captains' homes lining Main Street, looks much the way it did in the early 1800s. **The Valley Railroad,** Railway Avenue, Route 9, exit 3, offers passengers an old-fashioned, 12-mile steam-train ride through the Connecticut River Valley to Deep River. There you can connect with an optional riverboat cruise or return to Essex. The round-trip train ride takes just under an hour. The combination train and boat trip takes two hours, ten minutes. The regular season is May through October. Fall foliage trips go through late October, and a North Pole Express ride with Santa on board operates in December. Call (860) 767-0103 for schedules.

If you're heading to New York from Mystic, take a break and stop by the **Barnum Museum,** 820 Main Street, Bridgeport. (Take 1-95, exit 27 in Bridgeport.) This lively place is housed in the newly restored original building provided by showman and circus impresario Phineas Taylor

(P.T.) Barnum in 1893 as a home to local historical and scientific societies. Barnum was a local boy, born in Bethel, Connecticut. Among the highlights: a hand-carved scale model of Barnum's "Greatest Show on Earth," a re-created library from Barnum's first Bridgeport mansion, a simulation of Tom Thumb's Bridgeport home, a Punch and Judy Show (Barnum was the first to introduce the puppets to American audiences), plus an exhibit devoted to clowning. One section of the building houses temporary exhibits. Call (860) 331-1104 for information.

FOR MORE INFORMATION

Mystic Chamber of Commerce and Convention and Visitors Bureau, P.O. Box 143, Railroad Depot, Mystic 06355 (860-572-9578), provides information and literature. You may also stop by the Mystic and Shoreline Visitor Information Center, Olde Mistick Village; (860) 536-1641. A map and guide of Mystic coast and country is available from Southeastern Connecticut Tourism District, P.O. Box 89, 27 Masonic Street, New London 06320; (800) 222-6783.

Emergency Numbers

Ambulance, fire, and police: 911

Twenty-four-hour pharmacy: CVS, Long Hill Road (860-446-0912), Groton

Mystic Pharmacy, 17 East Main Street (860-536-8615), is open from 8:00 A.M. to 8:00 P.M. weekdays and 8:00 A.M. to 6:00 P.M. weekends.

Poison Control: (800) 343-2722

Twenty-four-hour emergency room: Lawrence and Memorial Hospital, 365 Montauk Avenue, New London, about 9 miles from Mystic; (860) 442-0711

PORTLAND

In the harbor city of Portland, Maine, seagulls' cries float above the downtown office buildings, and boats take you out to look for whales, to admire the lighthouse, and to sigh at views of the coastline islands. Portland is a family-friendly harbor town that your kids will like. Combine a maritime seaside tour with a day trip to nearby Freeport or Kittery for discounted clothes at the scores of outlet shops.

GETTING THERE

Portland is accessible by land, sea, and air. The Portland International Jetport (207-775-5809) is just ten minutes from downtown and has direct flights from most major cities on the East Coast. A Metro City bus (207-774-0351) will take you from the airport to downtown.

By land arrive via Vermont Transit/Greyhound bus (207- 772-6587), although most bus routes are lengthened by frequent stops. A car is the more convenient option since Portland is just off I-95. For Maine Turnpike travel conditions, call (800) 675-7453.

To spice things up Canadians might want to try taking the M.S. *Scotia Prince* ferry from Nova Scotia. Call (800) 482-0955 in Maine or (800) 341-7540 out of state. Those with their own boats are welcome to stay in private marinas; the harbormaster can be reached at (207) 772-8121.

GETTING AROUND

Portland's old port can and should be explored on foot. To reach points out of walking distance in the greater Portland area, Metro bus services (207-774-0351) and taxis are available. Town Taxi runs twenty-four hours a day; (207) 773-1711. If you want to explore greater Portland by car, several rental agencies are located near the airport, including Avis (800-225-9065), Budget (207-774-8663), and Thrifty (207-772-4628).

WHAT TO SEE AND DO

Museums and Historical Sites

One of the best things to do in Portland is to meander around Old Port, exploring the harbor by foot and boarding one of the tour boats. (See Shopping and Special Tours.)

Downtown Portland also features several historical buildings that are open to the public. Most are only open seasonally from June to October, so be sure to call in advance.

Portland Museum of Art, 7 Congress Square, Portland; (207) 775-6148. Come here to view artists' renditions of the surrounding sea and landscapes. Maine's largest art museum, it features works by Winslow Homer, Edward Hopper, and Andrew Wyeth.

The Portland Head Light, 1000 Shore Road, Cape Elizabeth; (207) 799-2661. The oldest lighthouse in the state towers over a classic Maine scene: a windswept rocky coast with waves breaking into sprays of whitecaps. This impressive structure, located just outside Portland in Cape Elizabeth, is the most photographed light in the world. The lighthouse, which George Washington ordered to be lit in 1791, has a new museum that opened in July of 1993. Located in the former keeper's house, the museum at Portland Head Light details the history of this lighthouse as well as that of Fort Williams, the adjacent park that was once home to the Coast Artillery Core.

Kids will like listening to the boom of the foghorn and browsing through the small exhibit to uncover such secrets as the details of famous wrecks, how the lenses magnified the light, and what life as a keeper was like in the nineteenth century when Joshua Freeman Strout and his family tended the beacon. According to newspaper reports of the day, keeper Strout gave visitors "as fine a glass of wine as ever was poured down the neck of an alderman."

Other finds: Fresnel lenses, photographs of storms, and a series of —what else—lights illustrate the location of other Maine lighthouses. Allow time for the gift shop with its kid-pleasing array of stickers and magnets. Be sure to bring a picnic lunch to take advantage of the adjacent park with its sea views and acres for romping.

Portland Observatory, 138 Congress Street, Portland, (207) 774-5561. This signal tower, built in 1807 for merchants and shipowners,

---

Portland at a Glance

- Coastal fun and great shopping in a New England port city

- Portland Head light, the most photographed lighthouse in the world

- Several harbor cruises to choose from

- L.L. Bean and dozens of outlet stores are in nearby Freeport

- Day trips to many coastal towns

- Convention and Visitors Bureau of Greater Portland, (207) 772-5800; Maine Office of Tourism, (207) 289-5710

---

offers a great view of the city, bay, and the White Mountains. It is open from June to October.

Children's Museum of Maine, 142 Free Street, Portland, (207) 828-1234. It features hands-on art and science exhibits.

Tate House, 1270 Westbrook Street, Portland (207-774-9781), provides another glimpse into Portland's maritime history. Take a tour of this Georgian house, constructed in 1755 by George Tate, for an inside view of a Colonial merchant's home.

The Victoria Mansion, 109 Danforth Street (207-772-4841), is also known as the Morse-Libby House. With its stone towers it reminds some kids of the manse in "the Addams Family." Built 1858-1860 this Italianate home with its elaborate staircase and furnishings will interest your kids if they go wide-eyed at the sight of mansions.

Wadsworth-Longfellow House, 485 Congress Street, Portland; (207) 774-1822. Poetry enthusiasts might want to visit the childhood home of poet Henry Wadsworth Longfellow. Built in 1785 by his grandfather, the home still includes family furniture.

The **Maine Narrow Gauge Railroad Co. & Museum,** 58 Fore Street; (207) 828–0814. Preschoolers and grade-schoolers like the ride aboard these historic trains and enjoy looking at the railroad cars built for narrow-gauge rails.

Other Attractions

Fun places to take the younger children are **Funtown U.S.A.,** 774 Portland Road; Saco (207–284–5139 or 284–7113), with Kiddie Bumper Boats, the longest and tallest log flume ride in New England, and Canoe Adventure River; at **Discovery Zone,** Foden Road and Western Avenue (207–772–KIDS), children twelve and under climb foam mountains, swim in the giant ball baths, and test their orientation skills in the maze.

Performing Arts

Add some culture to your visit. The Portland Concert Association, 262 Cumberland Avenue, Portland (207–772–8630 or 800–639–2707), offers dance, opera, theater, and music presentations. Theater buffs should check out Portland Stage Company, 25A Forest Avenue; (207) 774–0465. The Portland Symphony Orchestra performs at 30 Myrtle Street; (207) 773–8191 or (800) 639–2309.

Don't forget the **State Theatre,** 609 Congress Street (207–897–1112), located in Portland's Arts District, a premier concert hall and dinner theater with concerts, movies, and theater performances. The ninety-seat intimate atmosphere of **Oak Street Theatre,** 92 Oak Street (207–775–5103), holds professional theater performances for adults and children alike.

Special Tours

Harbor Cruise. What's a Maine vacation without some time on the sea? Seasonally—from about June through Columbus Day—several ships offer either scenic or whale-watching cruises. Check out the kiosks along Commercial Street for a line and a time that suits your schedule. Bay View Cruises, 184 Commercial Street (207–761–0496), adds a nice touch to their scenic tours by bringing bread on board for the kids to feed to the seagulls who swoop down, catching the pieces in mid-air to the giggles of all. Casco Bay Lines, Commercial and Franklin Streets, Portland (207–774–7871), is another option. Scenic autumn

A trip to Portland Head Light is a treat for the whole family. (Courtesy Portland Convention and Visitors Bureau)

foliage cruises (dress warmly) let you admire the coast as our Founding Fathers did—from the deck of a ship.

A cruise is a wise option for the afternoon, a time when kids are often tired and cranky. Instead of dragging them off to yet another museum, lounge on deck by the rail, listen to the ninety-minute narrated tour, and admire the scenery, including the ruins of the old forts and the panoramic sea view of the Portland Head Light. Along the way look for seals and admire the shoreline.

Take the family to sea with **Olde Port Mariner Fleet,** Commercial Street (207-775-0727, 642-3270, or 800-437-3270), which departs from Long Wharf. Three boats offer whale watches, with chances to spot white-sided dolphins, humpbacks, and finbacks, as well as a dinner cruise of a pre-prepared buffet, and other excursions.

The adventurous may want to go wild or mild with **Crab Apples Whitewater,** HC 63 Box 25, The Forks (800-553-RAFT or 207-663-4491), which has a great trip for families. Raft on the Dead River from June through August. Minimum age is nine years. For more rafting try **Eastern River Expeditions,** Box 1173, Moosehead

Lake, Greenville (800-634-RAFT), with four to six passenger rafts and kayaks. Even the inexperienced can receive skilled instruction from guides.

A unique way to tour Maine's wilderness is through **Captain Steve Randall,** 16 Thomas Drive, Scarborough (207-883-2148), an official Maine Guide. His twenty-year outdoor experience—and a background that includes degrees in photography and electronics, as well as graduation from Hurricane Island Outward Bound—will unmistakably leave a lasting memory. Explore tidal pools in the 15,000-year-old Salt Marsh, or try fishing for bass and trout in Maine's secret fishing spots.

Shopping

Old Port. Be sure to meander through Old Port, an area of boutiques, interesting shops, and restaurants just across Commercial Street from the harbor. This is the place to let your kids spend their allowance on inexpensive pleasures. Stroll along Exchange Street to **Something Fishy,** 22 Exchange Street (207-774-7726), for a fine selection of T-shirts. Try **Abacus American Crafts,** 44 Exchange Street (207-772-4880), for unusual and affordable pins, platters, boxes, and other crafty pleasures.

Stein's Glass Gallery, 20 Milk Street (207-772-9072), sports an eye-catching array of swirled and rainbow-colored goblets, bowls, and sculpture. **The Maine Potters' Market** at Fore and Moulton streets (207-771-1633) is a cooperative shop representing people from around the state. They sell a wide selection of mugs, dishes, candle holders, and lots more. **Painted Horse,** 184 Middle Street (207-871-1770), has unique high-quality toys, while **Skytoyz,** 388 Fore Street (207-828-0911), has kites and playthings.

SPECIAL EVENTS

Fairs and Festivals

When the long Maine winter finally comes to a close, Maine is ready to celebrate. Festivals abound in the summertime, and the visitor's guide has a complete calendar.

June: The Old Port Festival features crafts, food, and entertainment for the family. Explore Maine's rich maritime heritage at the Waterfront Festival.

July: Maine Summer Fest and the Yarmouth Clam Festival, often a classy affair, offer clams galore and quality entertainment. The Maine Lobster Festival in Rockland in August is for lobster lovers.

August: The Maine Festival of the Arts, Thomas Point Beach, Brunswick (207-772-9012), includes demonstrations and live music. Six-Alive's Sidewalk Arts Festival features artists from around the country. Spring Point Festival includes a mock Civil War encampment. There's also the Italian Street Festival, and Art in the Park, which brings together artists from the Eastern Seaboard.

Other summer activities include noontime performances through the downtown area: music, mime, and dance. Call (207) 772-6828.

September: Fall brings the Thomas Point Beach Bluegrass Festival in Brunswick (207-725-6009); call for a listing of performers. Country fairs abound, including the Common Ground Country Fair in Windsor and the Cumberland Fair.

October: Fall for Art (207-772-9012). Maine Audubon Society's Apple Cider Day offers a taste of autumn.

November: Try the United Maine Craft Shows for holiday shopping.

December: The holiday season puts Portland back in a festive mode. Tree-lighting ceremonies in most towns, Portland Symphony Orchestra Christmas Concerts, and Christmas at the Victoria Mansion. If you're in town for the new year, go to New Year's Portland downtown for a nonalcoholic celebration for the whole family.

WHERE TO STAY

Portland offers a variety of accommodations. The **Portland Regency,** 20 Mile Street, Portland (207-774-4200 or 800-727-3436), is in the heart of Old Port. It offers family-friendly lodging in a renovated century-old armory. Another possibility is the **Radisson Eastland Plaza Hotel,** 157 High Street (207-775-5411 or 800-333-3333). Recently renovated, it offers a harbor view. The **Hotel Everett,** 51A Oak Street, Portland (207-773-7882), has low rates.

Many major chain hotels are in Portland including the **Holiday Inn by the Bay** (207-775-2311 or 800-HOLIDAY), **Sheraton Inn** (207-775-6161), **Marriott** (207-871-8000), and **Howard Johnson's** (207-774-5861).

Bed and breakfast lodgings are available too. Try the **Inn on Carleton,** 46 Carleton Street (207-775-1910), and **Keller's B & B,** Island Avenue (207-766-2441). Both welcome children. For more information on places to stay, call the Maine Convention and Visitors Bureau at (207) 272-5800.

If you're roughing it, the Maine State Parks has campground reservations; call (207) 287-3824 or (800) 332-1501 in Maine. The Maine Campground Owners Association can be reached at (207) 782-5874.

Mountain Spring Farm, 429 Elmwood Road, Pownal (207-688-4023), is a bed and breakfast in a twenty-acre country setting 4 miles from Freeport. Year-round activities include a skating pond, trails for horseback riding, hiking, or cross-country skiing, and a Kid's Room.

WHERE TO EAT

Hungry? **DiMillo's,** on Long Wharf (207-772-2216), is a floating, somewhat touristy restaurant, but it offers a dockside array of reasonably priced sandwiches and soups. Your kids may like the novelty of eating on deck. At **Carbur's Restaurant,** 123 Middle Street (207-772-7794), grab a moderately priced hamburger and some Victorian ambiance in this renovated 1877 commercial building. Other recommended Portland restaurants include **Village Cafe,** 112 Newbury Street (207-772-5320), for steaks and seafood at reasonable prices, and for wholesome family food, try **Raff's** and **Emily K's Rotisserie Chicken,** 285 Forest Avenue (207-773-7763).

Try **Two Lights Lobster Shack,** 225 Two Lights Road, Cape Elizabeth (207-799-1677), offers lobster stew and fried seafood, and, for other offerings, **Eastside Marios,** 390 Gorham Road, South Portland (207-772-0700).

A more extensive listing of area restaurants can be found in the Greater Portland, Maine Convention & Visitor's Bureau visitor's guide.

DAY TRIPS

Portland is an excellent base for day trips to quaint old villages dotting the shoreline as well as to the mountains of Maine and New Hampshire.

Freeport, Maine. Freeport is outlet heaven. About twenty minutes north of Portland, you can get discounts on almost everything. Some back-to-school bests include J. Crew, at Down Outlet. Parents will find such fashion staples as Calvin Klein, Coach, and Polo/Ralph Lauren. And if you've spent time all these years browsing through the catalogues and imagining yourself a stalwart Mainelander, be sure to visit L.L. Bean (207-865-4761 or 800-341-4341), which is open twenty-four hours a day, 365 days a year. For a Freeport map call the Freeport Merchants Association at (207) 865-1212.

Kittery, a little farther than Freeport, is about an hour south of Portland on routes 95 and 1. Kittery offers more discount stores for the die-hard outlet shopper.

Kennebunkport, a household word after George Bush's presidency, is only about thirty minutes away. This nineteenth-century village created by merchants and seamen boasts authentic Victorian mansions. Stroll around Dock Square, stocked with shops, art galleries, and restaurants.

Ogunquit, forty-five minutes away on routes 95 and 1, is a village option for art enthusiasts. An artists' colony today, there is also a beach, so don't forget your bathing suit.

Maine Maritime Museum, 243 Washington Street, Bath; (207) 443-1316. About a forty-minute drive this museum is worth a stop. Located on ten acres along the Kennebec River on the site of a former shipyard, the museum offers both wildlife cruises and lobster bakes in-season, along with several buildings of nautical lore. Some of the buildings offer intriguing exhibits, such as one on lobstermen: Boats, traps, buoys, and a video tell the story of this Maine folk staple. Other buildings may disappoint with static displays and cursory explanations, but your kids will learn something by browsing in the Mill and Joiner's Shop, which tells how a keel was built and what riggers' tools were needed.

The Maritime History Building has an eclectic collection that includes ship models, art, and several early navigational devices. Be sure to find the World Trade Game, a kid-friendly way to learn about nineteenth-century sea trade. Spin the pointer and your trade ship may face such perils as desertion, mutiny, or man overboard.

The Calendar Islands, scattered throughout Casco Bay, once numbered 365, bringing about their name. These tiny worlds can be toured with the Casco Bay Lines ferry; call (207) 774-7871.

Western Mountains and Lakes Region. It takes less than an hour on Route 302 to reach the White Mountains. Take a hike in summer or fall for a new perspective of the Atlantic Ocean and wash the salt off your body in the freshwater lakes. For more information call Maine State Parks at (207) 287-3824 or (800) 332-1501 in Maine; and also the Department of Inland Fisheries and Wildlife at (207) 287-2871.

Bethel, Maine. Steve Crone, proprietor of the **Telemark Inn,** RFD 2, Box 800, Bethel, Maine 04217 (207-836-2703), offers wonderful outings for families. In summer he has three-day llama trek trips, which take families through nearby New Hampshire's White Mountains. Encouraged by Crone, even four-year-olds enjoy leading their own llama. The comforts in camp—guides pitch your tents, cook your food, and even awaken you with hot coffee and warm towels—make the backcountry accessible to a wide range of ages from kindergartners to octogenarians. Crone also combines a llama trek with a canoe expedition. In winter at his plain but comfortable inn, he offers cross-country skiing and dog-jorring (dog sledding without the sled).

FOR MORE INFORMATION

Be sure to obtain a visitor's guide from the Convention & Visitors Bureau of Greater Portland, 305 Commercial Street, Portland (207-772-5800). The guide includes a map and a calendar of events. Other sources of information are Portland Recreation (207-874-8793), the Maine Office of Tourism (207-289-5710), and the Maine Publicity Bureau (800-533-9595), which provides information on state events including foliage and ski condition reports. You can reach AAA at (207) 774-6377.

Local newspapers give a glimpse of less touristy events. The *Portland Press Herald* lists daily city events, and the *Maine Sunday Telegram* has a comprehensive weekly listing. Call (207) 791-6000.

Emergency Numbers

Ambulance fire, and police: 911

Maine Medical Center, 22 Bramhall Street, Portland; (207) 871-0111

Mercy Hospital, 144 State Street, Portland; (207) 879-3000

Poison Hotline: (800) 442-6305

Portland Police: (207) 874-8300

Rite Aid Discount Pharmacy (open until 9:00 P.M.), 713 Congress Street, Portland; (207) 774-8456

ALLEGHENY NATIONAL FOREST

The Allegheny National Forest offers families fresh air, recreation, and beautiful natural surroundings. Comprising more than 500,000 acres that stretch across the rugged plateaus of northwestern Pennsylvania's Elk, McKean, Forest, and Warren counties, the Allegheny National Forest has another bonus. Since this area isn't highly promoted, you'll find fewer crowds here than in the Poconos. To explore the forest choose between camping in one of its sixteen campgrounds or staying in one of the small communities on the fringes.

GETTING THERE

The forest's northern borders are just 40 miles south of the New York–Pennsylvania line. It's within easy driving distance from Buffalo to the north, Pittsburgh to the south, Erie to the northwest, and the Youngstown–Akron–Cleveland areas to the west. The following are considered gateways—areas where you can find food, lodging, and services.

Western gateway: the town of Warren, in Warren County, a major stop for visitors touring along U.S. 6, called "the Grand Army of the Republic Highway," or GAR, and considered one of the most scenic routes in the United States. In July 1994 the U.S. Department of Interior designated U.S. Route 6 as a National Recreation Trail. The transcontinental highway, U.S. 6, is the second longest highway and stretches from Provincetown, Cape Cod, to Bishop, California.

Eastern gateway: Ridgway, in Elk County.

Northern gateway: Bradford, in McKean County.

Southern gateway: Tionesta, in Forest County (twenty minutes from I–80).

Allegheny National Forest at a Glance

- 500,000 unspoiled acres in northwestern Pennsylvania

- 170 miles of forest trails

- Four beaches along the Allegheny River

- Sixteen forest-service campgrounds

- Several kid-friendly inns and B&Bs

- Forest service, (814) 723-5150

Commuter flights from Pittsburgh arrive at Bradford Regional Airport, Mount Alton, McKean County (814–368-4928). Rental cars and taxis are available at the airport. There is no Amtrak service to this area.

GETTING AROUND

Within the forest cars have access to more than 500 miles of roads. In addition, there are ATV trails, groomed snowmobile trails, hiking trails, and six boat launches. **Note:** Be particularly careful during rainy weather since about half of the forest region is served by dirt roads.

ATA (Area Transportation Authority, 800-822-3232—Pennsylvania or 814-965-3211) provides public transportation in Elk and McKean counties.

WHAT TO SEE AND DO

The Forest

First, get your bearings. The main forest office is at 222 Liberty Street, downtown Warren; (814) 723-5150, TTY (814) 726-2710 for the hearing impaired. Four ranger stations dispense maps and information about activities and facilities within their region:

Southwest: Marienville Ranger District, Highway 66; (814) 927-6628.

Northwest: Sheffield District, Kane Road, U.S. 6; (814) 968-3232.

Northeast: Bradford District, Kinzua Heights, Highways 59 and 321; (814) 362-4613.

Southeast: Ridgway District, Montmorenci Road, State Highway 94B; (814) 776-6172.

In addition, the U.S. Corps of Engineers, which operates the Kinzua Dam, run an information center at Kinzua Point (814- 729-1291), on Route 59, at the junction of 262 (Forest Road). This center is open from Memorial Day to Labor Day.

Swimming, Boating, Fishing

The 27-mile Allegheny Reservoir on the upper Allegheny River stretches over the border to New York's Allegany State Park. The Reservoir is the hub of summer recreation in the forest: Kinzua and Kiasutha, two of the forest's four beaches, are located here. (The other beaches are at Loleta and Twin Lakes.) No, you won't be alone. In summer this area is extremely popular with tourists, especially those who love boating and fishing. Some of the state's record fish were caught in reservoir waters. First, however, obtain a state fishing license.

An 85-mile stretch of the Allegheny River, from the Kinzua Dam to Oil City, is a recreational waterway, attracting pleasure and fishing boats. In April of 1992 Congress designated approximately 85 miles of the Allegheny River as a "wild and scenic river." A number of boat launches within the forest provide access to the reservoir's waters. Major sections of this stretch, including seven uninhabited islands perfect for picnics and wildlife viewing, are serviced by Allegheny Outfitters (814-723-1203), a Warren canoe-rental outfit. The company suggests three itineraries that range from 6^7/$_{10}$ to 15^7/$_{10}$ miles, or they'll be glad to plan a route that suits your needs. The 17-foot canoes accommodate two adults and two children.

The Kinzua-Wolf Run Marina, 11 miles east of Warren on Route 59 (814-726-1650), rents canoes, rowboats, and motorboats, and also offers forty-five-minute, scenic, narrated tours of the reservoir aboard

More than 170 miles of forest trails wind through the forest, meadows, and glens that comprise the Allegheny National Forest. (Courtesy Pennsylvania Bureau of Travel Marketing)

a twenty-passenger paddle wheeler, the *Kinzua Queen*. Visit Docksiders Cafe and enjoy casual dining, with a spectacular view.

The reservoir beaches are unsupervised, and parents are urged to keep a vigilant watch on their children because Kinzua's shorelines have steep, sudden drop-offs. In addition, because of fluctuating water levels, swimmers may encounter such hazards as submerged stumps, logs, and rocks, especially near the shoreline.

Families with young children are better off using the beach at Chapman State Park; (814) 723–0250. Although it's in the heart of the forest, the 805-acre park near Warren, off Route 6, is a separate entity. Chapman has a sixty-eight-acre lake on the west branch of Tionesta Creek. Its beach, which is free, is the only one within the forest region with lifeguards. Chapman is accessible to people with disabilities. There are two fishing docks for the handicapped at opposite ends of Chapman Lake. In the swimming area on the southeast side of the lake is a handicapped swimming pier, which can be accessed without a wheelchair. The carpeted deck and hand rails allow a handicapped person to slide down into the shallow water. The kids' area is 1 foot deep, and the adult area is 3 feet deep.

On busy days the park holds four designated sites with electric hookups for the handicapped until late in the day. Those with a state handicapped sticker can use all the service roads to drive up to activity areas. Stickers are available at the park's entrance. Several picnic sites have accessible picnic tables. Naturalists also tailor programs to be accessible.

In addition, Chapman hosts a variety of Junior Naturalist programs for kids and activities for families. Check the weekly newsletter for details.

Hiking

There are about 170 miles of forest trails that wind through dense forest, meadows, and glens. You're sure to spot some wildlife along the way, perhaps a muskrat, raccoon, or birds (even bald eagles have been spotted at Kinzua Dam).

White-tail deer, black bears, and wild turkeys also live here, and this is a popular spot for hunting from late October to early January. This is a good time to avoid hiking in the woods, or wear hunter orange for safety. In addition, there may be some kind of bird or game hunting throughout most of the year. May, for example, is spring gobbler season. Campsites have "safety zones," but exercise extreme caution. Before setting off for a hike, ask the park rangers about safety precautions and hunting seasons. For more information on hunting, contact the Pennsylvania Game Commission, 2001 Elmerton Avenue, Harrisburg 17110-9797; (717) 787–4250.

The North Country National Scenic Trail, 86⅔ miles, winds through the forest's rich landscapes and is part of a 3,200-mile National Scenic Trail which, when completed, will extend from Crown Point, New York, to Lake Sakawea, North Dakota. The trail is divided into ten segments that range from 2³⁄₁₀ to 13³⁄₁₀ miles. A map listing services and toilet facilities is available from the forest's headquarters. Young children—or anyone who prefers shorter, "tamer" walks—will enjoy the interpretive trails at many of the campgrounds.

Scenic Overlooks

The forest is beautiful to explore year-round, particularly during the brilliant fall foliage season, and in June when the fragrant laurel, Pennsylvania's state flower, blossoms. Both Jakes Rocks and Rimrock scenic overlooks, above the Kinzua Dam east of Warren, offer fabulous views of the Allegheny Reservoir, Kinzua Dam, and the forest. Both have walking trails, rest rooms, and picnic facilities. These overlooks are day-use areas; camping is not permitted.

Camping

The Forest Service operates sixteen campgrounds. Of the ten located along the Allegheny River shoreline, six can be accessed only by boat. You can reserve sites in most campgrounds by calling the national Reservation Service at (800) 280–2267. Some campgrounds, however, are on a first-come basis. Reservations for family sites can be made ten to 120 days in advance. Obtain local campground information by calling the Kinzua Point Information Center at (814) 726-1291. The Kiasutha Recreation Area is particularly popular, with ninety-two sites, flush toilets, showers, a play area, swimming beach, and interpretive trails. Some facilities remain open before and after the regular summer season (Memorial Day to Labor Day weekends) but with limited service.

Some families prefer camping in Chapman State Park (see above) since no alcoholic beverages or pets are allowed, creating what some feel is a more wholesome family atmosphere.

Winter Sports

Treat the kids to a sleigh ride in the forest's Tidioute area every January and February weekend, snow permitting. Call (814) 484-3441 or 484-7484 to reserve. For downhill sledding and tobogganing, Chapman State Park keeps a hill lit until 10:00 P.M. nightly. Snowmobiling is permitted on designated routes within the forest from December 20 to April 1. Snowmobiles and ATVs must be registered with the state or be registered in a state that is reciprocal. Registration dollars are used to maintain ATV and snowmobile trails and provide groomed snowmobile trails. A trail connects to New York's Allegany State Park. There are numerous cross-country ski trails, such as those in Forest County, where the Buzzard Swamp Cross-Country Ski Area offers $7\frac{2}{5}$ miles of ungroomed beginner's trails in a forest studded with ponds. To get here take the road in the center of Marienville, the road between the Uni-Mart and the Bucktail Hotel. This is Forest Road 130. Follow this for 3 miles and turn onto Forest Road 376.

Performing Arts

The Library Theatre Summer Playhouse, 102 Third Avenue, West Warren, is a professional troupe that performs musicals and dramas from late June to late July. Call (814) 723-7231.

Shopping

It's great fun browsing around **America's First Christmas Store,** Main Street, Route 6, Smethport (McKean County). What started as a pharmacy in 1932 turned into a Christmas display business, which, at its peak, shipped outdoor displays to every state in the United States. Four rooms feature decorated trees, dolls, bears, stained-glass scenes, and other holiday delights. Call (814) 887-5792.

SPECIAL EVENTS

Contact the individual county tourist associations listed below for more information on activities in their area. Here's a sampling.

June: Forest Fest, activities centered in and around the Allegheny National Forest. Free camping and swimming the first weekend, picnicking, fishing contests, nature hikes, boat rides, interpretive walks.

July: Elk "Hunt," Benezette, Elk County. Twelve elk silhouettes are hidden in the forest. The hunt starts at dawn until midafternoon; successful "hunters" receive prizes. Black Cherry Festival, Kane, McKean County, parade, family and children's activities, entertainment.

August: Elk County Fair, Fairgrounds, Kersey, includes magic shows, music, rides, games, food, and more. Warren County Fair, Pittsfield, large agricultural fair includes tractor and horse pulls.

WHERE TO STAY

If camping isn't your family's forte, visit the forest by day and stay at night in comfortable lodgings in nearby towns. There are several lodgings on the forest's borders—ranging from national chains to cozy bed and breakfasts that welcome kids.

McKean County

Blackberry Inn Bed & Breakfast, 820 West Main Street, Junction U.S. 6 and PA 59, Smethport, is a restored Victorian home with five guest rooms that share two full bathrooms. There's a parlor with TV, two large porches, and a yard where the kids can romp. Full breakfasts are included. Call (814) 887-7777.

Kane Manor Country Inn, 230 Clay Street, welcomes families to its 1897 inn with ten guest rooms. The gathering room has a grand piano, loads of books, and great views of the mountains and the Kinzua Valley. On weekdays a continental breakfast is served, while on weekends there's a full breakfast, including teddy bear pancakes for the kids. Hiking and cross-country trails are nearby. Call (814) 837-6522.

The Christmas Inn, Route 6, Smethport, one of the area's mansions, is now an inn. Call (800) 653-6200.

Warren County
Holiday Inn, Routes 6 and 62, Warren, has an indoor pool, restaurant, and a nightclub; (814) 726-3000.

WHERE TO EAT

You'll find a selection of eateries in all gateway areas. In Kane (McKean County), **Papa Nick's Family Restaurant,** 316 Chase Street, offers casual Italian American meals, plus a kid's menu. Call (814) 837-6652. At Ridgway, 25 miles from I-80 (exit 16) at the southeastern corner, grab a burger, fries, or submarine sandwich at **The Original Italian Pizza,** 161 Main Street; (814) 772-7576. There's a jukebox, too. **The Jefferson House and Pub,** 119 Market Street, U.S. 62, Warren, serves mainly mesquite grilled food in a restored 1890 home. There's a kid's menu. Call (814) 723-2288.

In Elk County the **Bavarian Inn,** which is also a motel, 33 St. Mary's Street, St. Mary's (814-834-2167), serves German food. In Bradford, McKean County, **Shady Point Family Restaurant,** North Farley Street, Route 6, offers daily specials, homemade soups, and pies. The only drawback is the sometimes slow service. Call (814) 837-7361.

DAY TRIPS

Knox, Kane, Kinzua Railroad operates June through October. This steam-and-diesel train travels through the peaks and valleys of the Allegheny National Forest and across the historic Kinzua Bridge. Built in 1892, this bridge is one of the world's highest railroad bridges. If you leave from Marienville in Forest County, the round trip is 96 miles; from Kane in McKean County, the round trip is 32 miles, a better option with young kids. You can order a box lunch for a small additional fee. Call (814) 927-6621.

The train stops before crossing the bridge so that those passengers afraid of heights may disembark. Then the train turns around and picks those passengers up.

Evergreen Enchanted Playground, Evergreen Park, Chestnut Street, in the town of Kane (McKean County), is delightfully creative. Your kids will love the dragon, wolf den, tire net, tree fort, pirate ship with gangplank, suspension bridge, and several mazes, slides, swings, and ramps.

FOR MORE INFORMATION

For National Forest information and literature, contact: Forest Service, USDA, P.O. Box 847, Warren, Pennsylvania 16365; (814) 723-5150, TTY (814) 726-2710. For information on Chapman State Park, located within the forest, contact RD 1, Box 1610, Clarendon, Pennsylvania 16313-9607; (814) 723-0250.

The tourist associations in gateway areas provide information on lodging, restaurants, and local attractions.

Elk County Visitor's Bureau, P.O. Box 838, St. Marys, Pennsylvania 15857; (814) 834-3711.

Seneca Highlands Association (McKean) Box G, Custer City, Pennsylvania 16725; (814) 368-9370.

Forest County Tourist Promotion Agency, P.O. Box 608, Tionesca, Pennsylvania 16353; (814) 927-8818/(800) 222-1706 in Pennsylvania only.

Northern Alleghenies (Warren County), 315 Second Avenue, P.O. Box 804, Warren, Pennsylvania 16365; (814) 726-1222/(800) 624-7802.

Emergency Numbers

As some of these areas may be switching to 911 numbers, consult the front pages of the phone book in the area where you are staying for the most up-to-date information on ambulance, fire, and police.

Elk County Police: (814) 776-6136

Elk County fire and ambulance: (814) 772-0000

Emergency Rescue Squad: (814) 723-4220

Forest County Police: (814) 755-3565

Forest County fire and ambulance: (814) 755-3200

McKean County Police: (814) 778-5555. Most, but not all of McKean County is tied into the 911 system for fire and ambulance. Check the front of the phone book.

Warren County ambulance, fire, and police: 911

Warren County Sheriff: 723-7553

Warren County State Police: (814) 723-8880

If you are in a National Forest campsite, the site's host can summon emergency help. Area hospitals with a twenty-four-hour emergency room include:

Elk County: Andrew Kaul Memorial Hospital, 763 Johnsonburg Road, St. Marys; (814) 781-7500; Elk County General Hospital, Ridgway; (814) 776-6111

McKean County: Bradford Regional Medical Center, 115 I-Parkway, Bradford; (814) 368-4143

Warren County: Warren General Hospital, Two Crescent Park, Warren; (814) 723-3300

Poison Control: (412) 681-6669 (Pittsburgh)

There are no twenty-four-hour pharmacies in the area, although several have after-hour emergency numbers. Ott & McHenry, 102 Main Street, Bradford (McKean County), is open weekdays from 8:30 A.M. to 8:00 P.M., closing at 6:00 P.M. on Saturday. Sunday hours are 10:00 A.M. to 1:00 P.M. Call (814) 362-3827. After-hours emergency number: (814) 368-7361.

Maryland

BALTIMORE

Baltimore, nicknamed "Charm City," has lots to recommend it, including personality. With its dazzling Inner Harbor, new but old-style baseball stadium, top-notch art museums, the winding waterfront of Fells Point and lots of ethnic neighborhoods, Baltimore is very different —but no less alluring—than its neighbor, Washington, D.C., less than one hour away. Instead of a planned, grand design for the ages, Baltimore exudes a down-to-earth hominess that adds, what else, charm to the historic sites, children's attractions, and educational museums.

GETTING THERE

The Baltimore/Washington International Airport (410-859-7100) is a fifteen-minute drive from downtown Baltimore. The BWI Airport Van Shuttle (410-859-7545) escorts visitors to many Inner Harbor hotels for reasonable rates. Taxis are also available.

Amtrak trains stop at Baltimore's Penn Central Railroad Station, North Charles Street, between Oliver and Lanvale streets. Call (800) 872-7245. For day trips to points between Washington, D.C., and Baltimore during the week, including Camden Yards and Penn Station, the MARC commuter train (800-325-RAIL) offers inexpensive service and frequent departures.

Bus travelers arrive at the Greyhound/Trailway terminals, 210 West Lafayette Street, and the Baltimore Travel Plaza. For information call (410) 744-9311.

By car Baltimore is easily reached by I-95 from the north or south, and I-70 and U.S. 40 from the west.

GETTING AROUND

Much of Baltimore, including the newly renovated waterfront and Fells Point, can be reached on foot. For cold days and weary feet, however, there are several transportation possibilities. To avoid the challenge of navigating the many one-way streets in Baltimore by car, visitors should consider the Metro, a limited subway system that runs until midnight, or the Mass Transit Administration (MTA) bus lines, which run twenty-four hours. MTA offers a one-day Tourist Passport for unlimited travel downtown. For fare and route information, call (410) 539-5000.

The Water Taxi (410-563-3901 or 800-658-8947) is an enjoyable way to reach points along Baltimore's Inner Harbor, including Fells Point, Little Italy, and the Aquarium. Inexpensive all-day passes are available for adults and children. Another entertaining possibility for children is the trolley servicing the downtown region. Call (410) 752-2015 for more information.

A car is also handy. Driving around Baltimore is easy, as street signs are easy to read, and routes are marked. The trick to remember is that many of Baltimore's main streets are one-way.

WHAT TO SEE AND DO

Inner Harbor Attractions

If you have limited time in the city, head for the Inner Harbor, where many of the family attractions are located. Park the car, as you can walk to everything. You will easily find a day's worth of attractions here, if not more.

National Aquarium in Baltimore, Pier 3, 501 East Pratt Street; (410) 576-3800. This world-class aquarium alone merits a trip to Baltimore's Inner Harbor. The several stories of exhibits in this aquarium offer everything from shark tanks to a rain forest, and the facility houses more than 5,000 specimens.

Discover the world's aquatic life at the twelve major displays. Highlights include Wings Under Water, the largest ray exhibit in the nation, featuring cow-nose rays and blunt-nose rays, among others. The Open Ocean exhibit, a.k.a. the Shark Tank, is home to sand tigers, nurses, and sandbar sharks; the kids will love this one for its easy-but-safe access to the ferocious-looking fish. The Atlantic Coral Reef, a coral reef re-created in fiberglass, features colorful tropical fish, and the South American rain forest demonstrates a wealth of plant and animal

---

Baltimore at a Glance

- A charming, down-to-earth city with lots of personality

- The National Aquarium in Baltimore and the Maryland Science center are just two of Inner Harbor's attractions

- Tons of trains at the B&O Railroad Museum

- Four first-rate art museums

- Two professional sports teams

- Baltimore Area Convention and Visitors Bureau, (800) 282-6632 or (410) 837-4636

---

life with more than 600 species of tropical plants, plus parrots, sloths, and a fish tank that includes piranha. Maryland: Mountains to the Sea displays such local creatures as bullfrogs, softshell turtles, flounders, and blue crabs.

Be sure to take in an enlightening dolphin show at the Marine Mammal Pavilion's 1.2-million-gallon pool, where you'll learn about the behavior of beluga whales and bottle-nose dolphins.

Maryland Science Center, 601 Light Street (410-685-5225), entertains all ages with its hands-on exhibits. At the exhibit on Maryland's Chesapeake Bay, look at tiny baby crayfish under a microscope, and find out about the life of a blue crab. The Hubble Space Telescope opens kids' eyes to the skies while Energy Place lets them use their bodies to generate electricity.

Take young children, ages two to seven, to K.I.D.S., a room with blocks, play areas, and appropriate hands-on items. The Davis Planetarium's sky show will leave your kids starry-eyed, and any of the educational, but usually entertaining, movies at the IMAX Theater are a big hit since the screen is five stories tall. The programs at both the planetarium and the IMAX theater are included in the price of admission.

Three of the friends you will meet at the National Aquarium in Baltimore.
(Photo by George Grall/courtesy National Aquarium in Baltimore)

What's an Inner Harbor without some maritime lore and actual ships? Baltimore has three noteworthy vessels that the curious can board. The **Baltimore Maritime Museum,** Pier 3, Pratt Street (410-396-3854), is a floating museum that consists of three ships: a 1940s submarine, U.S.S. *Torsk,* and the Lightship *Chesapeake,* and the Coast Guard cutter the *Taney,* the last remaining ship to have survived the attack on Pearl Harbor. All are open for self-guided tours. The *Torsk* submarine is distinguished for sinking the last Japanese warship in World War II. A walk through these narrow corridors lets kids know just how cramped life under the sea can be. The *Chesapeake's* beacon lantern served as a floating lighthouse in areas where rocks or shoals made the construction of a stationary lighthouse impossible. Quarters were tight here, too, and talk was often punctuated by the blast of foghorns.

The U.S. frigate *Constellation* should be back at the Inner Harbor Constellation Dock soon. This National Historic Landmark, the first commissioned ship of the U.S. Navy, launched in 1797, is in dry dock.

For some pure play try **Art Links Baltimore,** at the Power Plant, 601 East Pratt Street (no phone). The artist-designed holes at this miniature golf course feature such regional themes as a crab feast, a Preakness winner's circle, and Edgar Allan Poe's Nevermore.

For a literal overview of Baltimore, check out the view twenty-seven stories up at the Top of the World observation level and museum in the World Trade Center, 401 East Pratt Street; (410) 837-4515. The museum features exhibits on the port and the city's history and economic development. Top of the World often holds special events geared to kids, especially around holidays. Activities include puppet shows, storytelling, and face painting. Call ahead to check out the schedule.

Now that you've seen the top, try a bottoms-up view at the **Baltimore Public Works Museum and Streetscape,** 751 Eastern Avenue at Fallsway (410) 396-5565. Housed in the Eastern Avenue Pumping Station, a plant that originally processed the city's sewage, the museum demonstrates the city's public utility services from street lighting to trash removal to plumbing. The brightly colored outdoor Streetscape gives an insider's glimpse of the workings beneath the city streets. Children enjoy picking out the underground phone lines, water, and gas pipes by color. An activity center for ages three to ten, Construction Site, is open on weekends and by request.

Isaac Myers Shipyard, Inner Harbor. Baltimore's first black-owned and -controlled shipyard was established after the Civil War by Isaac Myers. Visit the historic beginnings of the man who went on to establish the National Labor Union for blacks in 1869.

The **Columbus Center of Marine Research and Exploration,** piers 5 and 6 (administration phone: 410-576-5700), is a new Inner Harbor attraction dedicated to marine biotechnology. The Columbus Center has three facilities: the Science and Technology Education Center (SciTEC), the Center for Marine Biotechnology (COMB), and the Hall of Exploration, the only facility open to the general public. SciTEC offers laboratory experience and educational outreach to groups, COMB houses the center's scientists, and the Hall of Exploration offers interactive exhibits for the public. "The Lighthouse," an interactive system, registers visitors into a database, maps out an individualized tour through the hall, and then directs them to other educational centers. Seven laboratories offer sightseers the opportunity to participate in authentic marine biotechnology research.

Also slated for the Inner Harbor is **Port Discovery—The Children's Museum,** the Brokerage at Marketplace. This hands-on children's facility, scheduled to open spring 1998, will have exhibits designed by the Walt Disney Company.

Museums and Historic Baltimore Sites

In addition to the prosperity brought to Baltimore by its port, Baltimore grew because of its railroad. With the laying of the Baltimore and Ohio tracks at the Mount Clare station in 1827, the city solidified its importance as a commercial distribution center.

Often overlooked is the **B & O Railroad Museum,** 901 West Pratt Street (410–752–2490), located at the site of the former Mount Clare Station. It's worth a stop, especially if toy trains, tracks, and thoughts of steaming around the countryside in a locomotive keep your child, or the child within you, happy.

Upstairs this museum displays a priceless collection of model trains, including a Lionel freight set from the 1920s, and some rare locomotives. Enjoy the elaborate display of tracks that wind through a replica of a 1940s city and of Maryland's mountains. Downstairs—save that for last—is the real thing, restored trains in an authentic roundhouse. As you listen to the taped sounds of whistles, chugs, and clanking, climb on and ogle such railroad darlings as a mail car, a caboose, and a big "mountain hauler."

After you explore the museum's three buildings, take a train ride to the nearby Mount Clare Mansion. Dating back to about 1756, this Georgian estate was home to Charles Carroll, founder of the Baltimore and Ohio Railroad.

For more city history visit the **Baltimore City Life Museums,** 33 South Front Street; (410) 396–3523. This conglomeration of eight historic sites gives a rounded view of Baltimore history. Four of the museums—the Carroll Mansion, the Center for Urban Archaeology, the 1840 House, and the Morton K. Blaustein City Life Exhibition Center —are located on Museum Row near Inner Harbor, with a single entrance at the above address. The other three are located elsewhere.

Start at the **Carroll Mansion** (410–396–3523) where Charles Carroll, the last surviving signer of the Declaration of Independence,

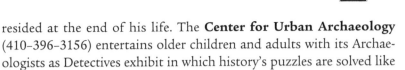

resided at the end of his life. The **Center for Urban Archaeology** (410–396–3156) entertains older children and adults with its Archaeologists as Detectives exhibit in which history's puzzles are solved like a classic mystery. The center also features a working laboratory and a life-size excavation pit. The **Courtyard Exhibition Center** (410–396–3524) illustrates Baltimore's historic revitalization from the 1930s to the present.

The **1840 House** (410–396–3279), a reconstructed row house recreates nineteenth-century life in Baltimore with its living-history theater performances and weekend tours. The 1840 House also features three unique programs for the entire family. For children ages five to twelve, the 1840 House staff conducts a ninety-minute 1840 Birthday program with historical games, craft activities, and baking in the open hearth. Ages ten through adult are invited to join the staff for An Evening in 1840. Guests prepare an authentic meal at the hearth, dine in the upstairs parlor, then join in parlor games. The Overnighter is the most comprehensive program. Escape the twentieth century by delving into the nineteenth. This begins with a tour, then you prepare dinner 1840s style, eat, and enjoy parlor games before bedding down for the night. In the morning you fix your own breakfast and help out with the 1840s household chores. Reserve these programs ahead. Call (410) 396–3279 for more information.

Star-Spangled Banner Flag House and Museum, 844 East Pratt Street at Howard Street (410–837–1793), is the home of Mary Pickersgill, the woman who sewed the flag that flew over Fort McHenry, inspiring Francis Scott Key to write "The Star-Spangled Banner." Pickersgill, a widow, paid nearly $200 of her own money to purchase the 400 yards of material for the 30-by-42-foot flag, the largest in the world at the time. Working more than 1,000 hours, she received $405.90 for sewing this flag and another, smaller version. The receipt is showcased in the museum.

Fort McHenry, Fort Avenue; (410) 962–4299. The American flag flying here after a long night of British attack in 1814 inspired Francis Scott Key to write "The Star-Spangled Banner." Visitors can explore the fort restored to its pre–Civil War appearance, walk o'er the ramparts, and see where the British invaded. From Memorial Day through Labor Day, there's shuttle boat service to the fort from Baltimore's Inner Harbor.

Baltimore is an industrial city, and its laborers—garment workers, oyster canners, printers, and others—come to life in the **Baltimore Museum of Industry,** 1415 Key Highway; (410) 727-4808. Housed in a former 1870 cannery, the hands-on exhibits teach kids about the labor in these laborers' days. Kids feel the muscle it took to operate a printing press, sample a foot-operated sewing machine, and—against a sweatshop display—see a photo of the real women who worked cramped together at their machines. At Children's Motorworks kids join a scaled-down assembly line learning firsthand about the benefits, and boredom; at the Cannery they take part in shucking and canning oysters in a simulated 1883 factory.

Slated to open in 1997 is the **Maryland History Center,** Centre Street and Park Avenue. Located in the renovated Greyhound garage, this museum will offer exhibits on Baltimore's 350-year history.

Several famous people associated with Baltimore have historic sites in the city. Budding journalists may want to breeze through the **H.L. Mencken House,** 1524 Hollins Street (410-396-1149), home to the outspoken journalist Henry Louis Mencken, "The Sage of Baltimore." This nineteenth-century row house is furnished with Mencken's belongings and presents a short film on his life and works.

Westminster Hall and Burying Ground, West Fayette and Greene streets (410-328-7228), is where Edgar Allan Poe and his wife, first cousin Virginia Clemm, are buried. Many other notable Marylanders rest here as well. Tours are conducted the first and third Friday evening and Saturday morning each month with prior reservations. The **Edgar Allan Poe House,** 203 North Amity Street (410-396-7932), where Poe lived from 1831 to 1835, is open with abbreviated hours.

Another Baltimore legend is represented in Charm City. The **Babe Ruth Birthplace,** 216 Emory Street (410-727-1539), features exhibits on George Herman "Babe" Ruth as well as famous Orioles. Scheduled to open in 1997, the **Baseball Center,** Camden Station Passenger Terminal Building at Oriole Park at Camden yards (no phone yet), will pay homage to baseball and to the Babe with exhibits. Computer and laser technology will enable visitors to stand in a batter's box and swing at a pro's best curve or fast ball. Part of the station's corridor will be decorated to resemble a 1920s railroad car of the kind the Babe used to ride to games.

The town's new specialty museum, the **Dr. Samuel D. Harris National Museum of Dentistry,** 31 South Green Street (410-706-0600), is on the University of Maryland at Baltimore campus. Artifacts include George Washington's dentures and the dental instruments used to treat Queen Victoria.

Art Museums

Baltimore Museum of Art, Art Museum Drive between Charles and 31st streets (410-396-7101), is the city's premier art museum, featuring the Cone Collection, with outstanding works by Matisse, Picasso, and Cezanne, plus an entire wing devoted to modern art. Besides these paintings—and the gift shop—kids seem to enjoy the Arts of Africa—specifically the masks—and the Cheney Miniature rooms, whose scaled-down furnishings depict life-styles from the seventeenth to the nineteenth century and are guaranteed to elicit an "ooh" from anyone who appreciates miniatures.

Besides its permanent collection the museum is noted for its frequent, top-quality shows. Call and see what's being featured, and inquire about their children's classes, often scheduled on weekends.

The **Walters Art Gallery,** 600 North Charles Street (410-547-9000), boasts more than 30,000 items in its collection, which spans 5,000 years. Some kid-pleasing highlights include Byzantine silver and jewelry, an extensive arms and armor collection, jewelry by Fabergé, and an extensive Asian arts wing at Hackerman House, 1 West Mount Vernon Place. Some children love the delicate swirls, patterns, and colors of these works in porcelain and lacquer.

The Black American Museum, 1765-69 Carswell Street (410-243-9600), presents changing exhibitions of contemporary black Americans and Third World artists.

Your kids might like to see the innovative works at the **American Visionary Art Museum,** 800 Key Highway and Covington Street (410-244-1900), a museum that was designated by Congress to feature the "best in self-taught, 'outsider,' or visionary artistry." Past exhibits have focused on divine flight and unique wood sculpture celebrating earth and the spirit. The Wildflower/Sculpture Garden is a kid-pleaser, with its wedding altar created from woven tree limbs.

Zoos

The Baltimore Zoo, Druid Hill Park (410-366-5466), boasts a large colony of African black-footed penguins, an elephant compound, an African watering hole, and a chimp forest plus a nice children's zoo. Take the kids for a lesson on Maryland's Wilderness at the Children's Zoo, which features replicas of five Maryland ecosystems.

Performing Arts

Baltimore has an abundant selection of theaters. Among the choices are the **Theatre Project,** 45 West Preston Street (410-752-8558), featuring national touring groups; the **Morris A. Mechanic Theatre,** Hopkins Plaza, Baltimore and Charles streets (410-625-1400), which presents Broadway hits, and **Center Stage,** 700 North Calvert Street (410-332-0033), home of the state theater of Maryland, which hosts repertory and original shows. Go to the **Fell's Point Cafe,** 723 South Broadway Street (410-327-8800), for audience-participation theater, which may include improvisation or mystery theater. **The Arena Players,** 801 McCulloh Street (410-728-6500), feature mainly African-American productions, and the **Children's Theater Association,** in the Walters Art Gallery, 600 North Charles Street (410-225-0052), hosts children's productions.

The Baltimore Opera Company performs at the Lyric Opera House, 140 West Mount Royal Avenue; (410) 685-0693. The Baltimore Museum of Art is home to the Maryland Ballet, Art Museum Drive, (410) 467-8495. The Baltimore Symphony Orchestra plays at Joseph Meyerhoff Symphony Hall, 1212 Cathedral Street; (410) 783-8000. The Chamber Music Society of Baltimore presents monthly concerts at Meyerhoff Auditorium, the Baltimore Museum of Art, Art Museum Drive, (301) 486-1140.

Shopping

At **Lexington Market,** 400 West Lexington Street (410-685-6169), grab some lunch. This is the country's oldest continuously operating market, where 140 merchants offer fresh seafood, including Maryland crab cakes, meats, cheeses, wines, and anything else you can imagine. **Harborplace,** at the corner of Light and Pratt streets, offers more than 150 shops, eateries, and restaurants in two pavilions. When you tire of browsing, enjoy the water view from the terraces.

Tours

Several creative tours in Baltimore are worth a try. The **Insomniac Tour** run by Baltimore Rent-A-Tour (410-653-2998) is a fun tour of the city at night for adults and teens. **Trolley Tours** of downtown Baltimore run daily in the warmer months but only on weekends in winter. Call Baltimore Trolley Tours (410-752-2015) or Tres Bon Trolley at (410) 252-7001.

Available harbor and boat tours include the **Baltimore Patriot I and II** (410-685-4288), the **Clipper City/Baltimore's Tall Ship** (410-539-6277), and **Harbor Cruises** aboard the *Bay Lady* and *The Lady Baltimore* (410-727-3113).

SPECIAL EVENTS

Sporting Events

Oriole Park at Camden Yards, 333 Camden Street (410-685-9800), is open from April to October for Baltimore Oriole baseball games. Built in 1992, the park mixes an old-stadium feel with modern amenities. Be sure to purchase tickets in advance for this popular summer activity. The **Preakness,** one jewel in racing's Triple Crown, is run in May, Pimlico Race Course, Baltimore.

Football has returned to Baltimore. The **Baltimore Ravens** play at the renovated Memorial Stadium. For tickets write to the Baltimore Ravens, 200 St. Paul Place, 24th floor, Baltimore, MD 21202.

Sailing fans should know that Baltimore and Annapolis are stopover ports for the prestigious **Whitbread Round the World Race,** held every four years. The fleet is scheduled to arrive the week of April 20, 1998.

Festivals

January: First Day Celebration at Harborplace.

February: Celebrate Black History Month at city sites. Call the Visitors Center at (410) 836-4636 for a calendar of events.

March: Annual Street Performers Auditions, Inner Harbor. Public Works Museum Open House for Archeology Week.

April: Mayor's Easter Egg Hunt, Druid Hill Park.

May: Preakness Stakes horse race at Pimlico Race Course with a week-long celebration throughout the city, including a parade.

June: National Flag Day Celebration at Fort McHenry.

July: July Fourth Celebration at the waterfront. ARTSCAPE (410–396-4575) annual arts festival.

September: Harborplace Street Performers Festival. Kunta Kinte Heritage Festival, St. John's College, Waterfront, Annapolis, Maryland.

October: Baltimore on the Bay, the annual family festival of the city's maritime heritage. Annual Fell's Point Fun Festival. Kids on the Bay, a waterside children's festival. Port Fest.

November: Baltimore's Thanksgiving Parade from downtown to the Inner Harbor. Hottest winter.

December: Noontime Christmas concerts all month long, except on Sundays at Lexington Market. Parade of Lighted Boats at the Inner Harbor. Christmas at Harborplace. Baltimore's New Year's Eve Extravaganza, a nonalcoholic celebration geared toward the entire family and ending with fireworks over the harbor.

WHERE TO STAY

The Inner Harbor is a practical area to stay in since much of Baltimore can be visited on foot from here. Among accommodation possibilities are the **Holiday Inn-Inner Harbor,** 301 West Lombard Street (410–685-3500) and **Baltimore Marriott Inner Harbor,** 110 South Eutaw Street (410–962-0202). Ask about the Marriott's Two for Breakfast package. Try **The Inn at Pier 5,** 711 Eastern Avenue; (410) 783-5553. The **Harbor Court Hotel,** 550 Light Street (410–234-0550) on the harbor, offers a Baltimore on Ice wintertime package where children stay free. The **Hyatt Regency at the Inner Harbor,** 300 Light Street (410–528-1234), has easy access to Harborplace and the Convention Center, plus special packages for families. The **Stouffer Renaissance Harborplace Hotel,** 202 East Pratt Street (410–547-1200), is a convenient lodging. The **Omni Inner Harbor,** 101 West Fayette Street (410– 752-1100), offers seasonal family packages, often with discounted attraction tickets and $1.99 children's menus. The **Sheraton Inner Harbor,** 300 South Charles Street (410–962-8300), also features seasonal packages.

The **Brookshire Inner Harbor Suite Hotel,** 120 East Lombard Street; (410-625-1300), is an all-suite hotel. The **Comfort Inn** at Baltimore's Mount Vernon, 24 West Franklin Street (410–727-2000), is located near the Walters Art Gallery.

For reservations in bed and breakfasts that welcome children, call **Amanda's Bed and Breakfast Reservation Service,** 1428 Park Avenue (410-225-0001). The **Biltmore Suites,** 205 West Madison Street (410-728-6550), is an all-suite property in the Mount Vernon historic district.

WHERE TO EAT

Baltimore is a great place to taste the Chesapeake Bay region's seafood specialties, among them crab cakes, steamed crabs, steamed shrimp, and fresh oysters. Suggestions for family-friendly restaurants include **Phillips,** 301 Light Street (410-685-6600 or 410-327-5561), for seafood near the Inner Harbor. If you're looking for lunch at the Inner Harbor, the fast-food eateries at **Harborplace,** Pratt and Light streets (410-332-4191), offer enough choices to please any picky eater. An amphitheater within the glass pavilions often provides free entertainment while you munch. Nearby, **Freddie's of Water Street,** 106 Water Street (410-752-5757), is a coffeehouse with a selection of sandwiches and salads.

Little Italy, 6 blocks east of the Inner Harbor, is the place to be for authentic Italian food in one of the oldest neighborhoods in the city. Try out **Velleggia's,** 829 East Pratt Street (410-685-2620) or **Sabatino's,** 901 Fawn Street (410-727-9414). For seafood in Fells Point, locals like the **Fishery,** 1717 Eastern Avenue; (410) 327-9340. If you're downtown and just want a sandwich, get one at **Lenny's Deli of Lombard Street,** 1150 East Lombard Street; (410) 327-1177.

Baltimore's official *Quick Guide* offers a comprehensive list of restaurants.

DAY TRIPS

Annapolis
About an hour away from Baltimore, Annapolis, at the picturesque junction of Chesapeake Bay and the Severn River, is a worthy day trip. Settled in 1649, much of the city has been designated a National Historic Landmark District. Stroll along its narrow streets, admiring the architecture and the shops, and grab a bite to eat. A kid-pleaser is a tour of the bay. Several are available from the forty-minute harbor tour aboard the *Harbor Queen,* to the seven-and-a-half hour tour aboard

the *Bay Cruise,* which passes the city landmarks en route to the Eastern Shore town of St. Michaels. For tour information contact **Chesapeake Maritime Tours,** city dock at Main Street; (410) 268-7600.

Be sure to tour the **U.S. Naval Academy,** bordered by King George and Randall streets; (410) 263-6933. Established in 1845, the Academy's museum in Preble Hall exhibits flags, ship models, and war relics. In warm weather watch the cadets muster in front of Bancroft Hall at noon. Older children may like visiting the historic houses such as the eighteenth-century **Hammond-Harwood House,** 19 Maryland Avenue, with its period pieces.

Before leaving the city take some time to romp at the **Neuman Street Playground,** an eclectic collection of climbing apparatus surrounded by green spaces for running.

Greenbelt

This Washington, D.C., suburb has **NASA's Goddard Visitor Center,** Greenbelt, Maryland (301-286-8981), where you can educate the family about space exploration at interactive exhibits created for children. Highlights include a Manned Maneuvering Unit, in which kids capture satellites in space, and a reproduction Gemini capsule with a mock take-off recording. Rockets are launched on the first and third Sundays of each month, and weekly grounds tours run every Thursday afternoon.

For additional day trips to points along the Eastern Shore, see the chapter on Washington, D.C. For a free Maryland Travel Kit, call (800) 543-1036.

FOR MORE INFORMATION

Visitor Information Centers

The Baltimore Area Convention and Visitors Association (BACVA), 100 Light Street, 12th floor; (800) 282-6632/(410) 837-4636. In 1997 the BACVA will open a new visitors center on the west shore of the Inner Harbor. Chamber of Commerce; (410) 269-0642. The Department of Recreation and Parks; (410) 396-7900.

Senior citizens will find the Waxter Center for Senior Citizens helpful. Call (410) 396-1341. Persons with disabilities can get referrals and information from the **Handicapped Services Coordinator** at the

Mayor's Office (410-396-1915) or from the **Disabilities Information and Assistance Line** (410-752-DIAL). The Easter Seal Society of Central Maryland has published a Baltimore guide for travelers with disabilities, *Bright Lights, Harbor Breezes*. For a copy call (410) 335-0100.

Emergency Numbers

Ambulance, fire, and police: 911

Block's Pharmacy, Baltimore Street at Linwood Avenue, is open from 9:30 A.M. to 9:00 P.M. Monday–Saturday and from 10:00 A.M. to 2:00 P.M. on Sundays; (410) 276-2312.

Johns Hopkins Hospital Emergency Room: (410) 955-5000

Maryland Poison Center: (410) 528-7701

BRANDYWINE VALLEY AREA

For more than 300 years—from the time of William Penn—people have sought refuge and renewal in the Brandywine Valley. This bucolic landscape on either side of the Brandywine River in Pennsylvania and Delaware offers the weekend sojourner an American sampler. Here, where southeastern Pennsylvania meets northern Delaware, you find extravagant country estates and simple farmhouses, fine art and nineteenth-century factories, Revolutionary War history, Colonial craft fairs, and pastoral backcountry roads.

GETTING THERE

Philadelphia International Airport (610-917-6937), the one closest to Brandywine Valley, serves most major airlines and has car rental agencies.

By car from the north, take Route 202 into the area. From the south I-95 north leads to Route 202. To visit by train take Amtrak (800-USA-RAIL or 302-429-6530) to the Wilmington, Delaware, station at the intersection of Martin Luther King Jr. Boulevard and French Street. The Wilmington station has car rental agencies.

GETTING AROUND

The best way to travel and tour the Brandywine area is by car. The Delaware Administration for Regional Transit (DART) provides transit service within northern New Castle County and the Greater Wilmington area. Call the DARTline at (302) 655-3381.

WHAT TO SEE AND DO

Parks and Green Spaces

Brandywine Battlefield Park, on Park Drive between the Augustine and Market Street bridges (610-459-3342), is a historic site. On September 11, 1777, when the morning mist rose over these Pennsylvania meadows and apple orchards, one of the most significant battles of the Revolutionary War began. By day's end 25,000 British and Revolutionary soldiers lay dead in the fields. Despite General George Washington's defeat by British General William Howe, the nascent Revolutionary forces scored an important psychological victory: Washington prevented Howe from capturing the iron forges that supplied ammunition and muskets for the soldiers, and Washington proved his forces were capable of sustaining a difficult attack by the skilled British. This helped Washington obtain official support from the French the following spring.

September is an especially good time to visit. During **Brandywine Battlefield Days** the park stages a reenactment of this battle, complete with cannon, cavalry, a horse unit, 300 soldiers in period dress, and camp followers. At night enjoy the troops' encampment, featuring demonstrations of eighteenth-century tenting, cooking, and wound dressing.

For more Revolutionary spirit during fall, board the shuttle bus for the quick ride to Chadds Ford for a Colonial crafts festival, called **Chadds Ford Days.** Stroll around the grounds and watch as blacksmiths, broom makers, weavers, potters, quilters, toy makers, and other costumed craftspeople demonstrate these essential eighteenth-century skills.

Longwood Gardens is at the junction of U.S. 1 and Route 52 near Kennett Square, Pennsylvania; (610) 388-6741. The gardens transport you from the rustic, rugged history of the Revolution to the tranquil, mannered society of the Du Ponts, Brandywine's nineteenth- and twentieth-century industrial heroes. The former summer estate of Pierre du Pont, the onetime board chairman of General Motors, Longwood features more than 1,000 acres of outdoor gardens, woodlands, and meadows, plus twenty indoor conservatories, several ponds, three acres of fountains, even an open-air water theater.

Brandywine Valley Area at a Glance

- Revolutionary War history and much more

- The battle of Brandywine is reenacted every September

- A mushroom museum and a Christmas museum

- An elaborate historic Christmas celebration

- The 15,000-acre Bombay Hook National Wildlife Refuge is close

- Brandywine Valley Tourist Information Center, (800) 228-9933 or (610) 388-2900

Walk among rows of trees, sit on a stone whispering bench, or stroll through conservatories bursting with orchids, roses, and blooming cacti. In summer watch a dazzling dance of colored fountains choreographed to classical music, capped by fireworks. Touring Longwood can take all day, but allow at least three hours. After an introductory slide show at the visitor's center, start your walking tour of the outdoor gardens under the towering beeches and ginkgoes planted by the original Quaker settlers in 1730. Walking tour highlights, depending upon the season, include tulips and rose gardens or fall gardens bright with red, yellow, and gold chrysanthemums. Throughout the gardens, especially along the woodland walk, enjoy the sunlight streaming through the sugar maples, beeches, and poplars.

For an *Alice in Wonderland* maze of outlandish shapes, tour the topiary gardens. Surrounded by a sundial that took Du Pont and his engineers five years to build, the carefully clipped yews assume unlikely geometric and animal shapes. The topiary garden even has a rabbit—reputedly created in tribute to Bunny du Pont, a relative of Pierre.

Be sure to allow time for a tour of the conservatories. These nurseries, with Palladian windows, house everything from bonsai, cacti, and palms to medicinal plants and rare orchids. The East Conservatory, where concerts are held, contains a 10,010-pipe organ. The Main Conservatory, an elegant pillared structure, provided shelter for Du Pont's garden parties. Pink bougainvillea drape the archways around the original dance floor.

Afterward enjoy the water displays mid-June through August. Legend has it that, as a child Du Pont would open the bathroom faucets to watch the water run—despite the reprimands of his parents. At Longwood Du Pont gave free rein to his water fantasies. Start with the Italian water garden, lined with linden trees, and based on the fountains of an Italian villa Du Pont loved. Four large fountains delicately frame a tranquil scene. Du Pont devilishly inaugurated the cascading staircase fountain: He positioned his nieces and nephews on the marble stairs, dressed in their Sunday best, then drenched them with water.

Check the schedule of events, as Longwood often features such family activities as Fabulous Fun Days for Children. Enliven a dreary winter day with a plant hunt amid acres of blooming plants in an indoor conservatory. Events are held periodically for the Wiggle Club, ages three to five, and Kool Kids, ages six to ten.

Museums

Nearby **Winterthur,** 6 miles northwest of Wilmington, Delaware (302-888-4600 or 800-448-3883), also features hundreds of acres of gardens and woodlands. From mid-April through October sign up for the tram tour, which is a great way to see the blooms, beeches, maples, and oaks, and save your feet.

The estate belonged to Pierre du Pont's cousin Henry Francis du Pont. Henry's passion was American furniture, and the furnishings at Winterthur will dazzle you and older kids, especially preteens in love with historical mansions. The 196 rooms of this magnificent country estate hold more than 60,000 antiques. From the William-and-Mary carved wardrobes to the eighteenth-century Pennsylvania blanket chests to the fine examples of Chippendale styling, Winterthur houses an astonishing collection of furniture, textiles, and other objects made or used in America between 1650 and 1850.

The galleries opened in October 1992 with a permanent exhibit, Perspectives on Decorative Arts in Early America. This is a good place to begin your tour with kids. They can choose one of six perspectives from which to look at objects. For example, Change Over Time shows how fashions changed in certain periods. Change Over Place shows how design and craftsmanship differed from one city to another. The Henry S. McNeil Gallery, opened in June 1993, intrigues future furniture builders with its tools, exhibits on the evolution of design styles, and lessons about furniture study. There is also a gallery for changing exhibits.

You can't see all of Winterthur in one visit. A popular overall tour is the Winterthur Experience, which includes a forty-five-minute tour of about twenty-rooms, plus a short tour of the gardens. Special tours focus on specific topics such as textiles, craftsmanship, folk art, or Queen Anne furniture. It's best to reserve these ahead of time.

Highlights of the museum include the elegant Port Royal parlor, with its matched Chippendale highboys and lavender-and-yellow color scheme; the Chinese parlor, noted for its vivid green Oriental wallpaper; the Baltimore drawing room, with its woodwork salvaged from a Baltimore mansion; and the Montmorenci stairway, a graceful curved staircase rescued from a North Carolina home built in 1822.

The Brandywine River Museum, U.S. Route 1, Chadds Ford; (610) 388-7601. This intimate museum on the banks of the Brandywine River is housed in a converted nineteenth-century gristmill. The pastoral setting and unpretentious galleries provide a low-key way for kids to enjoy art. This is an especially good place to introduce kids to American illustrators.

In the museum the American countryside comes to life. Those who have been captivated by three generations of Wyeth paintings—by patriarch N.C. Wyeth, son Andrew Wyeth, and grandson Jamie Wyeth —will especially enjoy these special exhibits.

View Andrew Wyeth's paintings: the wistful *Christina's World,* the weathered barns of *Night Sleeper,* the country boy by the roadside in *Roasted Chestnuts.* Enjoy Jamie Wyeth's whimsical *Portrait of Den Den,* a likeness of his pig. You also can see such American illustrations as N.C. Wyeth's drawings for *Kidnapped* and *Treasure Island,* Howard Pyle's Brandywine settings, William Smedley's New York scenes, and Harrison Cady's lion drawings.

After your tour take a Wordsworthian turn through the grounds to experience firsthand the countryside you've viewed in the museum.

Follow the trail along the banks of the winding Brandywine River where lush birches and maples grow near fields of wild flowers. Pack a picnic lunch or buy one from the museum's cafe, where you may dine overlooking the Brandywine. In fall the museum's cobbled courtyard comes alive with a crafts festival and harvest market each weekend from mid-September to mid-October.

The Hagley Museum and Library is off State Route 141, in Wilmington; (302) 658-2400. The Du Pont fortune that nourished Longwood and Winterthur began at the Hagley in Greenville, Delaware, 3 miles north of Wilmington. The Hagley is strung along the banks of the Brandywine River on 230 acres. Here nineteenth-century industrial history is set against a sweep of centuries-old trees, including such unusual ones as blue Atlas cedars transplanted from Africa and Chinese empress trees from the Orient. After all, in 1799 when E. I. du Pont emigrated to America, he listed his occupation as "Botaniste." The careful cultivation of these grounds was his lifelong interest.

To the rustle of the river and the wind, this mostly outdoor museum tells the story of nineteenth-century America's booming need for explosives, and the birth of the Du Pont Company. The new nation demanded black powder not only to fight the War of 1812, but to blast its way west—clearing farmland, developing mines, and building railroads. Here along the Brandywine River, Eleuthère Irénée du Pont built gunpowder mills in 1802 to supply the United States Army.

With prosperity came the mansion and the workers' village, blacksmith's shop, machine shop, and schoolhouse. All are restored and open to the public. This industrial park displays the stark contrasts of wealth and poverty that characterized nineteenth-century industrial life.

Start with the exhibits in the Henry Clay Mill. Once a cotton-spinning mill, it was converted by the Du Pont Company to barrel manufacturing and is now a museum. The exhibits offer an overview of eighteenth- and nineteenth-century Brandywine Valley industry and include explanations of tanning, water turbines, and an interesting model of Oliver Evans's 1819 automatic flour mill. This Rube Goldberg-looking device of conveyors, descenders, and elevators greatly increased a mill's efficiency.

At the mill purchase a ticket for the five-minute jitney ride to Eleutherian Mills, Du Pont's first property. With borrowed money E.I.

du Pont began the family's American fortune. The house, completed in 1803 and later enlarged, was home to Du Ponts for nearly one hundred years. A tour reveals the tasteful antiques of the last occupant, E.I.'s great-granddaughter, Louisa Evelina du Pont Crowninshield, who received the house as a wedding gift from her father in 1923.

But the drawings lining the ground floor hallway and the view from the veranda reveal the most. Instead of the terraced garden that now sweeps down the hill, the pictures depict rows of billowing smokestacks. E. I. du Pont built this home in the European tradition of close proximity to the factory. This pastoral landscape once bustled with workers, smelled rancidly of sulphur, and rang with frequent blasts from the mills just below.

Before heading to the heart of the museum—the Hagley Yard—tour the original office, and visit the barn, with its cooper shop, cars, carriages, and a Conestoga wagon. Reboard the jitney to visit the engine house where, upon request, volunteers demonstrate the 1870 slide-valve box-bed steam engine used to power the pack house where the finished powder was packaged. Take the quarter-mile walk along the tree-lined river bank to the sixteen-foot wooden waterwheel, which was used prior to the 1840s when the family switched to water turbines.

At the Millwright Shop in Hagley Yard, an interpreter explains the manufacture of black powder. Displays show how saltpeter imported from India and sulphur from Sicily were heated, purified, and blended with local charcoal to create the volatile substance. Stamping mills were originally used to mix these materials, but by 1822 more efficient rolling mills replaced them. A rolling mill ground the mixture between its two eight-ton cast-iron wheels for three to eight hours, depending on the consistency required.

The rolling mills are the paired, granite curiosities lining the river banks. Several stand tall, and some are just foundations covered by plants. With 3-foot-thick walls, a thin roof, and a gaping opening, these buildings were designed to channel the force of any explosion toward the water. Just one rolling mill, originally built in 1839 and rebuilt in 1886, survives intact. The others sacrificed their iron wheels for World War II.

Still powered by a water turbine, this one mill operates at selected intervals. A guide explains how Du Pont used the millrace, a man-made canal, to harness the natural power of the 17-foot drop in water level. Then the guide opens the sluice gate to set the force in motion.

But the rolling mill was just one step in the production process. Before the powder could be sold, the mixture still needed to be compressed in the pressing house, broken into chunks and ground in the graining mill, polished in the glazing mill, dried in the dry house, and screened and packed in the pack house.

Take time to stroll along the millrace and to follow the river path to the creek banks. With its contrast of stone, water, and rows of trees, this area is among the nicest spots at the Hagley. Stop by the machine shop as well. Inside, hear the slap and leathery hum of belts that drive nineteenth-century lathes, planers, and presses used in repairs.

Blacksmith's hill and other areas hold periodic demonstrations, including living history interpretations. Check the schedule. Spring and summer are beautiful at the Hagley, but autumn is a special gift as the grounds fill with brilliant foliage.

Delaware Art Museum, 2301 Kentmere Parkway, Wilmington; (302) 571–9590. This respected museum is known both for the works of Howard Pyle and his disciples and for its Pre-Raphaelite collection, the largest collection on permanent view in the United States. As an intriguing aid in your tour, pick up *Take Apart Art,* a booklet with fill-in blanks that helps kids and parents talk about such components of art as color, line, shape, and texture. The booklet makes the illustrations and paintings more accessible to kids. Pyle, born in Wilmington in 1853, is an important American illustrator credited with training such soon-to-be-famous students as N.C. Wyeth and Maxfield Parrish, whose works are also here. Most kids respond to the techniques, colors, and subject matter of these noted American illustrators.

Take younger children to the Pegafoamasaurus, otherwise known as the Children's Participatory Gallery. Kids create their own artwork from foam pieces of various shapes and colors. January features the annual Children's Event, a festive affair that in the past has included tea parties and teddy bear picnics. Summer offers "Jazz-On-Tap" in the early evenings.

The **Delaware Museum of Natural History,** on Kennett Pike, Route 2 (302–658–9111), is 5 miles northwest of Wilmington. Must-sees here include the 500-pound clam shell; the world's largest bird's egg; and the

Kids can create their own works of art at the Children's Participatory Gallery in the Delaware Museum of Art. (Courtesy Delaware Tourism Office)

re-created natural habitats, such as an African watering hole and the Great Barrier Reef. For some hands-on exploration, take younger children to the Discovery Room, open to the public weekday afternoons and weekends.

Ask about the museum's special event Children's Weeks in spring and winter, usually coinciding with holiday school breaks.

Rockwood, 610 Shipley Road, Wilmington (302-571-7776),is an 1851 Gothic-style country estate, on seventy acres. The period furnishings here will probably appeal only to older children with an interest in antiques, but the landscaped grounds offer a pleasing place for a family romp, especially during the mid-July Old Fashioned Ice Cream Festival when Victorian bicyclists, jugglers, clowns, and interpreters in period dress take over.

The American Christmas Museum, Route 1, Chadds Ford (between Longwood Gardens and Brandywine River Museum); (610) 388-0600. Closed mid-January to mid-March.

Phillips Mushroom Museum, Kennett Square on Route 1 south of Longwood Gardens (610-388-6082), is a definite must-see for any mushroom lover.

SPECIAL EVENTS

May: Winterthur Point-to-Point Races, an equestrian event with tailgate picnics and a parade.

July: Rockwood Museum sponsors its annual Ice Cream Festival on the first weekend following the Fourth of July. The **Philadelphia Eagles** host their summer camp in the Brandywine Area from mid-July through August at West Chester University's football stadium.

September: Revolutionary Times at Brandywine Battlefield Park features a battle reenactment.

October: Chadds Ford Pumpkin Carve, at the Chadds Ford Historical Society Fairgrounds, features professional carvers showing their skill at carving jack-o-lanterns, plus food and drink for the public.

November–December: A Brandywine Christmas is an areawide celebration with concerts, and decorated house and museum tours.

December: Old-Fashioned Christmas in West Chester, Chester County Historical Society, is a fun-filled CCHS open house with music and entertainment and family activities, plus a Holiday Treasures hunt. **Patchwork Puppet Theater, Chester County Historical Society,** encourages audience participation from all ages with adapted stories with a nineties twist of Rapunzel and Jack and the Beanstalk.

WHERE TO STAY

A nice way to experience the bucolic Brandywine Valley is by staying at a bed and breakfast inn. **Bed and Breakfast of Philadelphia** (800–220–1917) offers several places that welcome families with children of all ages. Among the finds:

Lenape Springs Farm (call 800–220–1917 for reservation information), located on thirty-two acres along the Brandywine Creek in Pocopson, is an 1850 three-story farmhouse. Kids love seeing the horses and cows in the pasture, and parents like the hot tub. The carriage house offers two rooms that share a bath, and the farmhouse has a family suite with two rooms and a hall bath. Children of all ages are welcome.

Pheasant Hollow Farm (800–220–1917) is in Thorndale, about a half-hour's drive from Longwood Gardens and the Chadds Ford area.

This colonial home is furnished with country antiques. The grounds have a pond, stream, and gardens.

Wilmington offers a range of accommodations, from the posh **Hotel du Pont** at Eleventh and Market streets (302–594–3100), to the **Days Inn** at 1102 West Street (302–429–7600 or 800–325–2525). The **Best Western Brandywine Valley Inn,** 1807 Concord Pike, Wilmington (800–537–7772), frequently offers sampler packages that include lodging and admission to several area attractions. Brandywine Valley packages are also available from the **Holiday Inn,** 4000 Concord Pike, Wilmington; (302) 478–2222 or (800) HOLIDAY.

Summerfield Suites Malvern-Great Valley, 20 Morehall Road; (610) 296–4343 or (800) 833–4353. This chain offers one- or two-bedroom suites with kitchen facilities and a daily continental breakfast plus breakfast buffet. There are also children's videos to rent (the two-bedroom units have three televisions plus a VCR) and a twenty-four-hour convenience store on-site. Ask about special weekend rates.

For bed and breakfast accommodations in Delaware, contact **Bed and Breakfast of Delaware** at (302) 479–9500 or (800) 233–4689. Many of their properties are best suited to families with older children and teens.

Fairville Inn, Route 52 south of Longwood Gardens and Chadds Ford, Mendenhall (610–388–5900), just fifteen quiet minutes away from the business district, has a uniquely home feel, with antiques and country decor; rooms are individually decorated.

WHERE TO EAT

The Chadds Ford Inn, Routes 1 and 100, Chadds Ford, Pennsylvania; (610) 388–7361. This Wyeth family favorite is just up the street from the Brandywine River Museum. Established in 1763 for travelers fording the Brandywine River, the restaurant offers Continental and American fare and is a good choice for families with older children and teens.

Buckley's Tavern, 5812 Kennett Pike, Centreville; (302) 656–9776. Housed in a 160-year-old building in the historic town of Centreville, near Winterthur, Longwood, and the Brandywine River Museum, the tavern has everything from burgers for the kids to grilled salmon for their parents.

For seafood servings head to **Dinardo's Restaurant,** 405 North Lincoln Street, Wilmington; (302) 652-9503. Try their hard-shelled crabs, lobster tails, or fisherman stew. **Arthur's Family Restaurant,** 215 North Dupont Highway, New Castle (302-322-3279), offers good seafood and homemade pastries.

DAY TRIPS

Easy day trips include Philadelphia and Valley Forge (see the chapter on Philadelphia) and the Amish areas near Lancaster and Hersheypark (see the chapter Hershey and the Pennsylvania Dutch Country).

Bird lovers and nature lovers should visit the **Bombay Hook National Wildlife Refuge,** RD 1, Box 147, Smyrna, Delaware; (302) 653-9345. The refuge includes 15,122 acres, three-quarters of which are tidal salt marsh. In fall and spring thousands of migratory birds fill the skies over the refuge. In October and November look up to see peak populations of snow geese, Canada geese, and ducks. Shorebirds arrive in quantity in May and June. Obtain a map for a driving tour—kids enjoy the comfort—and a trail guide. Some trails are easily conquered by young kids.

FOR MORE INFORMATION

For more information on the Brandywine Valley area, visit the Brandywine Valley Tourist Information Center at Longwood Gardens or write to them at P.O. Box 910, Dept. VG, Route 1, Kennett Square, Pennsylvania 19348; (610) 388-2900 or (800) 228-9933. For information about Delaware attractions, contact the Greater Wilmington Convention and Visitor's Bureau, 1300 Market Street, Suite 504, Wilmington, Delaware 19801; (302) 652-4088 or (800) 422-1181.

Emergency Numbers

Ambulance, fire, and police: 911

Medical attention in Delaware: Medical Center of Delaware, 4755 Ogletown Stanton Road; nonemergency (302) 733-1000, emergency (302) 733-1601

Medical attention in Pennsylvania: Crozer-Chester Medical Center, 1 Medical Center Boulevard, Upland; (610) 447-2000

Poison Control in Delaware: (800) 722-7112

Poison Control in Pennsylvania: (610) 386-2100

Pharmacy in Delaware: Brandywine Drug Center, 4605 North Market, Wilmington (302-762-6940), open Monday to Saturday from 9:00 A.M. to 8:00 P.M. and Sunday from 9:00 A.M. to 4:00 P.M.; Eckerd Drugs, 2003 Concord Pike, Wilmington (302-655-8866), open daily from 8:00 A.M. to 10:00 P.M.

Twenty-four-hour pharmacy in Pennsylvania: CVS Pharmacy, 246 Concord Road, Aston; (610) 497-2225

CATSKILL MOUNTAINS

Mention the word *Catskills,* and many people envision the large hotels in Sullivan County where families from New York City once flocked by the carload. While a number of these resorts exist today (most have modernized their images along with their facilities), there's much more to this area than stereotypes. The Catskill Mountains cut across four counties, each with its own personality: Ulster in the east, Sullivan in the south, Delaware in the west, and Greene in the north. The 386,000 acres of unspoiled state-owned Catskill Forest Preserve and the 705,000 acres of privately- and state-owned Catskill Park offer a variety of simple, natural pleasures: miles of hiking and skiing trails, plus creeks and streams for fishing, canoeing, and tubing. Much of this pristine area is in western Ulster and southwestern Greene counties, although Sullivan and Delaware counties have their share of natural places as well.

Whether your lodging choice is simple, fancy or in-between—and there's a wide selection of each—the Catskills afford your family a wonderful opportunity to get in touch with the outdoors any time of the year. The What to See and Do section includes some attractions in Ulster, Sullivan, and Greene counties—in addition to just hiking and enjoying the scenery—that you might enjoy during a stay in the area. Delaware County, largely rural, also provides beautiful scenery, particularly during fall.

GETTING THERE

The area is served by a number of commuter and regional airlines, with limousine service to Albany International, New York City's JFK and La Guardia airports, and Stewart Airport in Newburgh. Commuter flights are available from Stewart Airport to Sullivan County International Airport in White Lake; (914) 583-6600.

Amtrak currently doesn't serve the Catskills. Closest stops: Rhinecliff and Hudson, New York; (800) USA-RAIL. Adirondack Trailways, Trailways, Short Line, and Mountain View serve various areas of the Catskills. By car the Catskills are accessed via exits 16 through 21B of I-87, the New York State Thruway. The Route 17 "Quickway," beginning at exit 16, stretches westward to Lake Erie, passing through Sullivan and lower Delaware counties.

GETTING AROUND

Some Catskill cities have their own local bus service, although vacationers invariably rely on their cars to get around.

WHAT TO SEE AND DO

Ulster County

More than one-third of northwestern Ulster County lies within the Catskill Forest Preserve, which starts just west of the city of Kingston. The southern part of the county is in the Shawangunk Mountains, officially not a part of the Catskill mountains. But since this is also a popular vacation destination, attractions and lodging in the Shawangunk area are included here. The Hudson River runs along Ulster's eastern boundaries. A good place to start a tour is the Minnewaska State Park (10 miles west of New Paltz on U.S. 44 and U.S. 55; 914-255-0752) This park offers miles of hiking trails, some leading to waterfalls.

Tubing is a great way for older kids and adults to enjoy the **Esopus Creek,** located within the preserve. **Town Tinker Tube Rental** has a substation at the Mt. Pleasant Lodge, 3 miles before Phoenicia, where kids ages twelve and older can rent tubes and equipment. (Head protection and life vests are required for everyone under fourteen.) The novice section of the creek is about 2½ miles, or about a two-hour trip, and features one set of fast-moving rapids at the beginning. After that enjoy a slow, winding ride through gorgeous scenery. Call (914) 688-5553.

Catskill Mountains at a Glance

- Get in touch with the outdoors at any time of the year

- Stay in fancy resorts, simple motels, B&Bs, or cabins in the woods

- Tube down Esopus Creek

- See more than 2,000 animals at Catskill Game Farm

- Giant waterslides at Zoom Flume Waterpark

- Tourist information, (518) 943-3223

Opus 40 and the Quarryman's Museum, High Woods, Saugerties; (914) 246-3400. Opus 40 is an environmental sculpture made of tons of finely fitted bluestone and constructed over thirty-seven years by sculptor Harvey Fite. The creation spreads over more than six acres. You and the kids can walk through, around, and over it, past pools and fountains, and up to the monolith that is the summit of the work. Summer concerts of jazz, folk, and classical music are held on selected evenings. Fite's collection of tools (many hand-forged) and furnishings from a quarryman's household (stove, cupboard, and handmade dominoes) are housed in the museum. It's open from Memorial Day to November 1, but call first; some Saturdays are reserved for special events.

Visit the **Village of Saugerties'** sandy public beach on Esopus Creek, at the bottom of Hill Street. A lifeguard is on duty from July 4th weekend through Labor Day; (914) 246-2321.

Woodstock, just west of Saugerties, is at the foot of Ohayo and Overlook Mountains in the Catskill range. A brochure of area attractions, including hiking trails, is available from the Chamber of Commerce, P.O. Box 36, Woodstock 12498; (914) 679-6234. Stores that sell area hiking maps include the **Golden Notebook,** 29 Tinker Street (914-679-8000), which also has a children's book and cassette annex.

Woodstock is known for the 1960s music festival, although that didn't take place here. The festival was already named when the original deal fell through, and the site was relocated to Sullivan County. Woodstock—a community of writers, musicians, artists, and crafts-people—is worth a stop. Browse in the shops on and around Tinker Street. Don't miss **Tinker Toys of Woodstock,** 5 Mill Hill Road. Then take the kids for a romp in the **Woodstock Wonderworks,** a community-built playground on the grounds of the elementary school, Route 375. The complex is open to the public when school isn't in session, and it features tunnels and mazes, a dragon slide, Viking ship, a guitar car, and picnic tables. Just outside Woodstock, you'll find **Kenneth L. Wilson State Park,** Wittenberg Mountain Road, Mount Tremper; (914) 679-7020. A sandy beach on the park's shallow lake is perfect for tots. Nearby, marked trails wind through the woods. There are rest rooms, a picnic area, and overnight campsites by reservation.

Southeast of Woodstock the city of **Kingston,** along the Hudson River, was a leading nineteenth-century maritime center. At the Historic Rondout area—a revitalized nineteenth-century waterfront community with shops and restaurants—those days are relived. See the **Hudson River Maritime Museum,** 1 Rondout Plaza (at the end of Broadway) (914) 338-0071. The small museum tells the story of the Hudson through models, artifacts, photographs, and paintings. Exhibits change early. In the outdoor area antique vessels are displayed. Visiting vessels, such as the sloop *Clearwater,* are often tied up at the museum's bulk-head. The *Indie II* excursion boat leaves for a ten-minute cruise to the Rondout II Lighthouse, where you can climb to the top for river views. The museum, open from May to October, has a number of special events including the Shad Festival each May. Shad and shad roe are served along with music, puppet shows, and boat rides. The September Harvest Festival features crafts, harvest food, music, and boats.

Across the street is the **Trolley Museum,** 89 East Strand; (914) 331-3399. The big draw is the excursion ride that runs 1½ miles along the tracks of the old Ulster & Delaware Railroad to picnic grounds on the Hudson shores. The museum displays trolley, subway, and rapid-transit cars. It's open Memorial to Labor Day.

Rondout Landing is the departure point for Hudson River cruises aboard the excursion ship *Rip Van Winkle* from May through October. Two-hour sight-seeing tours of river estates and lighthouses are included, as are all-day sojourns down to West Point Military Academy in Orange County: The West Point round trip takes seven hours and doesn't stop, except to let off one-way passengers, so unless your kids love cruising, opt for the shorter tours. The boat has a snack bar on board. Reservations are suggested for evening music cruises, which feature local country and western or rock 'n' roll bands. Call (914) 255-6515/(800) 843-7472.

Shawangunk Area of Ulster County

Widmark Honey Farms, Route 44-55, 2 miles west of Gardiner (914-255-6400), has been producing honey on this working farm for more than one hundred years. Along with honeybees and livestock, the farm has three American black bears that wrestle and perform in ninety-minute shows from May to October, on Saturday, Sunday, and holidays at 3:00 P.M. The farm and apiaries are open all year. There's free honey tasting and goats, calves, and lambs to pet and feed. Picnicking is allowed.

Ice Cave Mountain, Route 52, Ellenville; (914) 647-7989. This national landmark can be seen via a self-guided driving and walking tour that includes well-marked nature trails, rugged rock formations, canyons, and mountaintop vistas of five states. The walkways slope gently, making this an easy hike for kids. (The paths are too narrow for baby strollers.) There's a snack bar, rest rooms, and a gift shop. It's open mid-August through November.

Winter pleasures include **Belleayre Mountain Ski Center,** NY-28, Highmount (914-254-5600), the county's largest downhill area. It's open Thanksgiving weekend to the end of March. The lower mountain is for beginners and novices. A nursery caters to ages eight weeks to twelve years (reservations suggested), and SkiWee lessons for ages four to twelve are available on weekends and holidays. Anyone purchasing a ticket gets a free lesson. Some 6.2 km of ungroomed cross-country trails are free. Lessons are available. At press time, Belleayre planned to stay open in summer, offering tennis, hiking, volleyball, and a swimming beach on their snow-making lake for a nominal entrance fee.

Consider taking a canoe trip on the Delaware River when you visit the Catskills.
(Copyright © 1993 New York State Department of Economic Development)

Sullivan County

This southwestern Catskill county, bordered on the west by Pennsylvania, has many of the big hotels and resorts long associated with these mountains. There are also more simple lodgings and plenty of family-friendly activities. The *Sullivan County Travel Guide* suggests several different driving tours; one includes the county's famous covered bridges.

This county was the site of the Woodstock Festival, held in Bethel. If your teens consider this a historic site, then drive by for a look. The farm is located off Route 17B on Hurd Road. You'll be close to the 1,409-acre **Lake Superior State Park** in Bethel, on Duggan Road, between Routes 17B and 55. This lake has a nice, sandy beach, lifeguards, rowboat rentals, and allows fishing and picnicking. Call (914) 583-7908, ext. 5002.

With older kids, consider a canoe trip on the **Delaware River,** located on Sullivan County's western border. The *Sullivan County Travel Guide* lists outfitters who plan day or overnight trips.

In the northern half of the county is **Apple Pond Farming Center,** Hahn Road, Calicoon Center; (914) 482-4764. Call for reservations. This is a working farm; all equipment is pulled by horses. On the horse-drawn wagon tour, you meet sheep, goats, lambs, and several breeds of horses. As you ride through the fields, you hear about farming in olden days. The farm is open year-round, so depending on when you visit, you may see wool spinning, beekeeping, or maple syrup-making. There are hayrides in the summer and sleigh rides in the winter. There's a picnic area. A guest house is available by the weekend or week; reserve in advance. Since this tour involves walking through fields, strollers aren't appropriate.

In the southern half of the county, stop at the **Fort Delaware Museum of Colonial History,** Route 97, Narrowsburg; (914) 252-6660. This is a no-frills (but interesting) re-creation of the first settlement in the upper Delaware River Valley in 1754. Costumed interpreters explain how these wilderness dwellers survived. The stockaded settlement comprises log dwellings, a blacksmith's shop, a weaver's shed, armory, pens for animals, and the fort. Demonstrations of spinning, candle dipping, and musket and cannon firing are held frequently. Open from Memorial Day weekend through Labor Day, there are a variety of special events in July and August.

Lucky Penny Riding Stables, Fosterdale, 20 miles west of Monticello on Route 17B; (914) 932-8348. At the free barnyard zoo, kids pet and feed baby goats, calves, lambs, ducks, pigs, geese, chickens, and rabbits. There are pony rides for younger kids and horseback trail riding for ages six and up. It's open May 1 to October 30.

Minisink Battlefield, Minisink Ford (SR-97 west to Route 168); (914) 794-3000, ext. 5002 (State Government offices). This is the site of the 1779 battle in which American militiamen were massacred by Tories and Mohawk Indians sympathetic to the British. Three flat interpretive nature trails wind through woodlands. Across from the entrance is the 1848 Roebling's Suspension Bridge, the oldest in America, created by John Roebling of Brooklyn Bridge fame.

Downhill ski from December to March at **Davos Ski Resort** (formerly Big Vanilla), Woodbridge, New York (exit 109 off Route 17 at

Rock Hill); (914) 434-1000. The twelve trails on the main mountain offer a good place for novices and some more advanced slopes, too. SkiWee is offered for ages four to eight.

Cross-country ski at **Morningside Park,** in the town of Fallsburg, Brickman Road, Route 52; (914) 434-5877. The park offers 2½ miles of marked, groomed trails and is open dawn to dusk.

Greene County

This northern Catskill county offers a variety of ethnic and music festivals, scenic trails, one hundred waterfalls (many with natural pools for swimming), and appealing family attractions. The city of **Catskill,** just off the New York State Thruway in the eastern central part of the county, has several of particular interest.

Eldred Preserve, P.O. Box 111, Route 55, Eldred (914-557-8316), is a 2,500-acre gold mine for fishing and hunting lovers. The preserve's two lakes hold rainbow, brook, and golden trout, as well as bass. Boats can be rented. A restaurant is on site.

Carson City and Indian Village, Route 32; (518) 678-5518. At this large "western" village, expect lots of gunfights, bank robberies, and other high jinks performed by "bad" and "good" guys. Cancan, magic and Native American shows, stagecoach and train rides, and a wagon museum with horse-drawn vehicles and sleighs add to the fun. Eat at their Chuckwagon or bring your own picnic lunch. Open Memorial through Labor Day.

Catskill Game Farm, off Route 32: (518) 678-9595. Families have been coming here for generations, and the appeal is obvious: 2,000 animals, including bears, tigers, lions, and performing acts such as monkeys who juggle and elephants who dance. Buy crackers to feed deer and llamas at the petting zoo, or bottle feed small baby pigs and lambs. A train heads from the petting zoo to the birdhouse. Have lunch either at the snack bars or the picnic area, and stay the day. It's open Memorial to Labor Day. Open from May 1 to October 31.

Clyde Peeling's Reptiland, Route 32; (518) 678-3557. Your kids will either be totally fascinated or completely repelled by the approximately one hundred reptiles ranging from little garden snakes to big king cobras. Reptiland is open Memorial to Labor Day.

Elsewhere in the county you'll find **Zoom Flume Waterpark,** Shady Glen Road, East Durham, northwest of Catskill: (518)

239-4559. This is the Catskills' largest, with giant waterslides, bumper boats, waterfalls, and a dry area with a moon walk and coasters that glide down a track on the mountain. It's open Memorial to Labor Day.

North-South Lake Public Campgrounds, County Route 18, Haines Falls, southwest of Catskill; (518) 589-5058 or 357-2234. This New York State-run recreation area has two sandy beaches on either end of the lake, plus boat rentals and fishing. Hike in the surrounding woods; one trail leads to the scenic Kaaterskill Falls. Call (800) 456-CAMP in advance for campground reservations, from Memorial Day to early December.

Winter pleasures include **Hunter Mountain,** NY 23A, Hunter; (518) 263-4223/(800) FOR-SNOW—taped ski report. This three-mountain complex covers forty-six slopes and trails. Machine-made snow keeps the place open from November through April. A Peewee program for infants up to age five combines child-sitting with skiing for the older tots. At SkiWee Frostyland ages five to twelve learn to ski on weekends and holidays from 9:30 A.M. to 3:30 P.M. (reserve). From July 1 to Labor Day, the mountain has ethnic and music festivals and a Sky Ride, with views of the Northeast from the Catskills' longest and highest chairlift.

There's also **Ski Windham,** Route 23 West, Windham; (518) 734-4300/(800) 729-SKIW/(800)729-4SNO—taped snow reports. Ski on twin mountain peaks with thirty-three trails. The Children's Ski School offers half- or full-day programs that include activities for non-skiers ages one to seven, for pre-skiers age three, for ages four to seven at Mini-Mogul Skiers, and two- or five-hour sessions on weekends and holidays for Mogul Master Skiers ages eight to thirteen. Reservations with full payment required. Area lodging can be reserved through their Lodging Service; call (800) 729-SKIW.

Performing Arts

In Ulster County, Kingston's **Ulster Performing Arts Center,** 601 Broadway (914-339-6088), features Broadway plays suitable for families, concerts ranging from symphony to rock, and second-run movies for reasonable prices. **Shadowland Theatre,** Ellenville (914-647-5511), has a professional company in residence performing Broadway-style productions, musicals, and children's plays from June to October. In Sullivan County **Catskill Actors Theatre,** County Road 47, Highland

Lake (914-557-6523), has professional theater in a historic church, July through September, including original kids' theater. In Greene County, **Bond Street Theatre,** Interarts Colony, Woodstock Avenue, Palenville (914-678-3332), offers original children's programs from June to September.

SPECIAL EVENTS

Fairs and Festivals

Contact individual tourist offices for more information on festivals in their area.

May: Woodstock–New Paltz Arts and Crafts Fair, New Paltz, Ulster County; Shad Festival, Maritime Museum, Kingston, Ulster County.

July: Fourth of July celebrations in Village of Ellenville, City of Kingston, New Paltz, and Saugerties in Ulster County. St. Joseph's Italian Festival, New Paltz, Ulster County.

August: Ulster County Fair, New Paltz. Antique and Classic Boat Show, Rondout Landing, Kingston, Ulster County.

September: Woodstock–New Paltz Arts and Crafts Fair.

July–October: A variety of ethnic and music festivals at Hunter Mountain, Greene County; with food, crafts, and entertainment.

August: Delaware County Fair, Walton. Old Franklin Day, Franklin, Delaware County, features crafts, flea markets, and activities.

October: Annual Apple Festival, Hensonville, Greene County.

WHERE TO STAY

Fancy resorts, simple motels, bed and breakfast inns, cabins in the woods: The Catskills have them all. Each county tourist office can supply a listing of lodgings. Here are a few to give you an idea of what's available for families.

Ulster County: Catskill

Frost Valley YMCA, Frost Valley Road, Claryville; (914) 985-2291. This splendid place is closed in late June (except Father's Day weekend) and in July and August, when it becomes a summer camp, but the facility is open the rest of the year to the public. Accommodations include some grand rooms in the "Castle," once the home of the industrialist who owned this property, where you share the house (and baths) with other guests. Lodges, much like motel accommodations, and basic cabins are also available. Everyone eats family-style in the main dining hall. When you check in, obtain a schedule of events, which include Junior Naturalist programs, crafts, group hikes, and orienteering. There's supervised swimming in a pond, rowboats, hayrides, bikes, evening entertainment (such as square dancing and sing-alongs), even cross-country skiing and sledding during winter.

Shawangunk Mountains

Mohonk Mountain House, Lake Mohonk, New Paltz; (914) 255-1000 or (800) 772-6646—from area codes 212, 516, or 718. This historic Victorian resort, situated on 7,000 acres of nature preserve, offers specialty, themed weekends fall through spring. During January's What's in the Winter Woods, you and your kids learn about forest animals and winter night skies; during the March Family Festival, listen to storytellers and join in sing-alongs.

When not busy with events, hike in the woods; if it's cold enough, skate on the frozen lake or the pond. When it snows, there's cross-country skiing as well. On weekends a modified kids' program operates for ages three to twelve. From Memorial Day to Labor Day, there are programs for kids ages two to seventeen. Baby-sitting is available at an extra charge. The rates include three meals a day. The rooms, remember, are not "hotel modern." Rather than glitz, you have lots of Victorian oak and many fireplaces.

Pinegrove Resort Ranch, Lower Chestertown Road, Kerhonkson, NY 12446; (800) 346-4626 or (914) 626-7345. This year-round dude ranch caters to families by offering day-long activities at an all-inclusive price. Located on 500 acres between the Shawangunk Mountains and the Catskill range, this ranch runs instructional horseback rides eight times a day. From 10:00 A.M. to 5:00 P.M. every day, a nursery cares for kids up to two years old, and a day camp keeps kids ages three and up happily busy feeding llamas, singing on hayrides, and riding ponies. Children under age seven learn to ride in the corral, and kids over seven go on trail rides with adults. Evening entertainment includes square dancing, scavenger hunts, and family games. The price includes three meals a day, an all-day snack bar, rides, and entertainment. Rates are half-price for children four through sixteen, and kids under four stay for free.

Sullivan County

Concord Resort Hotel, Kiamesha Lake; (800) 431–3850. This place is representative of the big, Catskill hotels: nightly entertainment, twenty-four outdoor and sixteen indoor tennis courts, indoor and outdoor pools, a health club, forty-five-hole golf, downhill and cross-country skiing, and day camps. Opt for the meal plan or go European. Food is an activity in itself here. Waiters bring you platefuls of things to try. While this bustling resort is not for everyone, some doubting Thomases come home with surprisingly fond memories.

Kutsher's Country Club, near Monticello, is another of the old-style resorts that has been trying to woo a new generation by promoting its kids' programs. These include a nursery for young ones, programs for ages three to five and six to nine, plus some activities for preteens and teens. With 450 rooms and more than 1,200 acres, Kutsher's is big. This Catskill's fixture offers tennis, golf, ice skating, and nightly entertainment. Call (800) 431–1273 or (914) 794–6000.

Greene County

Balsam Shade Farm, Route 32, Greenville; (518) 966–5315. This casual, country family lodging has pool, tennis, hiking, and lovely mountain views. There's nightly entertainment and three meals served daily with their own farm-grown vegetables.

Villagio, Route 23A, Haines Falls; (800) 834–4348. This year-round resort is set on 300 acres and has an Italian theme in food and entertainment. You'll find indoor and outdoor pools, movies, tennis, and 5 miles of cross-country trails. **Note:** Greene County has "pockets" of resorts with ethnic ambiance: Italian in Haines Falls/Tannersville area, Irish in East Durham, and Austrian-German in Round Top.

Albergo Allegria, Route 296, Windham (800–6-ALBERGO), is a hospitable Victorian bed and breakfast that welcomes families. Great for all seasons, the bed and breakfast offers Belgian waffles or gourmet omelettes (among other delicious foods) in their outdoor cafe. If you happen to stay during the ski season, warm yourselves by the fireplace during the Après Ski on Saturdays, when complimentary hot cider and hot chocolate are served.

Scribner Hollow Motor Lodge, Route 32A, Hunter (519-263-4211), has a rustic atmosphere with gorgeous Catskill views, sauna and Jacuzzi, an outdoor heated swimming pool, all-season tennis courts, and an indoor spa/pool.

Sunny Hill Resort and Golf Course, Route 32 or 82, Greenville (518-634-7693 or 518-634-7642), has 200 acres of open spaces and private woods as well as Lake Loree. The resort offers an eighteen-hole golf course, a video-game room, tennis courts, and an outdoor swimming pool.

WHERE TO EAT

Each county's travel guide offers dining listings. In Greene County **La Conca D'Oro,** 440 Main Street, Catskill, serves delicious Northern Italian food; (518) 943-3549. **Red's,** Route 9W, West Coxsackie, is known far and wide for its fresh seafood; (914) 731-8151.

Club 97, Route 97, Callicoon (914-887-5941), offers great family dining, with an available children's menu, serving dishes from Italian to seafood to prime rib, plus homemade desserts.

Eldred Preserve Restaurant, Route 55, Eldred (914-557-8316), is open every day from June to August; specialties include fresh trout and continental cuisine. Reservations are suggested in summer and fall.

DAY TRIPS

Wherever you stay, take a day trip to explore adjacent Catskill counties (Greene County, for instance, is about forty-five minutes north of Kingston). From Delaware County drive north to Cooperstown in adjoining Otsego County to the **National Baseball Hall of Fame;** (607) 547-9988. Most of Ulster and Sullivan counties are less than ninety minutes from New York City.

FOR MORE INFORMATION

Tourist Information in Greene County, Thruway exit 21, Catskill (518-943-3223), is open seven days a week, or call (800) 542-2414. For Ulster County information write to Public Information Office, P.O. Box 1800, Kingston, NY 12401; (800) DIAL-UCO. Sullivan County has two Information Center Cabooses. The first, on Broad Street, Roscoe, is also a mini railroad museum, open Memorial Day to mid-October. The Livingston Manor Caboose, exit 96 off Route 17, is open July and August on Friday, Saturday, and Sunday from 11:00 A.M. to 4:00 P.M. You can also call (914) 794-3000, ext. 5010 or (800) 882-CATS. Delaware County Chamber of Commerce, 97 Main Street, Delhi, New York 13753; (607) 746-2281 or (800) 642-4443.

Emergency Numbers

Since we're covering a wide area, we've listed county sheriff numbers. Much of the area will be tied into 911 in the near future. Consult the front of your area's phone directory for the latest information.

Greene County

Sheriff: (518) 943-3300

Catskill Community Care Clinic, 159 Jefferson Heights, Catskill: (518) 943-6334

Greene Medical Arts Center: (518) 943-1505

Ulster County

Sheriff: (914) 338-0939

Kingston City Hospital, 396 Broadway: (914) 331-3131

Sullivan County

Sheriff: (914) 794-7100

Community General Hospital has two branches: one on Bushville Road, Harris, in the center of the county (914-794-3300), and one in Callicoon, in the west, Route 97 (914-887-5530).

Poison Control: (914) 353-1000/(800) 336-6997 (from 518 and 914 area codes)

There are no twenty-four-hour pharmacies in the area. A number are open seven days a week, such as CVS, Route 9W, King's Mall, Kingston (914-336-5955), 9:00 A.M. to 9:00 P.M., Monday through Saturday, closing at 6:00 P.M. on Sunday. Some pharmacies post emergency numbers on their front doors for after-hours assistance.

CAPE MAY

Cape May, New Jersey, a born-again beach town, boasts a historic district with colorfully restored Victorian houses. Turreted, gabled, bay-windowed, and laced with gingerbread, these houses are a treat to the eye. How the town came to be is an interesting story.

The rich and the famous flocked to Cape May in its nineteenth-century heyday. Arriving by steamboat and railroad from Philadelphia, Baltimore, and Washington, political leaders such as Millard Fillmore, Franklin Pierce, Abraham Lincoln, and Ulysses S. Grant shook off the rigors of politics for sand and surf on Cape May's shores. Along these once-wide beaches, Louis Chevrolet and Henry Ford raced their automobiles. John Philip Sousa played at Congress Hall, one of the grande dame hotels, and Wallis Simpson, the future Duchess of Windsor, debuted at the Colonial Hotel on Ocean Avenue. In 1891 Benjamin Harrison took over Congress Hall, making it his summer White House.

Spurred by such high-society tourism, entrepreneurs built hotels like the Mount Vernon, which, though it burned just before its official opening, offered 2,000 rooms and stretched for blocks along the Atlantic. In 1878 a disastrous fire destroyed many of these grand hotels, particularly in the West End. The locals, hurriedly rebuilding for the coming summer season, eschewed costly and difficult-to-build large hotels for three-story Victorian "cottages" with plenty of spare rooms for summer guests. These now grace the streets of Cape May, still offering bed and breakfast in rooms filled with Victorian antiques, and polite conversation in elaborately draped parlors where afternoon tea is almost always served.

At the turn of the century, Atlantic City's modern accommodations had stolen Cape May's place in the sun, and the town experienced a gradual decline. But in the 1960s when urban renewal planners began tearing these old Victorian dwellings down to make way for modern motels, preservationists rallied. After a protracted fight in the early seventies, Cape May was designated a historical district. Restoration then began in earnest, and cottages formerly partitioned into boarding houses and apartments were born again as elegant guest homes.

GETTING THERE

Traveling by land, take either of two routes to Cape May: I-95 over the Delaware Memorial Bridge to Route 40 east, to Route 55 south, to Route 47 south, to U.S. 9 into Cape May; or, travel on I-295 to U.S. 322 south, to Route 55 south, to Route 47 south, to U.S. 9 into Cape May.

The Cape May–Lewes Ferry runs daily between Cape May and Lewes, Delaware. Kids really enjoy this boat ride because it offers a welcome break from being cooped up in a car. The ferry terminal is on U.S. 9, 3 miles west of the southern terminus of the Garden State Parkway. For schedule information call (800) 64-FERRY.

GETTING AROUND

The best ways to see Cape May are by foot or by bicycle. Self-guided tour maps outlining walking tours of Cape May are available at the Washington Street Mall's information booths. **Surrey Bicycles,** a four-seated bike with a canopy-hood—perfect for the family—can be rented at Victorian Village Plaza's **Village Bikes,** Ocean and Washington streets; (609) 884-8500. Carriage, trolley, and guided walking tours also originate at the Washington Street Mall. Call (609) 884-5404.

WHAT TO SEE AND DO

Nature: Beaches and Birds

Miles of beach lure summer crowds. The beach along Beach Avenue offers families the typical delights of sun and sand. Come early, as these shores get really crowded. Pick a spot and bring or rent a beach umbrella. Collect starfish, great cream-colored whelks, giant horseshoe crab shells, and driftwood. A time-honored tradition is strolling along the boardwalk and munching such beach delights as pizza and fries.

Fall, with smaller crowds, quieter beaches, and water temperatures still warm enough for swimming, may be the best time to enjoy this

Cape May at a Glance

- A restored beach town with Victorian flair

- Some of the best (and most popular) beaches on the coast

- Several zoos, farms, and nature preserves

- The largest ferris wheel on the east coast

- An authentic, old-time boardwalk

- Greater Cape May Chamber of Commerce, (609) 884-5508

historic beach town. Additional autumn attractions include a Victorian festival and a great migration of birds. Each fall the birds come by the tens of thousands to Cape May, funneling through here for food and rest before crossing Delaware Bay and continuing south. The beaches afford a perfect vantage point for such spectacular sights as a phalanx of Canadian geese in precise formation above the gray-blue surf, or thousands of hawks gliding on warm air currents before swooping down on their prey.

Besides the beachfront near the heart of town, three areas offer less crowded beaches and, in fall, the best spots for birding: **Cape May Point State Park;** the **Cape May Migratory Bird Refuge,** a stretch of beach and dunes along Sunset Boulevard; and **Higbee's Beach.**

Cape May Point State Park—take Sunset Boulevard to Lighthouse Drive—has 195 acres of nature trails, wooded areas, and a half-mile of beachfront. Check out the station headquarters for a modest display of birds and shells and for the schedule of beginner bird walks and demonstrations of hawk banding.

Walk along the boardwalk trails (wide enough for wheelchair access and strollers) through clusters of red cedars and shrubs to ponds where, especially in fall, snowy egrets hover like angels, and herons seem to walk on water. A special fall treat is the sight of thousands of hawks. A hawk-watch platform adjacent to the parking lot provides a good observation point for those with small children too weary to wander or climb the abandoned World War II concrete bunker that juts out into the ocean. This, incidentally, is a good place to glimpse the falcons gliding on an updraft.

Higbee's Beach, a wildlife area, is more isolated and features clusters of trees that lead to the water. Higbee's also provides a quiet space for birding and solitary strolls, where you can often hear the cries of laughing gulls. To get here take Route 7, called Bayshore Road, and continue for about 2 miles almost to the dead end sign, then turn left. (It's New England Road, but there's often no sign.)

For more information on birding, contact the **Cape May Bird Observatory,** New Jersey Audubon Society, 705 East Lake Drive, P.O. Box 3, Cape May Point 08212; call (609) 884-2736 or (609) 884-2626 (the hotline) for the latest information.

Nearby Nature

The **Cape May County Park and Zoo,** Route 9, Pinelane (609-465-5271), houses more than 250 species of animals. Located just 7 miles north of Wildwood via the Garden State Parkway, the zoo is an easy day trip, guaranteed to make little (and not so little) ones smile with delight. A highlight is the fifty-five-acre African savannah. From an overlook watch giraffe, zebra, ostrich, and antelope roam over the grasslands. Along the walkway listen to the mynah birds chatter. Other zoo highlights include a bear habitat, a reptile house, lions, tigers, and cougars. Bring a picnic lunch and spend several hours. After visiting the zoo, take time to enjoy the tennis and basketball courts and the nature trail.

Don't miss **Leaming's Run Gardens and Colonial Farm,** 1845 Route 9 North, Cape May Courthouse, New Jersey 08210, about 14 miles north of Cape May; (609) 465-5871. Open mid-May to mid-October, this garden offers thirty acres of beautifully sculpted, tranquil gardens and fern-carpeted woods.

Allow at least ninety minutes, preferably longer, to follow the winding path through each of twenty-five gardens, carefully planted

You and your family can climb the 199 steps to the top of the Cape May Point Lighthouse . . . the view will not disappoint. (Courtesy Cape May Department of Tourism and Economic Development)

with colorful annuals and graced with lily ponds, gazebos, and benches shaded by tall trees. By June the roses are best, and in October it's still warm, but the leaves are turning. The gardens, set above a forest bed of soft cinnamon ferns, each illustrate a color theme or solve such common gardening problems as hillsides and too much shade.

This kind of "education" is easy on the eyes. The English cottage garden pops into color with 140 varieties of flowers; the Serpentine Garden (demonstrating how to plant in a long narrow area) winds its way to the lake in a burst of red salvias; the Knoll Garden, with its wild flowers, illustrates planting at different levels; and the reflecting pond laced with water lilies demonstrates how to use water to mirror flowers.

As owner Jack Aprill intended, this is a garden for relaxing and sharing a pleasant moment. Just to be sure, Aprill has placed signs urging you to PLEASE LOOK BACK, RELAX HERE, and WATCH FOR HUMMINGBIRDS.

Another surprise is the occasional sound of roosters. Aprill has planted a Colonial farm that re-creates the world of Thomas Leaming, the whaler who originally settled this farm in 1706. There's a one-room log cabin, a barn with roosters, and a dooryard garden planted with such typical Colonial crops as cotton, tobacco, peanuts, okra, pumpkin, and squash. The gardens end at the Cooperage, one of the largest dried-flower shops in the East—and Aprill's main business. With artifice that would have been much admired by the Victorians, Aprill has masterfully blended art and nature.

Victorian Architecture

If you're a fan of whimsical architecture and the plutocratic lifestyle, be sure to stroll along Columbia Avenue, Hughes Street, Perry Street, and Ocean Avenue past some gaily painted structural dowager queens. Sit on the serpentine porches of the surviving grand hotels—the Chalfonte, Congress Hall, and the Colonial—or rest in a wicker rocker on the back veranda of an elegant inn and take in a view from the past.

The **Emlen Physick House,** 1048 Washington Street, is open for tours. Built in 1879, this home has the elaborate furnishings of its eccentric and wealthy resident, Dr. Emlen Physick. Sometimes, from Memorial Day to mid-June, *The Doctor is In* takes place in the evenings. Among the heavy drapes and rococo Victoriana, you'll find the good doctor himself, talking politics and town gossip.

Look for the Mid-Atlantic Center for the Arts' (MAC) weekly flyer *This Week in Cape May,* which highlights Cape May's upcoming attractions and events. For more information contact the Chamber of Commerce of Greater Cape May at (609) 884–5508 or MAC. Trolleys offer a wide variety of historic, architectural, and seasonal tours of Cape May throughout the year. Generally, there are special guided tours and open houses in May and during Victorian Week celebrations.

SPECIAL EVENTS

Festivals, Theater, and Cultural Events

April: Tour Cape May's Tulip Festival. The trolleys offer a great vantage point that's easy on little feet.

May: Cape May Music Festival, a six-week-long festival that showcases the talents of noted soloists and musicians. Almost all of the festival's numerous concerts are held at Congress Hall, Beach Drive at Perry Street.

June: Seafood-Kite Fest.

July–August: The **Cape May Kid's Playhouse** and the **Vintage Film Festival** offer entertainment for both young and old.

October: During Victorian Week this town throws a Victorian fete filled with vaudeville, a fashion show, an antiques fair, walking tours, and old-house restoration workshops.

November: During Victorian Holmes Weekend Cape May is the setting for amateur sleuths to solve Sir Arthur Conan Doyle's Sherlock Holmes mysteries.

December: Christmas Lights Trolleys tour the decorated streets. Coachmans Tour, Grand Tours.

WHERE TO STAY

Some of the best bets for family lodging in Cape May are motels and the handful of bed and breakfast inns that welcome families. Book as far in advance as possible, as Cape May is a very popular summer spot. And please be advised that most of the charming bed and breakfast inns do not really welcome children. In addition, many of these inns, in keeping with the period, either don't have air-conditioned bedrooms or have only one or two at most. Don't believe that stuff about cross-breezes and fans. Without this modern convenience in summer, you will be either hot or very hot. If this matters, ask ahead of time and find a lodging that accommodates your needs. A few inns, such as the Queen Victoria, are open year-round. Many close for the season in November.

The **Camelot Motel,** 103 Howard Street (609–884–1500) only 50 yards from the beach, has two-bedroom efficiencies complete with kitchenette. Another near-the-beach motel is the **Atlas Motor Inn,** 1035 Beach Drive (609–884–7000), which has a pool and restaurant, as well as efficiency apartments. **The Dormer House International,** 800 Columbia Avenue (609–884–7446), 3 blocks from the beach, rents one- and two-bedroom apartments with kitchens.

Featuring 1885 Victorian guest quarters, **Goodman House,** 118 Decatur Street (609–884–6371), is ½ block from the beach and also offers rental apartments with kitchens.

If you're traveling to Cape May with young children, a good bet is the **Chalfonte Hotel,** Box 475, 301 Howard Street; (609) 884–8409. The Chalfonte has special two-bedroom apartments and separate dining facilities for kids six years old and under. Parents can enjoy a romantic dinner while their kids eat and then play with newfound friends supervised by college-age counselors.

The Queen Victoria, 102 Ocean Street (609–884–8702), a nicely appointed bed and breakfast with Edwardian antiques, welcomes children and offers cot rentals for the little ones but has a limited number of rooms for families. According to the owners this bed and breakfast offers comfortable and functional antique furniture "sturdy enough to plunk down in, relax, and put your feet up on." Families may prefer the newly opened **Queen's Hotel,** Ocean and Columbia streets (609–884–8702) operated by the same family. More of a boutique hotel, this property's rooms all have private baths, refrigerators, coffeemakers, televisions, and telephones.

Congress Hall, Beach Avenue and Perry Street (609–884–8421), is one of Cape May's grand old hotels. Built in 1879, Congress Hall offers real variety in its 112 rooms—some with antique brass bed and ocean views and others with a more motellike feel.

The Virginia Hotel, P.O. Box 557, 25 Jackson Street (609–884–5700 or 800–732–4236), is an upscale Victorian inn, restored to its late nineteenth-century grace. Families can feel comfortable in rooms that come with oversize beds, down comforters, a television, and VCR. Children under ten stay for free, while kids over ten are charged a nominal fee per night. There's a free continental breakfast.

WHERE TO EAT

In high season—summer and during fall's Victorian Week—book your dinner reservations ahead; otherwise, the lines and the wait can be long.

For an Italian dinner try **God Mothers,** 413 Broadway; (609) 884-4543.

Dillons Restaurant, 524 Washington Street (609-884-5225), is open for breakfast, lunch, and dinner and serves light, cafe-style fare. The **Ocean View Restaurant,** Beach Drive and Grant Avenue (609-884-3772), is open for breakfast, lunch, and dinner; they serve diner fare. **McGlade's,** 722 Beach Drive (609-884-2614), offers seafood and American cuisine.

For fine dining families with older children should try **The Ebbitt Room,** in the Virginia Hotel, 25 Jackson Street; (609) 884-5700. Dishes combine French, Latin, and Euro-Asian touches. While at the Ebbitt Room, stop by the **Ebbitt Lounge,** a piano bar that offers nightly entertainment.

DAY TRIPS

Preteens and teens may urge you to spend some time at **Wildwood, N.J.,** a bustling beach town. Wildwood, along with attracting its share of college students and twenty-somethings, makes families feel at home. The beach is wide, the waves are manageable, and the 2-mile boardwalk comes replete with eateries, arcades, and amusements.

As any beach town aficionado knows, half the fun is enjoying the scene off the sand, and Wildwood's **boardwalk** is perfect. For kids the arcades and rides proffer a wonderland of fun; for parents it's a nostalgic stroll. Unlike the re-created midways being built at theme parks across the United States, Wildwood presents the real thing: T-shirt shops, saltwater taffy, arcade games of skill, and lots of boardwalk snacks. Treat the kid in you, along with those with you, to such time-tested beach fare as funnel cakes, pizza, and cotton candy.

You'll get nothing but "wows" from your kids when they see the **Ferris wheel at Mariner's Landing Pier** (Schellenger Avenue and the boardwalk). The largest in the East Coast at 156 feet high, this whirling bit of wonder serves as Wildwood's unofficial fun symbol. Known for its several amusement piers, Wildwood debuts a new one this Memorial Day: **Dinosaur Beach Adventure Theme Park** (Juniper Avenue and the boardwalk), at the former Hunt's Pier, sports rides based on these popular, prehistoric critters. Blast off in an inner tube pushed along by a jet spray of water; board a jeep for a safari ride through a jungle populated with high-tech, animated dinosaurs; and shriek with delight at the 40-foot drop on the log flume. Little kids aren't forgotten, either. They can dig for fossils, fly high on a Dragon Jet and Tilt, and take a spin on the carousel.

Your children will undoubtedly want to make the fun park rounds. Roller coaster enthusiasts find life's ups and downs thrilling on the **Great Nor'easter at Morey's Pier** (Twenty-fifty Street and the boardwalk), a suspended looping coaster that swirls you at speeds up to 55 mph. Both Morey's Pier and Mariner's Landing Pier feature a **Raging Waters Theme Park** for those who want more than ocean waves. Slide, slither, wiggle, and float, as well as get splashed and sprayed, at these kid-pleasing places. Although young children find pint-size pools and sprays at both parks, the **Raging Waters Theme Park at Morey's Pier** sports an expanded kiddie section themed to pirates.

Festivals, all free and all season long, add to the family fare. Two favorites include the **East Coast Stunt Kite Championships,** in late May, and the **Annual National Marbles Tournament,** in late June. At the kite display children grow wide-eyed at the high-flying maneuvers from team ballets to top-speed tricks. At the marbles matches kids gain inspiration (not to mention moves) from watching their peers ages eight to fourteen compete for scholarship money. Days when these hot shots aren't playing, your kids are free to try their skill on the ten permanent marbles rings, just another of Wildwood's bows to family fun.

Besides boardwalk browsing, sand-castle building, and swimming, a time-honored tradition is to get out on the water. Several companies offer **whale- and dolphin-watching cruises.** While you should be ready to yell

"Thar' she blows," you're more likely to encounter schools of playful dolphins than the great behemoths of the deep. Boats include the *Big Flamingo* (609-522-3934) and the speedboat the *Silver Bullet* (609-522-1919).

The Wildwood area offers more than 20,000 rooms in motels, hotels, and condominiums. For families, especially those with young children who want beachside access and more quiet than constant activity, Wildwood Crest, south of the boardwalk area, may be more appropriate. The **Reges Oceanfront Resort** (the beach at 9201 Atlantic Avenue; 609-729-9300) offers rooms with kitchenettes, an adult and kiddie pool, and some organized children's activities in season. Several rental agencies can book stays at homes and condominiums. For properties in Wildwood contact **Oceanside Realty** (4500 Atlantic Avenue; 609-522-3322); for Wildwood Crest contact **Century 21** (5604 Pacific Avenue; 609-522-1212). The **Greater Wildwood Chamber of Commerce** (800-WW-BY-SEA; 609-729-4000) offers a lodging guide.

Board the Cape May-Lewes ferry for a trip to Lewes, Delaware, another beach town. Within several hours of Cape May, you can be in Philadelphia or the Brandywine Valley, Pennsylvania. (See the appropriate chapters.)

FOR MORE INFORMATION

For more information on Cape May, New Jersey, contact the **Greater Cape May Chamber of Commerce,** P.O. Box 556, Cape May, New Jersey 08204; (609) 884-5508. For information concerning upcoming Cape May activities and cultural events, contact the **Mid-Atlantic Center for the Arts (MAC),** P.O. Box 340, 1048 Washington Street, Cape May, New Jersey 08204; (609) 884-5404.

Emergency Numbers

Ambulance, fire, and police: 911.

Poison Control: 911

Twenty-four-hour pharmacy and around-the-clock medical attention: Burdette Tomlin Hospital, Cape May Courthouse, exit 10 off Garden State Parkway; (609) 463-2000.

Hospital: The Burdette Tomlin Memorial Hospital is 11 miles away; (609) 463-2000.

GETTYSBURG

Take your family back to July of 1863 when Confederate General Robert E. Lee's army met the greater forces of the Northern army in a historic battle and turning point of the Civil War. The Gettysburg National Military Park, encompassing some 1,000 monuments and cannons, commemorates this important national event. Add a bonus to your visit by timing it to coincide with one of Gettysburg's popular festivals, such as the apple festival in May or the bluegrass music festival in May and September. A special time to visit is during the **Gettysburg Civil War Heritage Days,** the end of June through July Fourth, when battle reenactments and special events will add excitement to your visit. Besides visiting the battlefield, take time to enjoy driving and picnicking in the rolling countryside, dotted with apple orchards.

GETTING THERE

It's best to drive to Gettysburg. Several roads lead to the battlefield park, including U.S. 30 and 15, as well as state routes 134 and 116.

GETTING AROUND

There is no public transportation in Gettysburg. During the summer season a trolley runs every half hour; however, a car is a necessity.

WHAT TO SEE AND DO

Civil War History

Gettysburg National Military Park (Visitor's Center: Route 134, Gettysburg; 717-334-1124) is the site of one of the most significant, and bloodiest, battles of the Civil War. A visit here makes textbook history come alive, especially if you get your kids involved. Children ages

Gettysburg at a Glance

- Site of the Civil War's turning point

- Gettysburg National Military Park makes the war real for everyone

- A dozen other museums in the area

- Four historic walking and driving tours

- Civil War Heritage Days, held in July and August

- Gettysburg Travel Council, (717) 334-6274; Gettysburg National Military Park Visitor's Bureau, (717) 334-1124

five to thirteen can earn a Gettysburg **Junior Ranger** badge by completing activities in a free booklet available at the Visitor's Center. At the **Visitor's Center,** brush up on your history by reviewing the 750-square-foot electric map that illustrates the famous battle and is accompanied by a taped narration. Books and souvenirs are also available, some aimed at children.

From here there are three options for a comprehensive tour of the 25-square-mile battlefield. Obtain a Park Service tour pamphlet, and try a self-guided drive that takes you past the designated landmarks. Another option is to rent a narrated tape produced by a private company. The **CCInc. Auto Tape Tours** add voice, music, and sound effects to enliven your self-guided driving tour. The rental tapes are available for about $12 from the National Civil War Wax Museum, 297 Steinwehr Avenue (717-334-6245), or the tape can be ordered for about $13, including postage, by writing, CCInc, P.O. Box 631, Goldens Bridge, New York 10526.

The best way, we think, is to hire a National Park guide to accompany you in your car. A real guide makes dramatic history of what might be dubbed "boring stones and markers" by some kids. Guides,

Adults and children alike can learn what Civil War life was like at Gettysburg National Military Park. (Courtesy Gettysburg Travel Council)

who cost approximately $25 per car for families of up to five, add the vivid narrative and background necessary to turn these grassy slopes into important history. Ask and the guides will also tailor a tour to meet your family's interests. Ask where your state's unit or a distant relative's unit was positioned, and the guide will take you to the spot and tell you a more specific story.

Some guides cater to children, commanding them to disembark from their vehicle and assume the positions of an artillery crew in order to explain how a cannon was fired. Another kid-favorite place that a guide can easily lead you to is the monument for Sally the War Dog, who saw her share of battle.

But try to get out of your car for even a little bit. Walking along one of the several marked trails not only gives you a different perspective on the battle but also enables your kids to see the monuments and cannons up close. Trails vary in length from about 1 to 9 miles. Bring along a picnic lunch and break for food at one of the various picnicking sites. Maps of the trails and picnic areas can be obtained at the Visitor's

Center. A favorite path is the mile-long **High Water Mark Trail** that begins at the Cyclorama Center and takes you by regimental monuments, Union soldier territory, and General Meade's headquarters. Boy Scouts should ask about hiking on the Johnny Reb and the Billy Yank Trails, which, when completed, can lead to a Gettysburg Merit Badge.

Bicycling or horseback riding through the park adds fun to your visit as well. Biking trails wind through parts of the park, and an 8-mile horseback bridle trail meanders through the second- and third-day battle areas. Bicycle and horse rentals are available at the **Artillery Ridge Campground,** 610 Taneytown Road (717-334-1288) from April 1 through October 30.

The best time to visit the outdoor park is when the weather is good. Your kids will feel freer to roam outside, and from mid-June to mid-August the National Park Service presents a living history program, in which costumed interpreters act out Civil War roles. A nineteenth-century civilian carefully explains what it was like for him when the battle rolled into his hometown, and a soldier sitting next to him relates a different story of woe and worry.

The Cyclorama Center, also on the grounds of the national park, presents the *Gettysburg Cyclorama,* Paul Philippoteaux's painting of Pickett's charge, which is accompanied by an entertaining sound-and-light presentation. The center also displays exhibits and a ten-minute film.

Be sure to climb the **National Tower,** an observation tower, across from the National Park Visitor's Center, but not officially part of the park. The 307-foot tower affords a panoramic view of the battlefield. There's also a twelve-minute tape that details the battle.

If your kids aren't scared of graveyards, don't miss the **Gettysburg National Cemetery,** which encompasses twenty-one acres and contains nearly 4,000 graves of Civil War soldiers. It was at the dedication of this cemetery on November 19, 1863, that President Abraham Lincoln delivered his two-minute speech. Since then Lincoln's Gettysburg Address has been immortalized as inspired rhetoric and a moving speech about the sacrifices of war.

Additional Attractions

Adjacent to Gettysburg Park is the **Eisenhower National Historic Site;** (717) 334-1124. A tour of this site may interest older children who have some knowledge of former-president Eisenhower. A one-hour narrated tour takes visitors through the decorated rooms of the retirement home of Dwight and Mamie Eisenhower. Tours of the home are conducted from the Visitor's Center only. Be sure to get your tickets first thing, as there is a limited number of tours per day.

The following museums are not part of the National Park Service but are privately run; they expound on aspects of the famous battle and surrounding history. Some families like these; others find them not worth the trouble. If you plan to visit a number of these attractions, look into a package plan, which includes a two-hour bus tour and admission costs to either four or eight of the participating attractions. Package plans are available from the Gettysburg Tour Center; (717) 334-6296.

Jennie Wade House & Olde Town, Baltimore Pike; (717) 334-4100. This museum strikes a chord with children who can easily identify with the story of Jennie Wade, the only civilian killed in the battle of Gettysburg. Across the street in Olde Town, you'll find a gathering of old-fashioned crafts and merchant shops.

The National Civil War Wax Museum, Steinwehr Avenue (717-334-6245), is another favorite for kids. They can watch and listen to a full presentation, where two hundred life-size wax figures re-create the Battle of Gettysburg and Lincoln's Gettysburg Address.

Battle Theatre, Steinwehr Avenue (717-334-6100), presents a general overview of the battle as well as a multimedia reenactment on a 50-foot diorama screen. Visit **General Lee's Headquarters and Museum,** Route 30 West, 8 blocks west of Lincoln Square. In this old stone building, now displaying Civil War relics, General Lee and his advisers planned for the Battle of Gettysburg. **The Lincoln Room Museum,** Wills House, Lincoln Square (717-334-8188), is the former home of David Wills, where Lincoln revised his famous Gettysburg Address in November of 1863.

Lincoln Train Museum, Steinwehr Avenue; (717) 334-5678. Younger children and train enthusiasts will be drawn to this quaint museum where visitors take an imaginary ride from Washington to Gettysburg and eavesdrop on reporters and other distinguished guests. There are model trains to see as well. The **Hall of Presidents and First Ladies** (717-334-5717) offers more wax figures, this time presidents and first ladies, relating their visions of America. The kids might like the first ladies' inaugural dresses. **The Confederate States Armory & Museum,** 529 Baltimore Street (717-337-2340), displays rare and original Confederate edged weapons and small arms. The **Soldier's National Museum,** Baltimore Pike (717-331-4890), displays dioramas and exhibits of the Civil War from 1861 as well as the Charley Weaver Collection, miniature carved figures from ten major battles of the Civil War. **The State Museum of Pennsylvania,** Harrisburg, Pennsylvania (717-787-4978), located about 35 miles north of Gettysburg, documents the history of the state and presents The Keystone of the Union, an exhibit on Gettysburg and the Civil War.

Gettysburg Land of Little Horses, off Route 30 West; follow signs; (717) 334-7259. Here's a good rainy-day activity. Watch these 3-foot tall horses race, jump, and perform in the indoor arena. Call in advance for performance times.

Special Tours

Downtown Historic District Tour of the more than one hundred recently restored buildings will give visitors a feel of the town that gave the battlefield its name. The walking starts at the Gettysburg Travel Council Office and includes the Wills House, where President Lincoln composed his Gettysburg Address, and Samuel Gettys' Tavern, originally owned by James Gettys, the town's founder. Tour brochures are available at the Gettysburg Travel Council; (717) 334-6274.

The Adams County Scenic Valley Tour is a self-paced driving tour covering 36 miles south, west, and north of Gettysburg. The estimated driving time is two hours. Tour brochures are available at the Gettysburg Travel Council (717-334-6274), and posted signs mark the route. Highlights of the tour, which covers some of the famous orchards in Pennsylvania, include the Civil War site "Cashtown Pass," the 1790 Lower Marsh Creek Presbyterian Church, and Biglerville, the "Apple Capital."

The **Historic Conewago Tour** is a 40-mile driving tour, about two hours, which weaves around the Conewago Creek on the eastern side of the county. Tour highlights include the East Cavalry Battlefield, the historic towns of New Oxford and East Berlin, and country farms, churches, and the Adams County countryside. Tour brochures are available at the Gettysburg Travel Council; (717) 334-6274.

Gettysburg Battlefield Bus Tours (717–334–6296) presents various battlefield tours, including a sunset tour on a double-decker bus. Tours are conducted by a cast of actors who use sound effects to act out the drama of the battlefield.

SPECIAL EVENTS

Antiques Shows

There are several large antiques shows in and around the Gettysburg area. For more information call the Gettysburg Travel Council at (717) 334–6274.

Festivals

May: Gettysburg Spring Bluegrass Festival the first full weekend in May. Join in the Apple Blossom Festival for a fuller appreciation of Adams County's outstanding apple orchards and enjoy magic shows, apple-bobbing contests, music, and dancing. Gettysburg Square-Dance Round-up is the real thing, featuring nationally recognized square-dance callers. Memorial Day Parade.

June/July: Civil War Heritage Days is a nine-day event including several days of a historically accurate reenactment of the Battle of Gettysburg. Festivities include band concerts and lectures by America's foremost historians. A fairly new addition is the Living History Camp, where soldiers set up a realistic Civil War camp on the premises and demonstrate Civil War tactics, infantry drills, loading their weapons, and other pastimes. Children will love the realism of this event and are welcome to ask the soldiers questions.

Younger children will be entertained at the Gettysburg Firemen's Festival, a week-long evening celebration held at the same time as the Heritage Days. The festival includes games, rides, and a July Fourth fireworks display.

In conjunction with the Civil War Heritage Days, a Civil War Book Fair is held on the first weekend in July, with book dealers selling new, used, and out-of-print Civil War–related documents. The Annual Gettysburg Civil War Collectors' Show features some 250 dealers displaying their Civil War memorabilia.

In order to have a choice of accommodations during Heritage Days and other events, especially during the most popular anniversary

days, July 1–3, families should make reservations at least three to four months in advance. Group packages are available. For more information call (717) 334–6274; for ticket reservations call (717) 334–6246.

August: South Mountain Fair. Enjoy one last hurrah at this country fair before school starts.

September: East Berlin Colonial Days is an eighteenth-century crafts and cultural fair. Gettysburg Fall Bluegrass Festival is for those who didn't get enough of the country sounds in May.

October: National Apple Harvest Festival, Biglerville, Pennsylvania. These two weekends are full of country music, crafts, rides, and, of course, apples. The festival is organized with kids in mind.

November: Anniversary of Lincoln's Gettysburg Address and Remembrance Day.

December: Yuletide Festival is a three-day festival of Christmas music, crafts, food, and religion, including tours of historical homes and crafts. Ask about special children's events.

WHERE TO STAY

Colonial Motel, 157 Carlisle Street (717–334–3126 or 800–336–3126), just north of Center Square, is centrally located and offers family rates. Kids stay free at the **Criterion Motor Lodge,** 337 Carlisle Street (717) 334–6268. Other family-friendly hotels where children stay for free are the **Quality Inn-Gettysburg Motor Lodge,** 380 Steinwehr Avenue (717–334–1103 or 800–221–2222) and the **Howard Johnson Lodge,** 301 Steinwehr Avenue (717–334–1188 or 800–654–2000). Teens and kids stay free at the **Holiday Inn Battlefield,** Routes 97 and 15 (717–334–6211), which also offers discount meals. Be sure to ask your hotel about special battlefield tour arrangements.

The Gettysburg region is well stocked with country inns and bed and breakfasts; however most prefer children ages twelve and older. An exception is the **Keystone Inn,** 231 Hanover Street; (717) 337–3888. They welcome children older than infants at this late-Victorian Inn. The **Doubleday Inn,** 104 Doubleday Avenue (717–334–9119), is located on the Battlefield. It's decorated with war artifacts and period furniture and offers free Civil War lectures. Children over the age of ten are welcome here.

The following inns prefer children twelve and older: The **Old Appleford Inn,** 218 Carlisle Street (717-337-1711), is a historic Victorian Inn downtown that dates back to 1867 and is filled with antiques. The **Baladerry Inn,** 40 Hospital Road (717-337-1342), was the site of a Civil War hospital. The **Homestead Guest Home,** 785 Baltimore Street (717-334-2037), is the Historic Dormitory of Civil War Soldier's Orphanage, and it offers family rates.

Campgrounds are another option. Try the **Drummer Boy Campground,** 1300 Hanover Road, Gettysburg (800-336-DBOY), or call the Travel Council (717-334-6274) for a longer listing.

Consider **Gettysburg Hotel,** 1 Lincoln Square (717-337-2000), in the heart of Gettysburg historical district, including attractions such as the Gettysburg National Park and the Gettysburg National Cemetery, with complimentary battlefield bus tours. The hotels' rooms have been renovated with 1800s decor. Family efficiency suites are available only during the summer season.

For a full listing of area accommodations, call the Gettysburg Travel Council at (717) 334-6274 for a visitor's guide.

WHERE TO EAT

Dobbin House Tavern, 89 Steinwehr Avenue (717-334-2100), combines history and food for the whole family. This 1776 tavern includes a country store, bakery, and underground railroad hideout that guests can tour. The **Herr Tavern Publick House,** 900 Chambersburg Road (717-334-4332), was standing as the Confederate troops attacked in 1863, and it offers good food. The **Farnsworth House Inn,** 410 Baltimore Street (717-334-8838), is open for dinner only and has children's menus. Among its Civil War food offerings are pie, peanut soup, spoon bread, and pumpkin fritters. **General Pickett's Buffets,** 571 Steinwehr Avenue (717-334-7580), is a good spot for lunch, as it has all-you-can-eat buffets and children's menus. **Hickory Bridge Farm,** west of Gettysburg in the Orrtanna orchard area (717-642-5261), features farm-style dinners.

DAY TRIPS

Hersheypark, a little over 50 miles from Gettysburg, has a full day's chocolatey adventure for every sweet tooth in your family, including roller coasters and live entertainment. (See the chapter on Hershey for more information.)

FOR MORE INFORMATION

The local newspaper, the *Gettysburg Times,* published Monday through Saturday mornings, is a good source of information about local events.

Visitor Information Centers

Gettysburg Travel Council, 35 Carlisle Street (717-334-6274), has free tour brochures and maps available to the public.

Gettysburg National Military Park Visitor's Center: (717) 334-1124.

Emergency Numbers

Ambulance, fire, and police: 911

Gettysburg Hospital, 147 Getty Street; (717) 334-2121

Poison Hotline: (800) 521-6110

Rite Aid Pharmacy, 236 West Street (717-334-6447), is open Monday through Saturday from 9:00 A.M. to 9:00 P.M., Sundays from 10:00 A.M. to 4:00 P.M.

Twenty-four-hour emergencies: (717) 337-HELP

HERSHEY AND THE PENNSYLVANIA DUTCH REGION

On a visit to Hershey, combine the thrills of a theme park with the sweet excesses of chocolate and enjoy a tour of the Pennsylvania Dutch countryside, with its simple lifestyle and scenic back roads. Easy day trips take you into Adamstown, the antiques capital of the state, to browse for treasures or to Reading, the self-proclaimed "Outlet Capital of the World," to search for bargains on clothing and housewares.

GETTING THERE

Twelve airlines offer more than ninety nonstop departures to Harrisburg International Airport. Amtrak trains and Greyhound/Trailways buses arrive at the Harrisburg Transportation Center, 411 Market Street (800–872–7245 or 717–232–4251). If you're staying at the Hotel Hershey or the Hershey Lodge, there's a complimentary shuttle from the airport and from the Amtrak and Greyhound/Trailways stations in Harrisburg.

Hershey is easy to reach by car, since many highways lead into town. From the north and east, take I–81 and I–78. From the south take I–83, and from the east and west take the Pennsylvania Turnpike (I–76).

GETTING AROUND

During the summer months Hershey provides a free shuttle service throughout the park, Hotel Hershey, the Hershey Lodge, Campground, and ZooAmerica.

WHAT TO SEE AND DO

Hersheypark, 100 West Hersheypark Drive; (800) HERSHEY. With more than fifty attractions on eighty-seven acres, the park offers a sweet day's outing for kids of all ages. The daring will want to ride some of the four roller coasters, including the self-explanatory SooperDooperLooper and the Sidewinder that twists and turns upside down. Beat the heat with the Canyon River Rapids white-water rafting ride and the Coal Cracker flume ride. For a slower pace go to Carousel Circle to sit astride one of the sixty-six hand-carved wooden horses that adorn this 1919 carousel. Preschoolers like this attraction as well as the Tiny Timbers ride.

Especially if you have young kids, book the Breakfast in the Park package (See Where to Stay). This special deal lets your kids cuddle with such Hershey characters as Mr. Hershey Bar and Ms. Reese's Peanut Butter Cup before the park's official morning opening. Another bonus: This package gets you beyond the turnstiles before the crowds, so your children have first crack at the kiddie rides.

For a respite from lines and rides, sit and enjoy the live entertainment, which often includes a barbershop quartet, dolphin shows, a Dixieland music band, and strolling performers.

The park is open from May to September. Part of the park reopens in mid-November through December for Christmas Candylane, a wonderland of 300,000 lights that puts holiday stars in your child's eyes. At Dinner with Dickens you dine with Scrooge and Tiny Tim, who recite key parts from the Dickens classic.

As part of the nostalgia trend sweeping theme parks, Hersheypark has added **Midway America,** a themed area that features classic boardwalk rides such as a Ferris wheel and arcade midway attractions. The area debuted in spring 1996 with the Wildcat, a newly constructed wooden roller coaster.

Considered the most popular attraction at Hershey Park, besides the rides, is **ZooAmerica,** an eleven-acre North American Wildlife Park. Open year-round, the park represents five North American ecosystems, including the Southern Florida Everglades, Cactus community from Arizona's Sonoran Desert, and Big Sky Country from the Rocky Mountain region. You'll most likely spot bison, white-tail deer, alligators, and eagles from among the 200 animals.

Hershey and the Pennsylvania Dutch Region at a Glance

- Chocolate galore and more surrounded by simple and scenic Pennsylvania Dutch country

- Rides, chocolate, entertainment—it's all at Hersheypark

- Tour Amish and Mennonite communities

- Many crafts and antiques stores

- Reading, the "outlet capital of the world" is a short drive

- Hershey information, (800) HERSHEY or (717) 534–3090; Pennsylvania Dutch Convention and Visitors Bureau, (717) 299–8091

Chocolate World Visitors Center, Park Boulevard; (717) 534–4900. On this twelve-minute tour, trace the creation of a candy bar from the harvesting of a cocoa bean to the wrapping in tinfoil. Follow up with lunch at the Hershey Cafe inside an enclosed tropical garden. Of course if it's past lunchtime, go straight to the Chocolate Fantasy dessert counter for a milk shake, hot fudge sundae, or delectable cookies.

The Hershey Museum, 170 West Hersheypark Drive, (717–534–3439), gives you the scoop on the man behind this chocolatey world. Trace the history of Milton Hershey from his beginnings as a farm boy to the sweet success of his dreams, and explore the Hershey collection of Pennsylvania German and Native American objects, including furnishings and folk art.

Founders Hall, south of Hersheypark, is the center of the Milton Hershey School. Founded in 1909 by Milton and Catherine Hershey as a school for orphaned or abandoned boys, it's now a coed facility for disadvantaged children. Pick up a brochure and take a self-guided tour of

The Hershey's Chocolate costumed characters greet guests with a chocolatey wave or hug. (Courtesy Capital Region Chamber of Commerce)

the school beginning with a twenty-minute video, *The Vision,* on the Hersheys' mission to provide top-notch education to disadvantaged children.

Hershey Trolley Works Tours (717–533–3000) escorts visitors on a forty-five-minute tour through "the sweetest place on earth" where even the streetlights look like chocolate kisses. Costumed players are on board to entertain with historic anecdotes as you ride by the gardens, Hershey's childhood home, and the chocolate factory. A separate ticket is necessary for these tours, which depart from Chocolate World mid-May through Labor Day and again in November through December. During Christmas Candylane the trolley has special rides with Santa.

Hershey Gardens, Hotel Road, Hershey; (717) 534–3492. Stroll through twenty-three landscaped acres including a Japanese garden and an area of dwarf conifers. Spring brings forsythia, magnolias, and 25,000 tulips. Take time to smell the award-winning roses, at their best in June.

SPECIAL EVENTS

Performing Arts

Hersheypark Arena and Stadium regularly hosts the Ice Capades (which were founded at the Hotel Hershey), Disney on Ice, Sesame Street Live, and the circus, plus musicians and comedians. Call the Arena Box Office at (717) 534–3911 for information.

Hershey Theatre, a classic and classy old cinema, has clouds that literally float across its star-studded ceiling. The theater regularly hosts touring Broadway shows, dance performances, classical music recitals, and, most appropriately, vintage films. Call (717) 534–3411 for general information and (717) 534–3405 for tickets.

Sports

Hersheypark Arena hosts the Hershey Bears hockey team most Wednesday and Saturday nights from October through March. For tickets and game schedules, call (717) 534–3911.

Festivals

Make your visit to the Hershey area extra fun by arriving for a special themed weekend. For more information on all Hershey events, call (800) HERSHEY. For Lancaster and Pennsylvania Dutch area events, call the Pennsylvania Dutch Convention and Visitors Bureau at (800) 735-2629.

January: Winter Fantasy at Chocolate World, when kids learn to ski indoors on a 32-foot-long skiing deck, then ice skate, and break for a hot chocolate.

February: At Chocolate Lover's Extravaganza, Hotel Hershey, sample chocolate, learn to create chocolate desserts, and play chocolate games with your valentine. Pennsylvania Dutch Food Festival, Lancaster.

March: Great American Chocolate Week featuring kids games, live entertainment, and, of course, scrumptious desserts. Murder Mystery Weekend, Hotel Hershey. Annual Quilters' Heritage Celebration, Lancaster. Berks Jazz Fest, VF Factory Outlet, Reading.

April: Family Easter in the Country, Hotel Hershey and the Hershey Lodge. Easter Bunny Express, Blue Mountain & Reading Railroad; (717) 562-2102 or (717) 562-4083.

May: Hersheypark opens for the season with live entertainment.

June/July: The Kutztown Folk Festival celebrates the Pennsylvania Dutch way of life with old-time art, hand-woven coverlet displays, and food.

July: All American Ragtime Festival and Contest, Strasburg. Scenic River Days, Reading, with music, arts, and children's events.

July–October: Pennsylvania Renaissance Faire, Cornwall.

October: Antique Auto Show, Hershey. Balloon Classic, Hershey. Take a hot air balloon ride or stay on ground for arts, crafts, and entertainment. Oktoberfest, Blue Mountain & Reading Railroad; (717) 562-2102 or (717) 562-4083.

December: Christmas Candylane in Hersheypark.

WHERE TO STAY

Hershey

Hotel Hershey, Hotel Road, Hershey, Pennsylvania; (800) 533-3131 or (717) 533-2171. If you're looking to travel in style, Hotel Hershey, a four-diamond resort, offers several family packages including admission and shuttle service to the park and ZooAmerica. A Breakfast in the Park package allows little ones to breakfast with the Hershey cast of characters and enter the park before the crowds.

Although Hersheypark is closed from late September to early May, the fun continues at the Hotel Hershey with a host of themed weekends. Besides the month-long Christmas Candylane for the holidays, just after New Year's the Teddy Bear Jubilee—have your children dress up their favorite fuzzy for the parade—is a "beary" good pageant. Kids are Special Weekend in mid-February jam-packs two days of fun with cupcake decorating, T-shirt designing, pony races, and storytelling. In April try a Family Easter in the Country featuring a springtime trolley ride, a country fair, and, of course, the Easter Bunny.

Spring through Labor Day there is a Kids' Kiss Kamp on Saturday mornings from 9:30 to 11:00 A.M. with lots of crafts, sing-alongs, and games For a complete listing of packages and reservations, call (800) 533-3131.

Hershey Lodge, West Chocolate Avenue and University Drive, Hershey (800-533-3131), is more casual than the hotel but features such family-friendly amenities as indoor and outdoor pools, tennis courts, a nine-hole pitch-and-putt golf course and nightly movies in the Lodge Cinema. Family packages are available including admission and transportation to Hersheypark and ZooAmerica. Go on a chocolate egg hunt on Easter or breakfast with Santa on Christmas.

Hershey Highmeadow Campground, Hershey; (717) 566-0902. When the weather turns warm, families that love to camp should consider this campground with 296 sites on fifty-five acres. Roughing it is easy when there's a country store, playgrounds, a game room, picnic tables, grills, and two outdoor swimming pools. Bring an RV, a tent, or stay in a cabin that comes with laundry service.

Lancaster County

The Village Inn of Bird-in-Hand, 2695 Old Philadelphia Pike, Bird-in-Hand; (717) 293-8369. This nineteenth-century Victorian Inn just east of Lancaster welcomes families. Be sure to take advantage of the complimentary tour of the close-by Pennsylvania Dutch country.

At the **Historic Smithton Inn,** 900 West Main Street, Ephrata (717-733-6094), you'll sleep soundly under Pennsylvania Dutch quilts in beds hand-crafted by co-owner Allen Smith. Then wake up to homemade waffles at this cozy bed and breakfast in the heart of Pennsylvania Dutch country. Kids are welcome, especially in the self-contained two-level South Wing suite that includes a kitchenette, a living area, a pull-out couch, and an upstairs bedroom with a sleeping nook for wee ones.

The **Swiss Woods Bed & Breakfast,** 500 Blantz Road, Lititz; (717) 627-3358 or (800) 594-8018. This inn is tucked in the woods about 10 miles north of Lancaster, and guests stay in chalet-style rooms by a stream. Outdoor enthusiasts and families are welcome to hike in the surrounding countryside.

As one of American Historic Inns' top 10, the **King's Cottage,** 1049 East King Street (717-397-1017), is a Spanish-style mansion built in 1913. It is elegantly decorated with nineteenth-century antiques, has a marble fireplace in the library, stained-glass windows, and a sweeping staircase. Meals include a full gourmet breakfast, served in the dining room, and an afternoon tea. The innkeepers will gladly arrange private dinners with Amish families, as well as sightseeing tours.

Two farms in the Pennsylvania Dutch area welcome families as overnight guests. **Smucker's Farm Guest House,** 502 Peters Road, New Holland (717-354-4375), run by Amos and Malinda Smucker, an Amish family, has a guest house across the street from their farm. The guest house has electricity, but there are no private baths. Rates are moderate. **Jonde Lane Farm,** 1103 Auction Road, Manheim (717-665-4231), is owned by a Mennonite family. Guests are invited to watch or share in farm chores and stay in the 1859 farmhouse. Rates are moderate, and there are no private baths.

For more lodging information and seasonal package deals, request a *Map and Visitors Guide* from the Pennsylvania Dutch Convention and Visitors Bureau; (800) PA-DUTCH (723-8824).

Reading

The Inn at Reading, 1040 Park Road, Wyomissing (610-372-7811 or 800-345-4023), and the **Sheraton Berkshire,** Route 422 West, Paper Mill Road Exit, Reading (610-376-3811) both offer special weekend rates in the off-seasons.

For recommendations and reservations to bed and breakfasts near Reading, call **Bed & Breakfast of Southeast Pennsylvania** at (800) 992-2632. Be sure to ask if children are welcome, if the guest rooms are comfortable, and whether the bathrooms are shared or private.

WHERE TO EAT

Lancaster County

Fill up on homemade breads, mashed potatoes, and fresh pies at the region's family-style and buffet restaurants.

The Family Style Restaurant, Route 30, 4 miles east of Lancaster (717-393-2323), features all-you-can-eat buffets, and kids pay according to their weight. It's open daily April through November, weekends only in the off-season. At **The Amish Barn Restaurant,** Route 340 between Bird-in-Hand and Intercourse (717-768-8886), taste the apple dumplings and other Pennsylvania Dutch specialties.

Reading

Visit one of Reading's oldest neighborhoods for outstanding wild mushroom dishes at **Joe's Restaurant,** 450 South Seventh Street (610) 373-6794. If the kids say "yuck" to mushrooms, then try **The Peanut Bar,** 332 Penn Street (610-376-8500); tykes can toss their peanut shells onto the floor while waiting for their burgers.

DAY TRIPS

Pennsylvania Dutch Country; (800) 735-2629. Lancaster County, about forty-five minutes from Hershey, is the heart of the Pennsylvania Amish and Mennonite locales. In addition to its religious past, the region made history as a station for both the underground and the aboveground railroad. Be sure to explore the region's famous covered bridges.

To decide which tourist attractions will interest your family, start at the **Pennsylvania Dutch Convention and Visitor's Bureau,** 501 Greenfield Road, Lancaster; (717) 299-8091. Here you will find information on attractions, accommodations, and restaurants. You'll also want to take in an introductory film *There is a Season* on the region's cultural history. The movie is presented daily from April to November. Call in advance for film times.

The town of Lancaster is rich with history and home to Franklin and Marshall College, the country's fourteenth oldest. A 1½-mile **Historic Lancaster Walking Tour** stops at the town's major community structures. Guides well stocked with historic tidbits leave daily from the **Lancaster Information Center,** 100 South Queen Street (717-392-1776), April through October, and by prior reservation from November through March. If visiting on a Tuesday, Friday, or Saturday, stop by the **Central Market** on Penn's Square. It is open from 6:00 A.M. to 2:00 P.M. Laying claim to be the nation's oldest continually operating farmer's market it offers truly farm-fresh vegetables, meats, and cheeses. This is a good place to buy those famous Pennsylvania baked goods from whoopie pies (cakes with filling) to shoo-fly pies (has gooey-but-good molasses and brown sugar). On the Square as well is the **Heritage Center of Lancaster County,** 13 West King Street; (717) 299-6440. It showcases such Pennsylvania Dutch arts and items as grandfather clocks and quilts. The **Landis Valley Museum,** 2451 Kissel Hill Drive, Lancaster (717-569-0401), is the largest outdoor museum that depicts Pennsylvania German life. Families enjoy the craft demonstrations and the Harvest Days festival in October.

In Northern Lancaster County the **Ephrata Cloister,** 632 West Main Street, Ephrata (717-733-6600), is the restored cloister established in 1732 by Conrad Beissel. Imagine yourself a part of this religious commune on a guided tour of the twenty historic buildings. For an entertaining living history of the cloister, families shouldn't miss the musical pageant *Vorspiel,* presented at the cloister's outdoor amphitheater on Saturday nights from July to August. Call (717) 733-4811 for performance information.

At the **Sturgis Pretzel Company,** 219 East Main Street, Lititz (717-626-4354), kids eat up the demonstrations of pretzel making. If you're interested in the history of this charming old Moravian village, stop by the Lititz Historical Foundation at the **Johannes Mueller House,** 137-39 East Main Street (717-626-7958), for a brochure and a walking tour. It's open from Memorial Day to October 31.

At the **Strasburg Railroad,** PA 741 East, just east of Strasburg (717-687-7522), come aboard for a steam train ride on one of the oldest operating train lines in the country. It's open daily from May through October and some weekends in the off-season. There are also special holiday theme rides.

But don't just go along for the ride; learn about the history of the railroad at the nearby **Railroad Museum of Pennsylvania,** PA 741 East; (717) 687-8628. Here train lovers find train cars from sleepers to diners. There's also a railroading film shown in the station.

If toy trains are more your speed, take a quick look at the **Toy Train Museum,** 300 Paradise Lane off PA 741, (717) 687–8976. Kids are enthralled by five toy train displays and a video presentation. The museum is open daily May through October and on limited weekends in the off-season.

Travel down the Route 30 Corridor in Eastern Lancaster County for an education on Amish and Mennonite culture. Begin at the **Mennonite Information Center,** 2209 Millstream Road, between Smoketown and Strasburg; (717) 299–0954. As a quick introduction to the religion and culture, watch the twenty-two minute movie *Morning Song,* which begins on the half-hour. The center provides information on Mennonite and Amish attractions as well as books. An exceptional way to learn about these hard-working people is with a two-or-more-hour **Farm Country Tour.** With prior reservations a Mennonite guide will hop in your car and narrate the region's rich history, answering any questions you may have along the way.

At the **Amish Country Homestead,** Route 340 (717-768-8400), tour the home of fictional Old Order Amish characters Daniel and Lizzie Fisher. The location was the site for the filming of *Jacob's Choice,* and you'll find propane-powered lamps as well as authentic Amish clothes hanging in the bedrooms. Experience a world without television, telephones, or Nintendo. Another Amish experience can be had at **Amish Farm and House,** 2395 Lincoln Highway East, south of Smoketown (717-394-6185), which includes a blacksmith shop with crafts. **The Amish Village,** PA 896, between Smoketown and Strasburg (717-687-8511), features a guided tour of an 1840 farmhouse and a self-guided tour of a working smokehouse, windmill, waterwheel, and schoolhouse.

If the little ones are in need of more entertainment, try **The People's Place and Quilt Museum,** P.O. Box 419, on PA 340, west of Route 30 in the tiny town of Intercourse; (717) 768–7171. Come here for movie action with the twenty-five-minute *Who are the Amish?* film. For older kids try the hour-and-forty-five-minute *Hazel's People,* a fictional documentary on the Mennonites. You'll also find arts and crafts, a bookstore, and Amish World, an exhibit area that gives kids an up-close view of the clothes, books, and objects of daily Amish life.

Also in Intercourse is the **Old Country Store,** 3510 Old Philadelphia Pike; (717) 768–7101. This shop features the work of more than

450 local craftspeople, including a fine collection of quilts. Be sure to browse in the **Quilt Museum** upstairs, where some of the finest Amish handiwork is displayed. For more crafts take your kids to the **Old Candle Barn,** Main Street (717-768-3231), to watch candles being dipped and to **Lapp's Coach Shop,** 3572 West Newport Road (717- 768-8712), to see buggies being restored. Abner Lapp also fashions fine hobby horses and beautiful little red wagons. (Be forewarned: Your children are going to want you to purchase at least one.)

Food lovers should plan their visit to Lancaster County around the Dutch Food Festival in mid-June, a three-day Amish taste-fest where you sample such regional specialties as whoopie pies, grape mush, and banana pickles. In March quilters patch together their own schedule of workshops and tour the Dutch country at the Annual Quilters' Heritage Celebration. Call (800) 723-8824 for more information.

Outlet Shopping in Reading

Reading, about an hour away from Hershey, is the outlet capital of the world. Here a bargain hunter has to smile while tracking the red-brick paths around the minimalls. Refurbished former factory mills now harbor more than 200 stores that promise 20 to 70 percent off retail prices.

Begin the adventure at the **Vanity Fair Factory Outlet,** Hill Avenue and Park Road, across the river in Wyomissing; (610) 378-0408. Start here because you may not wend your way out of this huge complex—900,000 square feet and nine factory buildings, until nightfall. Stay here if your nerves can take only one outlet complex per trip. In a slightly prettier part of town than Reading's urban milltown heart, the VF stores offer easy parking, clear signs, a McDonald's for burger lovers, and more floor space for goods. VF also has such kid-friendly names as Health-tex, Lee, and Wrangler.

If you can still stand, stop by the **Reading Outlet Center,** 801 North Ninth Street, Reading; (800) 5-OUTLET or (610) 373-5495. In this tired-looking former factory, sixty stores are tucked away in labyrinths of dead-end halls and narrow staircases. Finds include Izod/ Lacoste, Liz Claiborne, and J. Crew.

Not sated yet? Then buzz over to **Hiesters Lane,** 755 Hiesters Lane, Reading (610-921-9394), on the edge of town. The Flemington Fashion Outlet here sports a reasonable selection of Saville, Evan

Picone, and Kasper women's suits at 25 percent or more off. **Big Mill Outlet Center,** Eighth and Olney streets, Reading (610–378–9100), is also worth some time.

Outlets are pure Americana. Busloads of purchasers come seeking the promise of cut-rate goodies. Who shops here? The tourists, the pennywise, and, increasingly, the trendy. Some of your best friends probably met their Adolfo, Evan Picone, or Ralph Lauren suits in Reading's shops. While you may be shopped out, with any luck you'll come home saving lots of money on clothes for the whole family.

Manufacturers Outlet Mall, exit 22, Pennsylvania Turnpike, Morgantown; (610) 286–2000. Affectionately called MOM, this outlet is 12 miles, about twenty minutes, south of Reading. It features more than seventy stores, including Flemington Plus—a larger-size women's dress store—and Marlene Fashion Outlet, which sells some designer labels such as Adolfo. Discounts range from 25 to 75 percent.

Contact Berks County Visitor's Information Association at (610) 375–4085 or (800) 443–6610 for a full listing of outlet stores. Be sure to call the malls in advance to find out the hours and which shops, if any, take credit cards. Many accept only cash and personal checks, so be prepared.

Antiquing in Adamstown

If Reading is the outlet capital, then Adamstown, in the east of Pennsylvania's Dutch Country, is the state's antiques capital. You will find 1,000 antiques dealers within a 2-mile strip along U.S. 272 and U.S. 222. Head here to find antiques and collectibles ranging from scanty twenties satin camisoles to nineteenth-century pocket watches, oak rolltop desks, and even fifties Hopalong Cassidy mugs.

Bring along some quiet entertainment for the kids while you browse through the bargains, often 10 to 30 percent lower than in the city. Begin at **Ed Stoudt's Black Angus Restaurant and Antiques Mall,** U.S. 272, a mile north of Pennsylvania Turnpike, exit 21; (717) 484–4385. Among the 200 neatly displayed dealers' stalls. you'll find jewelry, linens, china, and furniture—all this within a pink fantasy Bavarian building filled with a wafting aroma of sauerkraut and lager from the adjoining cafeteria. **Renninger's** (717–267–2177), almost next door, is a single-story sprawl of gray cinder blocks packed with

400 booths. The kids can snack on pretzels and popcorn while you browse through cluttered aisles filled with quirky collectibles: dinner plates with Richard Nixon smiling demonically or Howdy Doody dolls. **Adams Antiques and Collectibles,** just down the strip (717-267-8444), features an array of 150 shops. Besides such small dealer staples as thirties music scores and old tins, browse through Adams for fifties furniture and a good selection of oak.

Take in some Civil War history at **Gettysburg,** a forty-five-minute drive from Hershey. (See the chapter on Gettysburg.)

FOR MORE INFORMATION

For Hershey information and reservations, call (717) 534-3090 or (800) HERSHEY. Request a *Vacation Guide,* which describes the various family packages available, park schedules, and event information. Harrisburg-Hershey-Carlisle Tourism and Convention Bureau, 114 Walnut Street, Harrisburg (717-232-1377 or 800-995-0969), offers a free visitor's guide.

The Pennsylvania Dutch Convention and Visitors Bureau, 501 Greenfield Road, Lancaster (717-299-8901 or 800-PA-DUTCH), publishes a comprehensive map and visitor's guide with information on attractions, events, accommodations, and dining. Stop by the downtown Visitors Information Center, South Queen and Vine streets, Lancaster.

The Berks County Visitors Information Association, VF Factory Outlet Complex, Reading (610-375-4085 or 800-443-6610) publishes a visitor's guide listing the area's outlet shops, plus local restaurants and hotels.

Emergency Numbers
Ambulance, fire, and police: 911

Medical emergencies: In Hershey contact the Hershey Medical Center, 500 University Drive; (717) 531-8521. The facility also operates a twenty-four-hour pharmacy. In Lancaster contact the Lancaster General Hospital, 555 North Duke Street, Lancaster (717) 290-5511. In Reading call the St. Joseph's Hospital, Twelfth and Walnut streets, Reading; (610) 378-2000.

LAKE GEORGE

Much different from bustling New York City in ambiance, Adirondack Park encompasses about two-thirds of upstate New York, including some six million acres of private and state-owned land, approximately 60 percent of which is wilderness. Forty-two mountains plus thousands of miles of lakes, ponds, brooks, and streams make this a recreational paradise.

Lake George stands out among the developed areas as the Adirondack's most complete family vacation destination. Summer is a prime season to visit. The 32-mile lake, ringed by green mountains, is truly striking and, although commercialism abounds downtown, just a short drive north are quiet lakeside villages and mountain retreats. The area is also a winter playground and fall foliage hotspot that caters to families.

GETTING THERE

The closest airport to Lake George is Albany County (518–869-9611), some 50 miles away. Car rentals are available at the airport.

Adirondack Trailways (800–225-6815), runs buses to Lake George, Glens Falls, Tupper Lake, and Lake Placid from Albany, with connections to New York City. In Lake George the bus stops at the Mobil Station, 320 Canada Street; (518) 668-9511. Greyhound travels from New York to Glens Falls, 10 miles away, stopping at All Points Diner, 21 South Street; (518) 793-5052. To reach Lake George passengers must hook up with an Adirondacks Trailways bus, which leaves from the Fiddlestix Restaurant on Hudson and Elm; (518) 793-5525.

Amtrak's *Montrealer* train stops at nearby Fort Edward; however, this small town provides no direct transportation to Lake George. You can take a local bus from Fort Edward to Glens Falls, then transfer to another bus for Lake George (June to Labor Day only). Call **Greater Great Falls Transit;** (518) 792-1085.

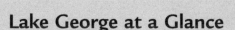

Lake George at a Glance

- The Adirondack's most complete family vacation destination

- A 32-mile lake surrounded by green mountains

- A variety of family-oriented ski areas

- A wide range of lake cruises

- More than 275 restaurants

- Warren County Tourism Department, (800) 365-1050 or (518) 761-6366

The village of Lake George is located off the Northway, I-87, near the junction of U.S. 9 and SR 9N, which travels north along the lake's western shore.

GETTING AROUND

A car is a must, as there's no public transportation within the Lake George area. Boat-rental facilities are located at various points along the lake (see the *Warren County Travel Guide* for specific locations). Lake George Village offers **trolley rides** on weekends from Memorial Day to late June. Call (518) 792-1085 for schedule and stops.

WHAT TO SEE AND DO

Museums and Historical Sights

Most people are so busy having fun in Lake George that they don't seem to notice the scarcity of museums. (We don't consider the House of Frankenstein Wax Museum on Canada Street a "museum" in the true sense of the word.) Many museums are small ones dedicated to local history and not terribly interesting to kids. Two area attractions do fill the bill, however.

The International Arts and Culture Association (IACA), 277 Glen Street, Third Floor, Glens Falls (518-793-2773), just opened in 1995, has fun interactive exhibits for kids of all ages. The museum also displays children's art from around the world.

Fort William Henry Museum, Beach Road and Route 9 entrances; (518) 668-5471. If your kids have seen or read James Fennimore Cooper's *The Last of the Mohicans,* they'll especially appreciate this restored Colonial fortress, which played an integral role in the French and Indian War. Costumed guide-historians conduct tours during July and August. The musket and cannon firings and demonstrations of musketball molding and grenadier bomb-tossing appeal to school-age kids and teens, though younger ages may wince at the noise from the firings. For some reason the dungeons and stockades are always the most popular exhibits with kids. During late spring and early fall, audiovisual displays take the place of the guides.

Parks and Beaches

Whatever type of trail you and your kids want to try—nature or hiking, easy or strenuous—you'll find it in or near Lake George. The Adirondack Mountain Club (518-668-4447) publishes *An Adirondack Sampler* in two volumes, with easy to moderately difficult hikes and backpacking trips of Warren County and Adirondack Park.

Easy nature trails through pines and hardwoods are just part of the attraction of **Crandall Park International Trail System,** south of Glens Falls city border on Route 9. Bring a picnic, Frisbee, and fishing poles and spend the afternoon: there's also a fishing pond, tennis and basketball courts, baseball field, and playground. A Fit-Trail has wooden exercise stations. Let the kids join in on some.

Prospect Mountain's entrance to its splendid hiking trail is on Montcalm Street, Lake George. Ages eight and up should be game for the moderate climb to the 2,100-foot summit for splendid views of the Adirondacks, Vermont's Green Mountains, and New Hampshire's White Mountains. If that's too strenuous, take the 5½-mile scenic highway to the parking lot, then ride the "viewmobile" to the summit.

A listing of area beaches appears in the *Warren County Travel Guide*. **Million Dollar Beach,** on the southern shore, east of U.S. 9 on Beach Road (518-668-3352), is the town's largest and best suited to families, with a lifeguard, bathhouse, picnic facilities, and volleyball nets. There's a small admission and parking fee.

Boaters can explore the lake's many islands, some with sandy beaches. A permit is required to picnic on Lake George Islands.

Other Attractions

Aqua Adventure Water Slide, Route 9, Queensbury; (518) 792-8989. Slide, splash, loop, curve—this water park is fun! There's a kiddie pool play area, too.

Great Escape and **Splash Water Kingdom Fun Park,** Route 9; (518) 792-3500. When your family wants to have fun, the state's largest amusement park is the place. Enjoy one hundred rides, shows, and attractions, such as Noah's Sprayground Water Area, Raging River Raft Ride, and Comet Roller Coaster.

Lake George Zoo, Route 9, Queensbury: (518) 793-3393. The kids can feed llamas and goats, then watch the captivating chimp show and live animal presentations.

Magic Forest, Route 9; (518) 668-2448. Younger kids may prefer this smaller, calmer park to Great Escape. With twenty-five rides, a Fairy Tale area, and Santa's Hideaway, this small park is just right for tots.

Rodeos are held at three area ranches weekly in summer: **Painted Pony Rodeo,** Lake Luzerne (518-696-2421); **1000 Acres Ranch and Rodeo,** Stony Creek (518-696-2444); and **Ridin Hy Ranch and Rodeo** (518-494-2742). (See Where to Stay.) For a list of area stables, consult the *Warren County Travel Guide*.

Special Tours

A guided horse-and-carriage ride is a fun way to see Lake George Village; (518) 668-9665. **Lake George Steamboat Cruises** (518-668-5777/800-553-BOAT) has narrated trips that range from one to four-and-one-half hours.

Lake George Shoreline Cruises, Kurosaka Lane (518-668-4644), offers daily narrated sight-seeing cruises. Other tours include guided walking tours such as **Mountainaire Adventures** (800-950-2194) and historical, educational, and environmental tours through **Overlook Tours, Inc.** (518–742–1735) or **Historical Makers** (518–668–5755). (See also Getting Around for trolley rides in Lake George Village.)

Shopping

Bargains abound in Warren County's more than eighty factory outlets, most located in what's known as the **"Million Dollar Half-Mile"** Factory Outlet Strip (take I-87 exit 20, then north on Route 9). **Aviation Mall,** I-87, exit 19, in Queensbury, is the area's largest mall and rents strollers.

Performing Arts

Lake George Dinner Theater, Holiday Inn Turf at Lake George, features Broadway show performances by professional Equity actors. Call (518) 668–5781 for program information. Renowned artists perform at **Luzerne Chamber Music Festival;** (518) 696–3892.

Adirondack Theatre Festival, French Mountain Playhouse at the Lake George RV Park, Route 149 (518–798–7479), offers children's workshops, solo performers, and more in June and July.

Magic Cabaret, 400 Canada Street, surfside on Lake George (518–668–2442), offers mystery and comedic entertainment for the whole family.

Thirty miles away, the **Saratoga Performing Arts Center** has top-named performing arts companies, such as the New York City Ballet and the New York City Opera, as well as popular entertainers. Call (518) 587–3330 for schedules.

SPECIAL EVENTS

Sporting Events

Adirondack Red Wings hockey team plays at the Glens Falls Civic Center, Route 9 (Glen Street); (518) 798–0202.

Adirondack Lumberjacks, AAA baseball at East Field, Dix Avenue; (518) 743–9618.

Fairs and Festivals

February: Warren County comes alive with winter carnivals. Lake George usually celebrates on weekends with a variety of races, including

A narrated cruise around Lake George aboard the Minne-Ha-Ha *is a great way to take in the scenery.* (Copyright © 1993 New York State Department of Economic Development)

one in which participants pull full-size outhouses (yes, outhouses). For the kids: Olympic games, clowns, contests, and Georgie the Snowman. The village of Hague's carnival is family oriented, with children's games and prizes, fishing contests, clowns, snow sculpture contests, and more. Lake Luzerne's one-day carnival has horse-drawn sleigh rides, clowns, arts and crafts, and other delights. Gore Mountain in North Creek, the area's largest downhill ski area, adds children's programs to their carnival's events. The Warren County Tourism Department can provide specific dates, as well as sites and listings of cross-country ski centers. Ask for details on these other seasonal events.

July–August: Family movies at Shepard Park, Lake George, Thursday nights.

August: Warren County Fair, Fairgrounds, Warrensburg. Family Festival Week, Shepard Park, Lake George, with entertainers, crafts, games, and more.

September: Hot Air Balloon Festival, Glens Falls–Queensbury.

October: Gore Mountain's Oktoberfest, with music, food, parade, and entertainment for kids. World's Largest Garage Sale, Warrensburg, has the town outfitted with vendors, garage sales, crafts, entertainment, and more.

WHERE TO STAY

If your family likes being in the middle of the action, the commercial strip of wall-to-wall motels on Route 9 will do. To appreciate the true beauty of the area, however, venture somewhat beyond. A complete chart of accommodations, ranging from rustic cabins to luxurious resorts, is included in the *Warren County Travel Guide* available from the Tourism Department; (518) 761-6366. Family-friendly possibilities include the following.

Cresthaven Resort Motel, Lake Shore Drive, Route 9N, is spread out on thirteen acres, with its own 300-foot sandy beach. Choose from log cabins, cottages, or efficiencies. A kiddie pool, game room, playgrounds, grills, and picnic tables are tailor-made for families. Call (518) 668-3332.

Roaring Brook Ranch and Tennis Resort, 2½ miles south on Route 9N, has one indoor and two outdoor pools, horseback riding, five tennis courts, and a playground, plus a children's counselor in July and August. Families appreciate the coin laundry on premises. Call (518) 668-5767.

Ridin Hy Ranch Resort is on 800 acres on Sherman Lake, Warrensburg. This year-round resort offers all-inclusive vacation plans. There's an indoor pool, beach, and playground area, and rodeos are held throughout the summer. Call (518) 494-2742.

Sagamore Resort sits on its own private island in Lake George, just ½ mile from the village of Bolton Landing. This luxury resort has efficiencies and hotel rooms, including junior suites, some with lake views. Although pricey (ask about packages), the resort has good facilities, including an indoor pool, spa, beach, tennis, golf, racquetball, and supervised kids' activities. Restaurants range from casual to gourmet. In summer the resort's wooden touring boat offers dinner and sight-seeing cruises. Call (518) 644-9400/(800) 358-3585.

Treasure Cove, Diamond Point, 4 miles north of town, is directly on the lake, with its own private sandy beach. Stay in two- or three-bedroom cottages, some with fireplaces. Two pools, a playground, lawn games, and row- and motorboats add to the appeal. Call (518) 668-5334.

WHERE TO EAT

With more than 275 restaurants in the area, your family need never go hungry. For restaurant listings check out the *Lake George Guide,* a weekly tourist paper available around town. When your taste for fast food begins to fade, try Log Jam, 4½ miles south on U.S. 9 at the junction of 149. This casual place has a rustic, log-cabin feeling and serves solid American fare, with a children's menu available. **Mario's Restaurant,** ¼ mile north on U.S. 9 and SR 9N, dishes out large portions of chicken, beef, seafood, and veal. They also feature a children's menu and valet parking. For older kids with sophisticated palates, or for a parent's night out, try the nouvelle American cuisine at **The Trillium** in the Sagamore Resort, Bolton Landing. This highly rated restaurant doesn't come cheap, but it's truly a fine dining experience.

DAY TRIPS

The touring possibilities in the Lake George area are numerous. The *Warren Country Travel Guide* offers some appealing possibilities.

Adirondack Park

If you decide to head northwest and explore the more remote parts of Adirondack Park, keep in mind that many mountain highways can be slow going, albeit scenic, so don't plan too much for one day. Two interpretive visitor centers offer indoor and outdoor exhibits and year-round programs about Adirondack Park. One is in Paul Smiths, New York, northwest of Lake Placid on SR 30, 1 mile north of SR 86 (518-327-3000); the other is in Newcomb on SR 28N, 14 miles east of Long Lake (518-582-2000). Blue Mountain Lake, northwest of Lake George, is home to the Adirondack Museum on SR 28N/30; it's worth a stop. The indoor and outdoor exhibits reveal area history and culture in an interesting way and include Adirondack guide boats, log hotel, blacksmith shop, and posh private railroad car. Open summer to mid-October, this is a splendid trip during the peak foliage period. Call (518) 352-7311/7312 for hours.

Lake Placid

You'll see some of the best scenery on the way to Lake Placid (I-87 north to exit 30; follow Route 73 west). The village, on the shores of Mirror Lake and Lake Placid, hosted the 1932 and 1980 Winter Olympics, and the game sites and facilities are open to visitors. Depending on the ages and stamina of your kids, you can either visit individual sites or purchase a complete self-guided auto tour package. Included are chairlift rides to the summit of Whiteface Mountain (site of the 1980 Alpine events), a trolley ride to the mile-long bobsled and luge runs, and visits to the Olympic Center ice complex and the Olympic Jumping Complex, where U.S. Ski Team freestyle aerialists polish their techniques in summer by jumping off ramps into a pool of water. For information call the Olympic Regional Development Authority at (518) 523-1655/(800) 858-7782—Eastern Canada/(800) 462-6236—United States.

In winter Lake Placid is a haven, and heaven, for snow enthusiasts. **Whiteface Mountain** offers the greatest vertical drop in the East, varied terrain, plus a play-and-ski program for ages three to six and a ski school for ages seven to twelve. In addition there's a nursery for tots one to six.

The **Mt. Van Hoevenberg Cross-Country Center,** a ten-minute drive from Lake Placid village, features 50 kilometers of groomed trails, including novice, intermediate, and expert loops. Next door to the center, try the bobsled and luge runs. The bobsled ride is generally offered Tuesdays through Sundays 1:00 to 3:00 P.M. Sign up for the luge ride Saturdays and Sundays from 1:00 to 3:00 P.M. In addition the **Jackrabbit Trail** offers nearly 25 miles of cross-country skiing that links the towns of Keene, Lake Placid, Saranac Lake, and the High Peaks region. Obtain a map from the Adirondack Ski Touring Council, P.O. Box 843, Lake Placid, New York 12946; (518) 523-1365.

For more thrills visit **Mirror Lake,** where Eric Heiden claimed five gold medals in 1980. Skate indoors at the Olympic Center or outdoors at the Olympic Oval. For something different try tobogganing and dogsledding across the lake.

For a schedule of winter events and ski conditions, call (518) 523-1655, or (800) 462-6236 in the United States or (800) 858-7782 in Eastern Canada. For Lake Placid lodging reservations, call (800) 44-PLACID, (800) 447-5224, or (518) 523-2445.

Wilmington

Santa's Workshop in Wilmington will delight preschoolers. Families have been coming to this nonglitzy attraction for generations to meet Santa at his home and workshop, pet his live reindeer, go on the rides (including a miniature railroad), and see puppet shows. For a taped message of the park schedule, call (518) 946-7838.

FOR MORE INFORMATION

Warren County Tourism Department, 5100 Municipal Center, Lake George 12845-9795; (518) 761-6366/(800) 365-1050, ext. 5100. Drop by their office or phone for a *Warren County Travel Guide* and other helpful information. Information on Adirondack Park can be obtained from Department of Conservation, 50 Wolf Road, Albany, New York 12233; (518) 457-3521. For the entire Adirondack Region. call (800) ITS-MTNS. If you're heading to Lake Placid, lodging and sight-seeing information can be obtained from **Lake Placid/Essex County Visitors Bureau,** Olympic Center, Lake Placid 12946; (518) 523-2445/(800) 44-PLACID.

Emergency Numbers

Ambulance, fire, and police: 911

Glens Falls Hospital, 100 Park Street, Glens Falls: (518) 792-3151
    (it has a twenty-four-hour emergency room).

Poison Control: (518) 761-5261

There are no twenty-four-hour pharmacies open to the public.

NEW YORK CITY

If your family loves the energy and excitement of a big-city vacation, there's no place like New York. Like many other cities, this one's not all polish and shine, but, with proper planning, a trip to the Big Apple can be one of your family's most memorable. If possible, come in spring, fall, or at Christmas, when the city is at its finest. But even sizzling summer comes with merits: Many New Yorkers head for the hills on the weekends, leaving behind a less crowded city.

GETTING THERE

New York is served by three airports: John F. Kennedy International (JFK) about 15 miles from mid-Manhattan; La Guardia, about 8 miles; and Newark (NJ) International, about 16 miles. Buses, limousines, and taxis are available at all three. Yellow medallion metered taxis are the most convenient mode into Manhattan if you're arriving with kids and baggage. Fares range from $30 to $50 to midtown, plus bridges, tolls, and tip; there's an extra $10 charge to Newark. Avoid the limousine drivers who appear near the baggage areas soliciting fares; instead, arrange service through Ground Transportation.

Amtrak (800–USA–RAIL) and a number of commuter trains arrive at either Grand Central Terminal, Forty-second Street and Park Avenue, or Penn Station, between Thirty-first and Thirty-third streets and Seventh and Eighth avenues. Taxi stands and public transportation are available at both.

Greyhound, Trailways, and other long-distance and commuter buses use the Port Authority Bus Terminal, between Fortieth and Forty-second Streets and Eighth Avenue. Taxis line up at the front entrance.

Manhattan is an island entered via bridges, tunnels, parkways, and expressways. The New York Thruway (Routes 287 and 87) leads to Manhattan's east and west sides. The New England Thruway (I–95)

New York City at a Glance

- There's just no place like the Big Apple
- Some of the best museums in the world
- Spend the day in Central Park
- Visit Ellis Island and the Empire State Building
- Catch a Broadway show
- New York Convention and Visitors Bureau, (800) NYC-VISIT or (212) 484-1200

leads, via connecting roads, to all five boroughs: Queens, Manhattan, Bronx, Brooklyn, and Staten Island. The western entry is accessed by I-80 (Bergen Passaic Expressway), while the south is served by the New Jersey Turnpike (I-95), which leads to the Holland Tunnel in lower Manhattan, the Lincoln Tunnel in midtown Manhattan, or the George Washington Bridge in upper Manhattan.

GETTING AROUND

The streets in midtown Manhattan, where most hotels are located (Thirtieth and Sixtieth streets from the East River to the Hudson River), are arranged in a grid, with streets running east and west and avenues north and south. Fifth Avenue separates the east from the west side. Once you figure out the avenues, New York is a surprisingly easy city to navigate; however, Lower Manhattan (with Greenwich Village, Chinatown, Little Italy, and the Financial District) doesn't adhere to this system. In midtown walking is often the best way to get around, particularly at rush hour. At night exercise common sense and stay away from streets that aren't well lit or well trafficked.

Public buses require exact fare ($1.50) in change or a token, sold mostly in subway stations. Request a transfer upon boarding. This entitles you to a free ride on a connecting line. Some buses have maps in a receptacle near the driver. Maps may also be obtained near the entrance of some major library branches.

The subway system is fast and extensive, but not aesthetically pleasing. Avoid it after dark. Tokens are sold by clerks near turnstiles, and children under 3'8" ride free. Request a map. Information for both the subway and buses is available from 6:00 A.M. to 9:00 P.M. by calling (718) 330-1234.

Taxis in New York are plentiful. Hail a cab on any street corner. Some taxi drivers may be annoying; if this is the case, feel free to step out and find another taxi.

Double-decker buses, operated by Gray Line Tours, are a good idea for avid sight-seers. Although traffic may be a problem at times, the buses stop at almost all attractions and parks. There is a flat fare for unlimited riding during one or two days. Call (800) 669-0051, (800) 876-9868, or (800) NYC-BUSO.

WHAT TO SEE AND DO

Museums and Historic Sites

New York has some of the best museums in the world. Since you could literally spend days—even weeks—exploring them, the following list includes only those with special kid appeal.

What kid doesn't like dinosaurs? Maker no bones about it; the **American Museum of Natural History,** Central Park West and Seventy-ninth Street (212-769-5100), has added two halls of these giants. The frames of such giants as *Tyrannosaurus rex* and *Apatosaurus* (formerly known as *Brontosaurus*) loom imposingly. Kids can finger the fierce nose horn of a *Triceratops,* flip through charts to find out how a dinosaur moves, walk about the skeleton of a *Barosaurus,* and check these giants' genealogy by using a computer.

Explore more skeletons in Mammals and Their Extinct Relatives, the largest exhibition of real fossils on view anywhere in the world. Fossil finds include the head and trunk of Effie, a baby woolly mammoth, a 57-million-year-old horse skeleton, and a block of Ice Age fossils from Agate

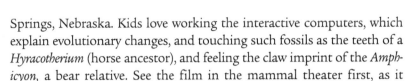

Springs, Nebraska. Kids love working the interactive computers, which explain evolutionary changes, and touching such fossils as the teeth of a *Hyracotherium* (horse ancestor), and feeling the claw imprint of the *Amphicyon,* a bear relative. See the film in the mammal theater first, as it explains the system used to organize and group this exhibit.

There's lots more to see: the gems and mineral gallery, with one of the largest pieces of crystallized gold ever found; the largest meteorite ever retrieved (which you can touch); a herd of wild (mounted) elephants; a 1,300-year-old giant sequoia, and lots more. At the Natural Science Center, kids can touch and explore fossils, shells, and other natural objects. The Naturemax Theatre boasts a four-story screen for interesting educational films.

Use the lower-level museum exit to connect to the adjacent **Hayden Planetarium,** Central Park West and Seventy-ninth Street; (212) 769-5920. This facility has two floors of exhibits, plus interesting sky shows, and evening laser light shows on the weekend. Kids love the scales, on which they can see how much they would weigh on other planets.

Children's Museum of Manhattan, 212 West Eighty-third Street; (212) 721-1234. While this doesn't rank with, say, Boston's Children's Museum, it has enough changing and permanent exhibits to keep kids of all ages busy. Older kids will head straight upstairs to the Media Center where they can work a TV camera or sit behind the mike and read the news. The outdoor urban environment area encourages kids to think seriously about recycling. For younger kids the family learning center has a grocery store, building blocks, and frequent supervised art activities. Special events and activities are constantly going on; call for a schedule. This facility is open on Monday when many other museums aren't. The museum closes on Tuesdays.

Intrepid Sea-Air-Space Museum, Pier 86, West Forty-sixth Street and Twelfth Avenue; (212) 245-0072. This 900-foot aircraft carrier is best appreciated by school-age kids, who will love the freedom to roam about and explore. The carrier was used in World War II, during the Vietnam War, and as a space program recovery ship. Along with peering through a periscope and exploring the deck, kids can see the cockpit of the world's fastest jet, historic aircraft, an Army armored tank display, and the world's only nuclear missile submarine open to the public (guided tours available). Call about Saturday afternoon workshops and hours. Multimedia presentations are offered Wednesday through Sunday.

Jewish Museum, 1109 Fifth Avenue at Ninety-second Street; (212) 423-3200. The four floors of exhibits, with frequently changing themes, family workshops, and special events, make this a worthwhile place to visit. Older children like the audiotaped vignettes of European immigrants and the collection of ornate torah scrolls.

Liberty Science Center, Liberty State Park, New Jersey; (201) 200-1000. This new hands-on science and technology museum, across the river from Lower Manhattan, is easily accessible by ferry. Particularly pleased are Manhattanites who find the excellent **New York Hall of Science** in Flushing Meadows, Queens (718-699-1341), less convenient. At the Liberty Science Center, three floors of exhibits center on the body. Kids love the pitch-black touch tunnel and labyrinth with mirrors and optical illusions. The environmental area includes a Bug Zoo and touch pool with horseshoe crabs. There's also a huge OMNI-MAX theater, the largest in the country. An added plus: a fabulous view of Manhattan and the Statue of Liberty. A ferry leaves from three points in Manhattan; call (201) 902- 8736/(800) 53-FERRY for information. People movers pick up passengers at the dock. Call the museum for other transportation options.

Lower East Side Tenement Museum, 97 Orchard Street; (212) 431-0233. This fascinating living-history museum is dedicated to immigrants and their experience on the Lower East Side. It offers walking tours, dramatizations, and special exhibitions. Orchard Street, with its bargain shops—some schlock, some name brands at hefty discounts—is an experience in itself. There's lots of local color in this area, and you're a short cab ride away from Chinatown and Little Italy.

Metropolitan Museum of Art, Fifth Avenue and Eighty-second Street; (212) 535-7710. As one of the world's greatest museums, the facility's enormity can overpower young ones, particularly during the crowded weekends. The key: Arrive early and focus on areas of particular appeal. Most kids are fascinated by the extensive Egyptian exhibits; wend your way toward the Temple of Dendur, housed in its own glass-enclosed wing. Nearby is the American Wing Garden Court, a peaceful place to sit and enjoy the stained glass (some of it by Tiffany), potted trees, and fountain. Off the court is the arms and armor area. In the second-floor Chinese Garden Court, watch fish swimming in pools and absorb the serenity of this magical place. In nice weather proceed to the pleasant rooftop sculpture gallery (it has its own elevator) with views of Central Park and the city. A recent renovation has expanded the Met's African Gallery. Especially attention-getting for kids are the fanciful masquerade masks of West Africa's Guinea Coast and the brass and ivory sculptures and adornments of the Benin collection. Weekend family programs are free with admission and include short films and lectures; call for information.

Museum of the City of New York, Fifth Avenue at 103rd Street; (212) 534-1672. You can combine a visit to the Jewish Museum with one here; it's just 11 blocks north, a nice walk on a pleasant day. The kids will be especially attracted to the toys and dollhouses and the costumes and accessories of another era. Half of the museum is devoted to changing exhibits, and there are frequent family workshops tied to these exhibits, plus seasonal walking tours of the five boroughs. Families who like to walk are cordially invited.

The museum is directly across from the beautiful **Conservatory Gardens** in Central Park, called "The Secret Garden" by some. Stop in for a peek—but note that this part of the park is a bit more desolate than the lower part below Eighty-sixth Street, so don't stray off the main pathways.

Museum of Modern Art, 11 West Fifty-third Street; (212) 708-9480. This museum bucks the trend and opens Mondays, closing instead on Wednesdays. Some kids enjoy the art here; others will be bored. Aim for a Saturday visit, when guides host special tours to introduce families with kids ages five to ten to the important aspects of the museum's collections. On Saturdays there are also workshops with games and activities, as well as a Family Films program that presents classic shorts. The museum is directly across from the New York Public Library's Donnell branch, which has one of the best children's rooms in the city (second floor) as well as frequent activities and performances for kids. Stop by for a schedule.

Museum of Television and Radio, 25 West Fifty-second Street; (212) 621-6600. An extensive collection of 20,000 radio and television program tapes is listed in a computerized file; select one and watch or listen to it in a console booth. Because of reruns and cable TV, kids think they've seen it all, but there are some gems they'll never catch on "Nick at Nite." Re-creating radio workshops for ages eight to thirteen are held on Saturdays during the school year. Kids read scripts and make sound effects to create their own classic show. Call (212) 621-6000 to reserve.

South Street Seaport Museum, Visitor's Center, 12 Fulton Street; (212) 669-9400. This isn't just a museum, it's a 12-block historic district in lower Manhattan where your family can easily spend most of the day. Stop by the Visitor's Center for information on what's going on, as special events are scheduled frequently. At the children's center kids interact with special exhibits and take part in weekend workshops. A number of historic ships anchored here can be boarded. Kids also enjoy strolling through the traffic-free, cobblestone streets lined with shops, restaurants, and inexpensive eateries.

One of New York's newest museums is the **National Museum of the American Indian, Smithsonian Institution,** 1 Bowling Green between State and Whitehall streets; (212) 668-6624. On display are North, Central, and South American Indian artifacts. The interactive computer terminals allow children to learn about these cultures' tales, leaders, values, and art.

Parks

Smack in the middle of the city, the green oasis called **Central Park** extends south to north from Central Park South (Fifty-ninth Street) to 110th Street and from Fifth Avenue to Central Park West. This is where the city comes to walk, jog, bike, play, roller-skate, and just have fun. Some places not to miss: the **Central Park Wildlife Center,** Central Park at Sixty-fourth Street; (212) 861-6030. Highlights include the penguins and puffins (arrive for their typical 10:30 A.M. and 2:30 P.M. feedings); the Tropic building, with its monkeys, poison dart frogs, and flight cage; and the polar bears, calm and cool in their Arctic pool. Close by, the **Wollman Rink** has ice skating in winter and miniature golf and roller skating in summer. The **Dairy,** a restored building that serves as a visitor's center, hosts weekend children's activities. From here it's a short walk to the wonderful **carousel.** Then head south to the **Hecksher Playground,** which has a wooden bridge, sandbox, slides, seesaws, and swings.

On the West Side the **Belvedere Castle** (near Seventy-ninth Street) is a learning center with nature exhibits and children's programs. Rent a rowboat at **The Boathouse** on East Seventy-second Street; then walk over to see the **Alice in Wonderland** statue, a favorite for climbing. **Note:** Stick to the main walkways during the day, and you will be safe. The park has a deserved reputation for being dangerous at night.

Attractions

So it's not the world's tallest building: Could you come to New York without seeing the **Empire State Building,** Thirty-fourth Street and Fifth Avenue (212-736-3100)? The view from promenades on the Eighty-sixth or 102d floor on a clear day is exhilarating. (While you're here, visit the Guinness World of Records, 350 Fifth Avenue and Thirty-fourth Street; (212) 947-2335. On exhibit are various human achievements in music, sports, outer space exploration, and more.

Farther up Fifth Avenue, **Rockefeller Center** (Forty-seventh–Fifty-second streets) has a sunken plaza where your family can ice skate in winter. **The benches at the Channel Gardens** on the Fifth Avenue side, with their always changing flower and plant arrangements, offer a pleasant place to sit and people-watch.

The **United Nations,** First Avenue at Forty-sixth Street, may be exciting for older kids (those under age five aren't allowed on tours). Free tickets to General Assembly and Security Council meetings are available on a first-come, first-served basis. Call (212) 963-7713. Downtown, the distinctive towers of the **World Trade Center** offer an Observation Deck; (212) 435-4170. Next door, the **World Financial Center** has shops, restaurants, a pleasing waterfront walkway, with a playground nearby, and free art and culture shows geared toward kids.

"The Lady in the Harbor," the **Statue of Liberty National Monument,** is reached via Circle Line Ferry from Battery Park in Lower Manhattan. There's an American Museum of Immigration in the base. Call (212) 269-5755 for ferry information: (212) 363-3200 for Statue information. Summer crowds are endless; arrive early and expect lines. Likewise for the nearby **Ellis Island Immigration Museum,** where the Great Hall has been restored to its 1918–1924 appearance and houses galleries filled with memorabilia, an oral history recording studio, two theaters, and a wall honoring immigrants who passed through. Ellis

Island is also reached via Circle Line ferry; a shuttle service runs between the two attractions.

Sports fans can see the locker rooms of the New York Knicks and the New York Rangers as well as catch the view from a luxury suite on a **Madison Square Garden Behind the Scenes Tour,** Madison Square Garden, Seventh Avenue between West Thirty-first and Thirty-third streets; (212) 465-5800.

At Chelsea Piers Sports and Entertainment Complex, Hudson River between 17th and 23rd streets (212-336-6666), athletic families can play minigolf, swim, ice skate, play basketball, climb a wall, and practice batting.

Television fans can attend free tapings of shows, that is, if they are sixteen years or older. The best way to obtain tickets for *Late Night with David Letterman* is to write *six months* ahead to Late Show Tickets, Ed Sullivan Theater, 1697 Broadway, New York, NY 10019; (212) 975-5853. For those persons who didn't plan ahead, the box office hands out one hundred standby tickets at noon on taping days. Only one ticket is given to each person, so don't send Mom or Dad to get them for the whole family. (Note that standby tickets don't guarantee admission.) Tapings are Monday through Friday at 5:30 P.M.

If you really plan ahead, you may get lucky and obtain free tickets to tapings of *Saturday Night Live.* Be part of the ticket lottery that is held each year at the end of August by mailing a postcard postmarked in August to *Saturday Night* Tickets, NBC, 30 Rockefeller Plaza, New York, NY 10112; (212) 664-3056. Standby tickets are given out at 9:15 A.M. at NBC on the mezzanine level of the Forty-ninth Street side of Rockefeller Plaza. Again, these tickets are limited to one person and do not guarantee admission.

On a calm day boat tours can be fun. **Circle Line Sightseeing,** Pier 83, West Forty-second Street at the Hudson River (212-563-3200), offers several tours.

Performing Arts

Show your children the bright lights of Broadway by taking them to a musical extravaganza. To find out what's playing, call the **Broadway Line** (212-563-2929) for a complete listing and description of Broadway and off-Broadway shows and to book tickets.

Other ticket services include **Tele-Charge** (212-239-6200 or 800-432-7250) and **TicketMaster** (212-307-4100 or 800 755-4000). If you're willing to wait in line (arrive early) you can save 25 to 50 percent on tickets for that day's shows by queuing up at the **TKTS** booth (Forty-seventh Street and Broadway in Times Square, or downtown at Two World Trade Center). Call (212) 768-1818 to hear what's available. **The Theater Development's Fund's Theater Access Project,** (212) 221-1103; (212) 719-4537 TTY, provides sign language interpreted performances of Broadway shows. **Hands ON** (212-627-4898 voice and TTY) offers the same service for off-Broadway productions.

New York has many kids-only presentations and theater groups such as **TADA! Youth Ensemble,** West Twenty-eighth Street between Sixth and Seventh avenues; (212) 243-6736. The **New Victory Theater,** 209 West Forty-second Street (tickets: 212-239-6200; schedules: 212-564-4222), presents plays, dances, films, and opera just for children. Consult the children's listings in the weekly *New York Magazine* for current performances. Seasonal treats include the **Marionette Theater,** West Seventy-ninth Street and West Drive (212-988-9093), which is held in the Swedish Cottage in Central Park. If you're here for the holidays, don't miss the Easter or Christmas shows at Radio City Music Hall, featuring the famous Rockettes (212-247-4777).

Lincoln Center for the Performing Arts, 70 Lincoln Center Plaza (Broadway at Sixty-fourth Street) is considered the Cultural Capital of the World. The complex frequently features musical performances for kids, such as the Little Orchestra Society and Young Peoples concerts, and the Metropolitan Opera's Growing Up With Opera program for kids five to fourteen and their parents. Other performances with kid appeal are held throughout the year, and, of course, *The Nutcracker* ballet is a perennial Christmas sellout. If you come to see Lincoln Center during the day, the public library branch at the east end of the complex has a nice kid's reading room on the second floor. For more information call (212) 875-5350.

Carnegie Hall, Seventh Avenue at Fifty-Seventh Street (212-247-7800) has better acoustics than ever. Its varied schedule of classical, jazz, symphonic, Broadway show tunes, and other performances please a wide range of musical tastes.

Shopping

New York shopping is legendary, from the tony department stores to the bargains sold by street vendors. There are simply too many shopping opportunities to mention all or even many of them. Famous department stores include **Macy's,** Thirty-fourth Street and Broadway, among the largest stores in the world; **Bloomingdale's,** Third Avenue at Fifty-ninth Street; and **Saks,** Fifth Avenue at Fiftieth Street. At Christmas the animated displays in the department store windows are guaranteed to delight kids. Here's a quick list of just a few special interest kid-pleasing stores.

F.A.O. Schwarz, 767 Fifth Avenue (212-644-9400), is an attraction as well as a store. This flagship of the chain is both fanciful and fun. Browse for stuffed animals of almost any variety, from cuddly dogs to a 9-foot bear big enough to require his own den and house to go with it. The Bookmonster has shelves of kid-pleasing volumes, the New York City section sports such souvenirs as a Statue of Liberty head dress, and NYC cockroach hand-puppets.

At the **Warner Brothers Store,** Fifty-seventh Street and Fifth Avenue; (212) 754-0300, find out what's up. Kids love the three floors of trendy 'toon stuff, from T-shirts to plush toys. **The Disney Store,** 39 W. 34th St., (212) 279-9890, is a kid-pleaser with its Walt Disney Company clothing, stuffed animals, video games, and collectibles. For comic collectibles as well as current funnies, the city has three specialty shops: the **Comic Arts Gallery,** Third Avenue between Fifty-sixth and Fifty-seventh streets (212-759-6355); **New York Comics,** Broadway and Forty-eighth Street (212-956-1133); and **Village Comics,** Bleecker Street between Sullivan and Thompson streets (212-777-2770).

Sports

New York fans are loyal to their teams. **Madison Square Garden,** Seventh Avenue between West Thirty-first and Thirty-third streets (212-465-5800), is home to the Rangers for ice hockey and to the New York Knicks for basketball. Call (212) 465-6741 for tickets. The Mets play baseball at **Shea Stadium** (718-507-METS), and the Yankees have their baseball diamond at **Yankee Stadium,** the Bronx (718- 293-6000). Football fans can watch the Giants and the Jets in **Giants Stadium,** the Meadowlands Complex, East Rutherford, New Jersey. Call (201) 935-8222 for Giants tickets and (201) 935-8500 for Jets tickets.

SPECIAL EVENTS

There's never a dull moment in the Big Apple. Check the Other Events listings in *New York Magazine* and the Friday Weekend section in the *New York Times* for the latest happenings. Here's a sampling:

January: Chinese New Year celebrations. Ice Capades, Madison Square Garden.

February: Westminster Kennel Club Dog Show, Madison Square Garden.

March: International Cat Show, Madison Square Garden.

March–April: Ringling Brothers Circus. Easter Show, Radio City Music Hall. Spring Flower Show, New York Botanical Garden.

Easter: Easter Parade, Fifth Avenue.

May: Ninth Avenue International Food Festival. Salute to Israel Parade. Ukrainian Festival, Lower East Side.

June–August: Central Park SummerStage.

July: Fourth of July Festivities with Harbor Festival and fireworks over Central Park and the East River.

July–August: Free Shakespeare in Central Park. Free Summergarden Concerts, The Museum of Modern Art. Free Summer Pier Concerts, South Street Seaport.

August: Lincoln Center Out-of-Doors.

September: Feast of San Gennaro, streets of Little Italy. Third Avenue Street Fair. New York is Book Country fair on Fifth Avenue. Atlantic Antic, Brooklyn Street Festival. Columbus Avenue Festival, Manhattan.

Thanksgiving: Macy's Thanksgiving Day Parade.

December: Lighting of giant tree, Rockefeller Center. Origami Christmas Tree, American Museum of Natural History.

WHERE TO STAY

Located in the theater district **Doubletree Guest Suites,** Forty-seventh Street and Seventh Avenue (212-719-1600/800-424-2900), offers a family-friendly Children's Center on the fourth floor. Rooms here have covers on electric outlets and plastic on furniture edges. If needed, the staff brings you diapers or other necessities. Also in the theater district, the **Millennium Broadway,** 145 West Forty-fourth Street (212-768-4400), offers upscale amenities. Ask about their lower weekend rates.

Loew's New York Hotel, 569 Lexington Avenue at Fifty-first Street (212-752-7000 or 800-23-LOEWS), has a Loew's Loves Kids program, which lets children under eighteen stay free with parents. The restaurant and room service feature kid's menus, kids get free ice cream dessert with any entree for kids, children under ten receive a gift bag upon check-in, and a second adjoining room is available at a discount. The **Grand Hyatt New York,** Park Avenue at Grand Central (212-883-1234; 800-233-1234), has kid's menus in the restaurant and for room service. A second room for children is available at a discounted rate.

At any of the nine **Manhattan East Suite Hotels** (800-ME-SUITE), you get more room for your money. All the accommodations, from studio suites to four-bedroom units, feature kitchen facilities. **Le Parker Meridien,** 118 West Fifty-seventh Street (212-245-5000), is a well-appointed hotel in a midtown location. **The Mark,** Madison Avenue at East Seventy-seventh Street (212-744-4300; 800-THE-MARK), is an uptown and upscale luxury hotel that combines the friendly feel of a small hotel with big hotel services and good-sized rooms, most of which have in-room refrigerators and a microwave—necessities for the all-important kids' snacks. The Upper East Side location puts you blocks from such New York City staples as Central Park and the Metropolitan Museum of Art.

Journey's End Hotels, 3 East Fortieth Street (212-447-1500/ 800-668-4200), offers limited services at lower than typical big-city rates. Other less expensive choices include the **Days Inn,** 440 West Fifty-seventh Street (212-581-8100/800-231-0405), where kids under seventeen stay free and those under twelve eat free as long as adults dine with them.

Don't forget to inquire about weekend deals at some of the upscale properties. Depending on the season you could be pleasantly surprised with a posh room at a good price.

WHERE TO EAT

New York has some of the finest restaurants in the world. *The Zagat Restaurant Survey,* available at all bookstores, is a handy objective guide to New York eateries, with special headings for indicating eateries appealing to kids and teens.

It seems all kids ten and up somehow gravitate to West Fifty-seventh Street, where they have a choice of the **Hard Rock Cafe** at 221 (212-459-9320) or **Planet Hollywood** at 140 (212-333-7827). Both have incredibly long lines during peak vacation times: arrive early to avoid the crunch. Also on West Fifty-seventh Street, between Fifth and Sixth avenues, is a high-tech **McDonald's** that's eye catching—and convenient after a trek to F.A.O. Schwarz or Central Park. In the same neighborhood, **Mickey Mantle's,** 42 Central Park South (212-688-7777), is a big hit with baseball fans. There's sports memorabilia, ten television monitors, and a kid's menu.

Hamburger Harry's, West Forty-fifth Street and Broadway (212-840-2756), serves great burgers and has a children's menu. This location is also convenient for many popular NYC attractions. The **Harley Davidson Cafe,** Fifty-sixth Street and Sixth Avenue, literally has motorcycles and biking memorabilia hanging from the ceiling. The menu features sandwiches, burgers, salads, and pasta. The **Brook-lyn Diner,** West Fifty-seventh Street between Seventh Avenue and Broadway (212-581-8900), with its shiny exterior, looks something like a traditional diner from the outside. The diner staples taste much better than standard diner fare, and the portions are large. You can get real chicken soup, sandwiches, burgers, pot roast, meat loaf and mashed potatoes, and chicken pot pie. The house special for dessert is a yummy Strawberry Blonde Cheesecake.

Serendipity 3, 225 East Sixtieth Street (212-838-3531), close to Bloomingdale's, is a favorite for ice cream concoctions. The place also has a funky gift/toy store. On Seventh Avenue the overstuffed sandwiches at the **Carnegie Deli,** at 854 (212-757-2245), and the **Stage Deli,** at 834 (212-245-7850), could feed an army. Both are good; the jury is still out on which has the best pastrami and corned beef.

The Olive Garden, Seventh Avenue and Forty-seventh Street (212-333-3254), may be a familiar restaurant, serving great Italian food at moderate prices, but its location and view of Times Square is worth seeing. (Be careful at night in this area. Although the streets may be full of people, the crowd is an easy diversion for pickpockets.)

Consider a trip to Chinatown for local color and good, inexpensive food. Try **20 Mott Street,** the name of the restaurant as well as the address; (212) 964-0380. They have superb dim sum and daily specialties. Next door, stop in the arcade to play ticktacktoe with a chicken (that's right, a chicken). Later, cross over Canal Street to Little Italy for a pastry at **Ferrara's,** 195 Grand Street; (212) 226-6150.

DAY TRIPS

Most people find so much to do in Manhattan that they hardly consider leaving it for a day. But if you're so inclined—or are on your second or third trip to New York—head straight to the **International Wildlife Conservation Park,** formerly called the **Bronx Zoo,** the largest urban zoo in the United States and home to more than 4,000 animals. Explore 265 acres of green parklands and naturalistic habitats. The Bengali Express monorail travels over 2 miles of tracks through the forests and meadows of Wild Asia, where you'll see rhinos, elephants, and Siberian tigers roaming about. At the Children's Zoo, kids imitate what animals do: crawl through a prairie dog tunnel or climb a spider's web, for instance. Perhaps the most impressive exhibit is JungleWorld, an indoor rain forest with tropical Asian plants and animals. You can easily spend a complete day at the zoo. Although this zoo is open all year, the zoo shuttle, camel rides, and Skyfari aerial tramway close during winter. Baby strollers can be rented at the entrance. Call (212) 367-1010 for information. Liberty Lines runs express bus service between mid-Manhattan and the Bronxdale entrance to the zoo. Call (212) 652-8400 for schedules.

Don't leave New York without catching a glimpse of the magnificent Brooklyn Bridge, which you can see from Manhattan's Seaport area. You can cross over to Brooklyn Heights, a pleasant residential area, where the esplanade provides a great view of Manhattan. Brooklyn's **Coney Island** area, once the city's fun spot, has seen better days. Home to the **New York Aquarium,** as well as an amusement park and beach, the area is sadly run down, but the Aquarium is modern and pleasant and has its own parking lot.

If it's sizzling hot and your family is in dire need of a beach, head to the Rockaways in the borough of Queens, where you'll find **Jacob**

A day trip to the Bronx Zoo will be a day well spent. (Copyright © 1993 New York State Department of Economic Development)

Riis Park (IRT #2 subway to Flatbush Avenue, then bus Q35). Manhattan area beaches are not world famous, but this one, part of **Gateway National Park,** has a nice sandy stretch. Note that the western portion is almost exclusively gay. Call (718) 318-4300. If you have a car, head out to the **Hamptons,** on Long Island, a much more scenic option, though the traffic on weekends is horrendous. The Hampton Jitney (516-283-4600) has express motorcoach service from New York City. At the easternmost tip of the island, the town of **Montauk** has a beautiful, clean public beach, a scenic lighthouse, and two large oceanside state parks. Passenger ferries leave daily for Block Island and Newport. Call the Montauk Chamber of Commerce at (516) 668-2428 for more information.

From New York you're also a day trip away from the sights in Mystic, Connecticut. (See the Mystic chapter.)

FOR MORE INFORMATION

New York Convention and Visitors Bureau, Inc. is at 2 Columbus Circle (Fifty-ninth Street between Broadway and Eighth Avenue), New York 10019; (212) 484-1200 or (800) NYC-VISIT. They have helpful literature, advice, and an information center that is open 365 days a year. For lodging availability during peak times, Sept. 1–Dec. 31, call the bureau's Peak Season Hotel Hotline (800) 846-ROOM, (212) 582-3352. Volunteers (not professionals) at Big Apple Greeters, (212) 669-8273, are glad to tell visitors about some of the city's highlights as well as pass on access tips to the physically challenged.

For information on the accessibility of public transportation, obtain the free *MTA New York City Transit Accessible Travel Brochure,* (call (718) 330-1234. Two additional resources: the free *Access Guide for People with Disabilities,* available from the **Mayor's Office for People with Disabilities** (212) 778-2830; and the *Access for All,* available from **Hospital Audiences Inc.;** (212) 575-7676. This offers details on access to the city's cultural institutions. Another helpful resource is the All Around Town listings in the front of the Yellow Pages phone directory, containing loads of basic information and phone numbers.

The Big Apple Parent's Paper (212-533-2277) and *New York Family* (914-381-7474) are publications that feature news and events of interest to families.

Emergency Numbers

Ambulance, fire, and police: 911

Poison Control Center: (212) 764-7667 or 340-4494

Twenty-four-hour pharmacy: Kaufman Pharmacy, Lexington Avenue and Fiftieth Street; (212) 755-2266

If your child has a middle-of-the-night ear infection, go to the twenty-four-hour emergency room at Manhattan Eye, Ear and Throat Hospital, 210 East Sixty-fourth Street: (212) 838-9200. For other emergencies head to one of the city's respected hospitals, which include Emergency Pavilion at New York Hospital Cornell Medical Center, 510 East Seventieth Street: (212) 746-5050.

PHILADELPHIA

Philadelphia, the site of America's first capital, is rich in history. Your kids will love seeing the sites they've read about, from the Liberty Bell to Independence Hall. After exploring the birth of American democracy, families can discover their personal heritage at the city's ethnic museums. There is more fun at the waterfront, which, in warm weather, hosts several cultural festivals that feature music, food, dance, and entertainment.

GETTING THERE

Philadelphia International Airport (215-492-3181 or 492-3000), 8 miles south of central Philadelphia, services all major domestic airlines and several international lines. The Southeastern Pennsylvania Transportation Authority (SEPTA) railway system is a good way to get downtown from the airport.

Amtrak train lines (800-USA-RAIL) run out of Penn Station on Thirtieth Street (215-824-1600), just across the Schuylkill River from downtown. Philadelphia is a regular stop on the northeast corridor line for the high-speed Metroliner that runs between New York and Washington. Train lines also connect the city to Atlantic City and Harrisburg. For more luxurious accommodations try the American-European Express (800-677-4233), a deluxe overnight train servicing Chicago, Indianapolis, and several eastern locations.

The bus that connects Philadelphia with New England, Chicago, St. Louis, and the rest of the country is another option. Intercity buses stop at the Greyhound Terminal, Tenth and Filbert streets (800-231-2222). Bus travel is a cheap alternative for short trips.

GETTING AROUND

You can tour the city by bus, trolley, or subway. For specific information call SEPTA at (215) 580-7800. Dial-A-Schedule (215-574-7777) will mail you a schedule in advance.

The commuter rail system circulates throughout the Center City and connects downtown with the airport, the Amtrak station, and the suburbs. The Port Authority Transit Corporation (PATCO) is an inexpensive way to travel to southern New Jersey. For more information call (215) 922-4600 or (609) 772-6900 in New Jersey.

SEPTA offers a day pass to all buses and trains, including a one-way trip on the airport line. Passes can be obtained at the visitor's center on Sixteenth Street and John F. Kennedy Boulevard (215-636-1666).

For information on parking within the city, call the Philadelphia Parking Authority at (215) 563-7670 or (215) 977-7275.

WHAT TO SEE AND DO

Historic Sites

Independence National Historical Park, with forty buildings on thirty-seven acres, is a must-see in Philadelphia. Stop off first at the **Visitor's Center,** Third and Chestnut streets (215-597-8974 voice, 215-597-1785 TDD), to get a map and to watch the short film *Independence.* Then choose the historic sites that interest you most. The Declaration of Independence was adopted and the Constitutional Convention was held at **Independence Hall,** which offers daily tours. The **Liberty Bell Pavilion,** on Chestnut Street between Fifth and Sixth streets, hosts talks on the nation's symbol of independence. **Carpenters' Hall,** at 320 Chestnut Street (215-597-8974), is the site of the first Continental Congress. Other attractions include an **Army-Navy Museum,** Chestnut Street between Third and Fourth, which details the development of these military branches; **Congress Hall,** Sixth and Chestnut streets, where the U.S. Congress met from 1790 to 1800; and **Declaration House,** Seventh and Market streets, where Thomas Jefferson drafted the Declaration of Independence in rented rooms.

Other sites of interest on the historic square mile include **Franklin Court,** Market Street between Third and Fourth streets (215-597-2761),

Philadelphia at a Glance

- History abounds in America's first capital

- See the Liberty Bell, Independence Hall, and the rest of Independence National Historical Park

- Several art museums, including the Norman Rockwell Museum

- A self-guided tour of the U.S mint

- Six ethnic museums and three professional sports teams

- Visitor's Center of Philadelphia, (800) 537-7676 or (215) 636-1666

with its museum, theater, and printing and binding exhibit, all dedicated to Benjamin Franklin; and the **Old City Hall,** Fifth and Chestnut streets, where the U.S. Supreme Court met from 1791 to 1800.

It won't take long to tour the **Betsy Ross House,** 239 Arch Street (215-627-5343) the restored Colonial home of the woman credited with the creation of the first American flag. The **Edgar Allan Poe National Historic Site,** 532 North Seventh Street (215-597-8780), is for Poe buffs. Here the author probably wrote "The Tell-Tale Heart" and "The Black Cat." Attractions include a reading room and slide show.

Art Museums

When you tire of history, enjoy the city's art. Turn this into a treasure hunt by asking your kids to find the great works in these galleries.

The Philadelphia Museum of Art, 251 South Eighteenth Street (215-763-8100), is the nation's third largest art museum, with works varying from paintings to furniture to period rooms. Some of many highlights include works by Renaissance masters and by the nineteenth-century Philadelphia artist, Thomas Eakins. Kids also like to browse in the collec-

The Liberty Bell is just one of the many historical attractions in Philadelphia kids can see first-hand. (Courtesy Philadelphia Convention and Visitors Bureau)

tion of arms and armor. Among the delights at the **Rodin Museum,** Twenty-second Street and Benjamin Franklin Parkway (215-787-5476), is the *Thinker* and a cast of the *Burghers of Calais.* This museum boasts the largest collection outside Paris of the famous sculptor's works.

An American favorite, the **Norman Rockwell Museum,** at 601 Walnut Street (215-922-4345), features the artist's familiar illustrations plus a video presentation. All Rockwell's cover illustrations for the *Saturday Evening Post* are here. For more art the **Institute of Contemporary Art,** Thirty-sixth and Sansom streets (215-898-7108), presents temporary exhibitions in all mediums including performance art. **The Museum of American Art of the Pennsylvania Academy of the Fine Arts,** 118 North Broad Street (215-972-7600), displays a wide variety of both older and contemporary artwork.

More Family-Friendly Attractions

Take a self-guided tour of the **U.S. Mint,** Fifth and Arch streets; (215) 597-7350. You will get an inside view of the money-making process. Watch as molten metal is cooled and rolled into thin sheets, blank coins are punched out, and coin designs are impressed. In summer the museum is open on Saturdays and during the week.

The Academy of Natural Sciences, Nineteenth and Benjamin Franklin Parkway (215-299-1002), is for dinosaur lovers. Here the kids and you get to finger replicas of bones and eggs. Check out the temporary shows, which are often designed for children.

The Franklin Institute Science Museum and Mandell Center, Twentieth Street and Benjamin Franklin Parkway (215-448-1208), has a host of hands-on science fun and merits a full day. Benjamin Franklin would be proud of the scientific achievements and exhibits displayed here, including a heart you can walk through, a 350-ton locomotive, a rooftop observatory, and an astronomy exhibit. The Mandell Center houses traveling exhibits, along with an Omniverse movie theater. The Fels Planetarium features fun-filled lessons in astronomy as well as less scientific laser shows.

The **Corestates Science Park,** a 38,000-square-foot urban garden, is just the place to romp between museums, and for that reason, it is located between the Franklin Museum and the Please Touch Museum, both of which operate this facility. The family fun here includes testing your balance on a high-wire tandem bicycle, playing tunes on a step-on organ, and climbing on a 12-foot tire.

Just for kids, the **Please Touch Museum,** 210 North Twenty-first Street (215-963-0667), offers interactive exhibitions for ages seven and under, including a Nature's Nursery for those under two years. These playful exhibits include lessons on the muscles of the body, the origin of the food we eat, and works of art. Children can design their own theater sets at the new Puppet Land theater.

At **RiverRink,** Penn's Landing, glide hand in hand with your children or practice figure eights and double axels at this hockey-size outdoor ice rink. Check the schedule for special performances.

Ethnic Philadelphia

The city of brotherly love offers a good place for you and your kids to explore your ethnic heritage. Begin at the **Balch Institute of Ethnic Studies,** 18 South Seventh Street (215-925-8090), with the Do Your Own Heritage computer. Visitors input one of nineteen ethnic groups;

the computer responds with a printout of that ethnic group's history and influence in the United States. The institute also presents regular educational programs on ethnicity. The Do Your Own Heritage computer program is found at four other sites as well. Call (215) 636–1666 for more information.

The **Afro-American Historical and Cultural Museum,** Seventh and Arch streets (215–574–0380), traces the history of African-American culture, displays African-American artwork, and talks about people who have made contributions to sports, theater, music, and the sciences. There's also a moving depiction of slavery in the United States. The **National Museum of American Jewish History,** at 55 North Fifth Street (215–923–3811), traces the Jewish experience in America since 1654. Other ethnic museums include the **American Swedish Historical Museum,** 1900 Pattison Avenue (215–389–1776) and the **Polish American Cultural Center Museum,** 308 Walnut Street (215–922–1700).

To learn about an interesting group that has no ethnic identity, visit the **Mummers Museum** at Second Street and Washington Avenue (215–336–3050). You'll find out there's more to them than their parade.

Waterfront Attractions

Take a walk down to **Penn's Landing** along the Delaware River to visit the historic ships in port. Among them are the cruiser *Olympia* and World War II submarine U.S.S. *Becuna,* at Christopher Columbus Boulevard and Spruce Street; (215) 922–1898. In the Basin check to see if *Gazela of Philadelphia* is in dock; this masted sailboat is more than one hundred years old. Call the Basin at (215) 923–9030 for visiting hours.

For a glimpse of the art of wooden boatbuilding, visit the Philadelphia Maritime Museum's floating **Workshop on the Water,** at the Boat Basin; (215) 925–5439. The **Independence Seaport Museum,** Penn's Landing, Columbus Boulevard and Walnut Street (215–925–5439), focuses on the maritime history of the Delaware Valley. Interactive exhibits let you unload a container ship, experience a general quarters drill aboard a naval destroyer, and try welding and riveting a ship's hull. Explore the undersea world with Divers of the Deep.

Parks and Zoos

You can't avoid history in this city. **The Philadelphia Zoo,** 3400 West Girard Avenue, Philadelphia; (215) 243-1100, established in 1874, was the nation's first. It now encompasses more than forty acres. Be sure to visit the Carnivore Kingdom, where animals wander around in simulated natural habitats; the Reptile House, for slithery snakes and slow-moving tortoises; the Jungle Bird Walk, where you stroll through an aviary where birds fly free. The Children's Zoo is great for little kids who love riding the camels, petting and feeding the goats, and exploring the Treehouse, with exhibits to climb through and touch.

The zoo is located in **Fairmount Park** (215-685-0000). This park, covering nearly 9,000 acres at the north end of the Benjamin Frank Parkway, is the world's biggest landscaped city park. Besides the zoo other highlights include the **Japanese House and Gardens** at North Horticultural Drive off Belmont Avenue (215-685-0104), a replica of a seventeenth-century home; and **Strawberry Mansion** at Strawberry Mansion Drive (215-228-8364), a Federal and Greek Revival mansion that houses some fine period furnishings and an antique toy exhibit. At **Boathouse Row** (215-686-2176) enjoy seeing for yourself this frequently painted and photographed image of Philadelphia. The kids might enjoy catching one of the rowing clubs at practice. Also, be sure to take a break from the city to hike or bike miles of trails.

Smith Memorial Playground, Reservoir Drive by Thirty-third Street, Philadelphia (215-765-4325), is fun for children of all ages and features an outdoor swimming pool and sliding board.

Performing Arts and Entertainment

The redevelopment of Broad Street in Center City added or reinvigorated 16 performance, visual and educational faculities to what's called Avenue of the Arts. Kids like the "street concerts" played on the 39 bronze bells on Broad Street between Chestnut and Carpenter streets. Check out the Annenberg Center at 3680 Walnut Street (215-898-6791) for international productions and a children's theater series. The Freedom Theatre, 1346 North Broad Street (215-765-2793), established in 1966, has been rated one of the top six theaters in the country. It's located in the historic Heritage House. Other options are the Merriam Theater, 250 Broad Street (215- 732-5446), the Philadelphia Theatre Company, 1714 Delancey Street (215-592-8333), and Society Hill Playhouse, 507 South Eighth Street (215-923-0210) for off-Broadway plays.

Children delight in the Philadelphia Marionette Theater; (215) 879-1213.

If music is more your style, you can listen to the Philadelphia Orchestra. Call (215) 893-1999 for performance information, including children's productions. For the city's Bach Festival, call (215) 247-BACH; for the Mozart Orchestra, call (610) 284-0174. The Curtis Institute of Music, 1726 Locust Street (215-893-7902), presents free student performances.

The Pennsylvania Ballet performs at the Academy of Music, Broad and Locust streets (215-551-7000), along with the Opera Company of Philadelphia (215-928-2110).

Sports

Philly is a town for sports lovers as well. In summer check out the Phillies baseball team at Veterans Stadium, Broad Street and Pattison Avenue; tickets and information: (215) 463-1000. In autumn the Eagles football team takes over Veterans Stadium. Call (215) 463-5500 for tickets and information. The 76ers basketball team plays at the Spectrum, Broad Street and Pattison Avenue, Philadelphia. For tickets and information, call (215) 339-7676. Hockey fans can watch the Flyers in season at the Spectrum. Tickets and information are available at (215) 465-4500.

The new CoreStates Center is the new home for the 76ers and the Flyers.

More Useful Numbers

For general entertainment and sports tickets, there are a few ticket sales bureaus: Central City Ticket Office, 1312 Sansom Street; (215) 735-1350 or 735-1351. Upstages, 2nd level, and The Shops at Liberty Place Sixteenth Street and John F. Kennedy Boulevard; (215) 567-0670. Wanamaker's Ticket Office, Thirteenth and Chestnut streets; (215) 568-7100. Call (215) 646-3566 for "The City Perks" coupon book, which offers discounts at Philadelphia area attractions.

Special Tours

Conduct your own walking tour of African-American history in Philadelphia with the *African-American Historical and Cultural Guide* published by the Philadelphia Convention and Visitor's Bureau; (215) 636-1666. Highlights include the Mother Bethel African Methodist Episcopal Church, founded in 1794 and considered to be the oldest piece of property continually owned by blacks in the country, and Heritage House, the oldest black cultural center. This helpful guide includes information on restaurants, shopping, and nightlife as well.

A guided walking tour of historic Philadelphia begins at Barry Statue, Sixth and Walnut streets. Call (215) 592-1971 for more information. If you prefer to go at your own pace, try Audio Walk & Tour, Sixth and Sansom streets (215-925-1234), for a self-guided cassette tour. Candlelight Tours (215-735-3123) offers a candlelight stroll with costumed guides on selected evenings.

If you're looking to get off your feet, old trolley tours of the historic district leave from the Visitor Center, John F. Kennedy Boulevard and Sixteenth Street; (215) 333-0320. For a trolley tour of Penn's Landing, call (215) 627-0807.

Horse and Buggy. The even more old-fashioned enjoy horse-drawn carriage rides available at Fifth and Market streets and South Street at Headhouse Square.

SPECIAL EVENTS

Festivals

The Visitor's Center publishes a calendar of events and has a twenty-four-hour event hotline; (215) 337-7777, ext. 2540.

January: Start off the new year with the Mummers Parade on New Year's Day. This world-famous event features 30,000 mummers. Later in the month enjoy Valley Forge Day and the Chinese New Year Celebration.

February: Presidential Jazz Weekend offers three days jam-packed with jazz for the whole family.

March: The Philadelphia Flower Show, the largest flower show on the East Coast. In March or April The Book and the Cook, a celebration of cookbook authors and fine food, is featured at many area restaurants.

Summer/Fall: Penn's Landing Summer Season sponsors more than sixty free concerts on the waterfront. Mann Music Center Summer Concerts are staged in Fairmount Park.

May: USAir sponsors a Jambalaya Jam, a festival of food and music on Memorial Day weekend. Other festivals include Africamericas Festival, Italian Market Festival, and International Choral Music Festival. Philadelphia International Theatre Festival for Children at the **Annenberg Center** features juggling workshops and an international atmosphere.

June: The Odunde Festival of the African New Year, Twenty-third and South streets, features live performances. Rittenhouse Square Fine Arts Annual Festival and Mellon Jazz Festival also are highlights.

July: Freedom Festival celebrates America's birthday. Philadelphia International Film Festival (Philafilm).

August: Polish Festival at Penn's Landing, Great Gospel Picnic Weekend in Fairmount Park, and African American Extravaganza.

September: South Street Seven Arts Festival. Annual Pepsi Penn's Landing Jazz Fest.

October: Freedom Fest sponsored by the Freedom Theatre.

November: Thanksgiving Day Parade.

December: There is no lack of holiday events. Attend the Presence of Kwanzaa, and bring in the New Year with First Night Philadelphia and fireworks on the waterfront.

WHERE TO STAY

Hotels

Philadelphia has a wide range of accommodations. Some upscale choices include the **Rittenhouse,** 210 West Rittenhouse Square; (215) 546-9000. Situated on historic Rittenhouse Square, it offers large rooms and luxurious bathrooms. **The Four Seasons,** One Logan Square (215-963-1500 or 800-332-3442), is a full-service luxury hotel including complimentary town-car service within the city. **The Ritz-Carlton** (215-563-1600) at Liberty Place in the business district features luxury accommodations, including a fitness center and three restaurants.

Less expensive choices, especially with weekend packages, include the **Sheraton Society Hill** at 1 Dock Street (215-238-6000) near Independence National Historical Park. The **Holiday Inn Independence Mall** at

Fourth and Arch streets (215-923-8660) is close to the Liberty Bell. The **Holiday Inn Select Center City,** Eighteenth and Market streets (215-561-7500), is centrally situated. The **Comfort Inn at Penn's Landing,** 100 North Delaware Avenue (215-627-7900), is on the waterfront and has relatively inexpensive weekend rates.

Near the airport are two all-suite choices. **Embassy Suites,** 9000 Bartram Avenue (215-364-4500), has five floors of suites and weekend packages. **Guest Quarters Suite Hotel,** 1 Gateway Center (215-365-6600), also near the airport, offers suite space.

Bed and Breakfast Accommodations

Bed and Breakfast homes offer an especially nice alternative for families in Philadelphia because many are located in historic districts. **Bed and Breakfast of Philadelphia,** 1530 Locust Street, Suite K (800-220-1917 or 215-735-1917), has several possibilities for families. **Rittenhouse Comfort** and **Rodman Renaissance** are both historic town houses. **Spruce Street Seclusion,** in Center City, offers a suite with two bedrooms, and two baths, perfect for families.

Another bed and breakfast registry to check out is **Bed and Breakfast Connections,** P.O. Box 21, Devon (215-687-3565 or 800-448-3619) **All About Town-Bed and Breakfast,** P.O. Box 562, Valley Forge (800-344-0123 or 215-783-7838), has listings for the Valley Forge region, in town, and in other suburbs.

WHERE TO EAT

You've got to have an authentic hoagie or steak sandwich while staying in Philadelphia. Two good suppliers are **Jim's Steaks,** 400 South Street. (215-928-1911), or **Pat's King of the Steaks,** 1237 East Passyunk Avenue (215-468-1546). **Tacconelli's,** Somerset Street and Aramingo Avenue (215-425-4983), has some of the best pizza in town.

A fun place to stop for a quick bite, coffee, or dessert is **Reading Terminal Market,** Twelfth and Arch streets, just off Market Street. Here you can put together a lunch, mixing fresh produce, deli meats, and cheeses available from a bustling array of individual food service booths. Or get some chicken pot pie from the Amish vendors who come to the market on Wednesdays and Saturdays.

When your stomach is growling in Independence Park, the **Food Court at Liberty Place** is not far away on the second floor of Liberty Place between Chestnut and Market streets in Center City. It's well stocked with fast-food spots.

If you're in the mood for Chinese food, Chinatown's the place, with a lineup of restaurants stretching from Ninth to Eleventh streets. Good picks are the **Imperial Inn,** 142 North Tenth Street (215-627-5588) and the **Harmony Vegetarian Restaurant,** 135 North Ninth Street (215-627-4520).

For fine dining with older kids and teens, **Le Bec-Fin,** 1523 Walnut Street, in Center City (215-567-1000), has excellent French cuisine. In the Historic District try **The Dickens Inn,** 421 South Second Street (215) 928-9307. Housed in a Federal-style town house with British owners, the restaurant is decorated with Dickens paraphernalia. For Italian cuisine and a waterfront view, go to **Ristorante Panorama** on Front and Market streets; (215) 922-7600.

DAY TRIPS

The **New Jersey State Aquarium,** Riverside Drive and Delaware River, Camden, New Jersey; (609) 365-3300. Take the *Delawhale Ferry* (800-634-4027), from Penn's Landing to the Camden Waterfront, right next to the Aquarium. If you prefer to be on land, take the PATCO train line, which connects downtown Philadelphia to the Aquarium by way of the scenic Ben Franklin Bridge. The Aquarium features a huge open-ocean tank, with fish species ranging from sharks to minnows.

Ocean Base Atlantic features 1,00 tropical fish, plus such "awesome" real artifacts as a 7-foot shark jaw, complete with 275 fossilized teeth. Interactive computers make learning about this sea life hands-on fun. Other fishy finds include a 3,000-gallon Rainbow Seas Caribbean reef tank, a trout stream, and a 170,000-gallon Seal Pool with nine seals.

Another treat in Camden is the **Blockbuster-Sony Music Entertainment Centre,** right across the Delaware River from Penn's Landing. Big-name concerts take place outdoors May through October at this 25,000-seat amphitheater. In winter walls create a climate-controlled theater.

The **Valley Forge National Historic Park,** Route 23 and North Gulph Road, Valley Forge (215-783-1077), is thirty minutes outside the city, and worth the trip. In 1993 the area celebrated its one-hundredth anniversary, and there's always something to celebrate at this Revolutionary War site where George Washington and 12,000 soldiers barricaded the British for six months. Take a self-guided tour of the reconstructed huts, headquarters, and fortifications of the encampments. Other attractions in the area include the 1770 **Isaac Potts House,** the **Washington Memorial Chapel,** a 1903 Gothic chapel with Sunday concerts, and the **Valley Forge Historical Society Museum;** (215) 783-0535.

Germantown, a historic Philadelphia district occupied since the 1680s, offers enough sight-seeing to justify a day's trip. Stop off at the **Visitors Center,** Sixteenth Street and John F. Kennedy Boulevard (215-636-1666), where you can obtain a map. The main sites are historic residences including the **Clivedon,** 6401 Germantown Avenue (215-848-1777), an old Georgian mansion; the **Ebenezer Maxwell Mansion,** 200 West Tulpehocken Street at Green Street (215-438-1861), a Victorian mansion; and **Stenton,** Eighteenth Street and Windrim Avenue (215-392-7312).

Bucks County, about an hour by car from Philadelphia, is well stocked with historic estates, antiques stores, and country inns. Call **Bucks County Tourist Commission,** 152 Swamp Road, Doylestown (215-345-4552), for more information.

A great place for families in Bucks County is **Sesame Place,** Oxford Valley Road, Langhorne, Pennsylvania; (215) 757-1100 for recorded information or (215) 752-7070. This theme park, aimed at kids ages three and older, delights with characters from Sesame Street plus lots of climbing and water activities.

The **Pearl S. Buck House** at Green Hills, 520 Dublin Road, Perkasie (215-249-0100), also in Bucks County, is a good place for a picnic. Relax at this sixty-acre farm, a National Historic Landmark and home of the Nobel and Pulitzer prize winner.

The **Pennsylvania Renaissance Faire,** on the grounds of Mount Hope Estate and Winery in Cornwall (717-665-7021), simulates a 1599 English country "faire" for fifteen weekends throughout the summer and fall beginning in late June or July. Activities in this thirty-acre spread include crafts, sporting events, music, and food. Many, including a petting zoo and marionette shows, are expressly for children. The faire runs Saturday through Monday during early September, and weekends only from then until October. Summer hours are 11:30 A.M. to 7:00 P.M.; fall hours are 10:30 A.M. to 6:00 P.M.

The **Brandywine Valley,** about an hour's drive from Philadelphia, mixes scenery and history. (See the chapter on the Brandywine Valley.)

FOR MORE INFORMATION

The Visitor's Center of Philadelphia, Sixteenth Street and John F. Kennedy Boulevard, Philadelphia: (215) 636–1666 or 800–537–7676

Twenty-four hour event hotline: (215) 337–7777, ext. 2540

The Philadelphia Convention and Visitors Bureau, 1515 Market Street, Philadelphia: (215) 636–3300

International Visitors Center: (215) 823–7261

Philly Fun Line: (215) 568–7255

Travelers Aid Society: (215) 546–0571 or 386–0845, for travel problems, lost luggage, etc.

The Philadelphia *Inquirer* puts out a Weekend section of entertainment events on Fridays. The *Daily News,* a paper with heavier local coverage, also lists events.

Persons with disabilities can get referrals and information from the **Mayor's Office for the Handicapped,** Room 143, City Hall, Philadelphia; (215) 686–2798.

Also, those of you who are wired into cyberspace can access Philadelphia information via the Internet: http://www.libertynet.org/phila-visitor.

Emergency Numbers

Ambulance, fire, and police: 911

Children's Hospital of Philadelphia: (215) 590–1000

Health Hotline: (800) 692–7254

Philadelphia Police: (215) 231–3131

Poison Control Center: (215) 386–2100

Twenty-four-hour pharmacy: CVS, 6501 Harbison Avenue; (215) 333–4300.

WASHINGTON, D.C.

In Washington, D.C., prepare to have fun and to feel proud, as our nation's capital is a city that belongs to all Americans. Even after more than 200 years, the city of Washington still sparkles. Pierre L'Enfant, the French architect who planned this city of wide avenues and open spaces, paved the way for a city of heroic proportions.

Spring is an especially good time to visit the nation's capital, for the city blooms with tulips and azaleas, and with any luck, you might catch the famous cherry blossoms. An autumn stroll through Rock Creek Park serves as a wonderful respite to life in the fast lane. Winter in Washington is lots of fun, too. After touring many of the museums' special exhibits, take the whole family ice skating on the mall.

GETTING THERE

Air travelers touch down at one of three airports in and around the District of Columbia. **Washington National Airport** is the closest to downtown, about 4.5 miles, or fifteen minutes away. Metrorail, Metrobus, and taxi service are available from the airport. **Washington Dulles International Airport,** approximately 26 miles from downtown, is a forty-minute drive, although during rush hour, the time and charges can increase significantly. From downtown Washington Flyer vans leave 1517 K Street, NW, for the airport every half-hour. Children under six ride for free. Call (703) 685-1400 (tape) or (703) 892-6800 for more information.

Baltimore/Washington International Airport (BWI), approximately 28 miles to downtown Washington, D.C., is about a fifty-minute drive in nonrush-hour traffic. Amtrak trains (800-USA-RAIL) and the Maryland Commuter train line (MARC) (800-325-7254) run frequently from BWI to Union Station in Washington.

For those traveling from major East Coast cities including Boston, New York, Philadelphia, and Baltimore, taking Amtrak is a convenient

---

Washington, D.C., at a Glance

- Fun and national pride in the city that belongs to all Americans

- Fourteen museums of the Smithsonian Institution

- Tour the Capitol and the White House

- Go to the top of the Washington Monument

- See the Jefferson, Lincoln, and Vietnam memorials

- Washington, D.C., Convention and Visitors Association, (202) 789-7000

---

way to access Washington. Amtrak is stationed at the beautifully restored Union Station, which has many boutiques, restaurants, and movie theaters; First Street and Massachusetts Avenue, NE. Call (202) 383-3067 for information or (800) USA-RAIL for reservations.

GETTING AROUND

An exciting town, Washington remains a manageable destination. Since the mall acts as the tourist hub, the must-see sites can be navigated more easily than in most cities. In pleasant weather and with a solid pair of sneakers, you can see the sights by walking from Capitol Hill, along the mall with its museums, to the memorials.

To get to other parts of the city, Washington Metropolitan Area Transit Authority's (WMATA) Metrorail, the city's amazingly clean and safe subway, is your best bet. It's easy to navigate, with five color-coded subway lines—Orange, Red, Blue, Yellow, and Green—that cover much of the city and surrounding suburbs. Obtain Metro maps at the Visitors Center, 1455 Pennsylvania Avenue, or at any Metro station. Call (202) 637-7000 or TTD (202) 638-3780 for more information. Up to two children ages five and under may ride free with a paying passenger. If you're darting all over the city, on any day except holidays, a One Day Pass allows unlimited travel after 9:30 A.M. WMATA also operates an extensive bus system. Call (202) 637-7000 for route and fare information.

The district's cab companies include **Diamond Cab** (202-387-6200), **Yellow Cab Company** (202-544-1212), and **Capitol Cab** (202-546-2400). Fares are based on a zone system, and the charge is generally $2.50 per zone passed, per person, plus added charges for baggage, number of passengers, and time of day.

Since public parking is scarce and parking lots fill up quickly, avoid driving downtown. You'll wind up frustrated. A popular and easy way to get around is to climb aboard either the **Old Town Trolley** or the **Tourmobile.** (See Special Tours.)

WHAT TO SEE AND DO

Museums

The largest and arguably most popular museum complex in the world, the **Smithsonian Institution,** is in Washington, D.C. Begun in 1846 with a $500,000 donation from British scientist James Smithson, the Smithsonian complex today consists of sixteen museums, fourteen of which are in Washington, plus the **Cooper-Hewitt Museum** and the **National Museum of the American Indian,** both in New York City.

The **Smithsonian Institution Building,** 1000 Jefferson Drive, SW; (202) 357-2700, the first to be completed in 1855, is affectionately called "the Castle" because of its architecture. Besides housing administrative offices, the building serves as the Smithsonian Information Center. Come here first to get oriented, find out about special exhibits, and plan your museum visits.

It's not likely that you'll be able to visit every one of the Smithsonian Museums, and if by some chance you did, you surely wouldn't spend enough time to do them justice. Your best bet is to choose a few that most interest you. The Smithsonian complex includes **The Arts and Industries Building,** 900 Jefferson Drive, SW; **The National Museum of American History,** Constitution Avenue between Twelfth and Fourteenth streets, NW; **The Museum of Natural History,** on

Constitution Avenue at Tenth Street, NW; **The Freer Gallery** (Asian Art), Twelfth Street and Jefferson Drive, SW; **The Arthur M. Sackler Art Gallery** (Asian Art), 1050 Independence Avenue, SW; **The National Museum of African Art,** 950 Independence Avenue, SW; **The Hirshhorn Museum and Sculpture Garden,** Independence Avenue at Seventh Street, SW; **The National Air and Space Museum,** Seventh Street and Independence Avenue, SW; **The Renwick Gallery** (American Crafts), Seventeenth Street and Pennsylvania Avenue, NW; **The National Museum of American Art,** Ninth and G streets, NW; **The National Portrait Gallery,** Eighth and F streets, NW; the **Anacostia Museum,** 1901 Fort Place, SE; the **National Zoo,** 3001 Connecticut Avenue, NW; and the newest addition to the Smithsonian, **The National Postal Museum,** 2 Massachusetts Avenue, NE. All can be reached by telephone at (202) 357-1300 or (202) 357-2020 for a recording of daily events and (202) 357-2700 for general information.

The Arts and Industries Building, 900 Jefferson Drive, SW (202-357-2700), was completed in 1881. Kids love the elaborate carousel out in front and will demand 75 cents to ride it. Inside you'll take a walk through American Victoriana, and in the southern area of the building, you can see how curators decide on display setups in the Experimental Gallery.

The National Postal Museum, 2 Massachusetts Avenue, NE, the Smithsonian's newest museum, is dedicated to the history and development of the United States mail. Here you can trace the route of the Pony Express and decide whether it's best to route a letter by land, rail, or sea; climb aboard a stagecoach; create your own greeting card; and watch stamps being printed. While stamp lovers will delight in the Smithsonian's philatelic collection, this museum offers a lot more, including actual mail artifacts. Gape at the 1920 airmail planes suspended in the atrium, and climb aboard a stagecoach. In one exhibit read actual letters sent by soldiers in wars from the Civil War to Desert Storm.

The Museum of Natural History, Constitution Avenue at Tenth Street, NW, presents wonders of another kind. In the Fossil Hall the 80-foot-long skeleton of *Diplodocus,* the largest land animal to have existed, renders kids as well as adults wide-eyed. Peruse the bony remains of such fear-inspiring beasts as the *Stegosaurus,* and in the Ice Age Hall, the Woolly Mammoth. A gigantic African bush elephant is your host at the front door, and check out the 45.5-carat Hope diamond. Visit the Insect Zoo, where glass tanks, filled with beetles, bees, and scorpions, buzz, chirp, and whir. Watch centipedes wriggle, and if you time it right, help feed the friendly tarantula—he professes a fondness for crickets.

At the **National Museum of American History,** Constitution Avenue between Twelfth and Fourteenth streets NW, be sure to see "Land of Promise/Land of Paradox," displaying the experiences of African Americans, Cherokee Indians, and Central and Eastern European Jews in nineteenth-century America. Another favorite is "First Ladies: Political Role and Public Image," which includes much more than the First Ladies' inaugural ball gowns. Kids like the Railroad Hall, with its locomotives, the exhibit on the machines that sparked the Industrial Revolution, and the coin collection in "Money and Medals." This is a good place to let your kids browse for hours, stopping briefly at whatever catches their fancy. Allow time to shop at the extensive gift and bookstore on the lower level, among the best of all the mall museums' shops.

The National Gallery of Art, 600 Constitution Avenue, NW (202-737-4215), is a gift to the eye. This museum consists of two buildings: the classically inspired West Wing, designed by John Russell Pope, and the East Wing, a dramatic asymmetrical trapezoid, designed by I. M. Pei. The museum houses a world-class collection of paintings, sculpture, and graphic arts from the Middle Ages to contemporary times. The huge Calder mobile suspended above the lobby of the East building especially charms children, as does the bold colors and lines of postmodern art. To turn the museum into an exciting treasure hunt for your kids, ask them to select several favorite postcards of paintings from the gift shop, or for those of you who are on-line, call up a painting from the Micro Gallery, the National Gallery's multimedia computer system; (202) 842-6681. Then set out in search of the originals as you meander through the galleries. Masterworks in the West Wing include paintings by Leonardo da Vinci, Rembrandt, and Van Gogh.

The most popular museum of them all is the **National Air and Space Museum,** Seventh Street and Independence Avenue, SW. Chronicling the story of flight, the museum presents a galactic lineup of aircraft, including such stars as the Wright brothers' *Kitty Hawk Flyer,* Charles Lindbergh's *Spirit of St. Louis,* John Glenn's *Friendship 7,* and the *Apollo 11* Command Module. Walk through the Skylab Orbital Workshop to see just how little room astronauts have in space. Allow time for the museum's famed, forty-minute movies, and stop in the gift shop for some astronaut ice cream on the way out.

The **Freer Gallery of Art,** Twelfth Street and Jefferson Drive, SW, houses a renowned collection of Asian art as well as an often overlooked wonder—the Peacock Room, the only interior-design scheme by noted artist James McNeill Whistler. Walk in here and you and your kids will be delighted by the intricate peacocklike swirls. The museum has a children's guide both to this room and to its Asian collection. Don't skip this museum, as the swirls, patterns, and colors of this type of art delight kids.

The **United States Holocaust Memorial Museum,** 100 Raoul Wallenberg Place, SW, between Fourteenth and Fifteenth streets near Independence Avenue (202–488–0400), which opened in April 1993, is a major addition to Washington's museums. It tells the story of the Holocaust through a series of moving exhibits composed of actual artifacts. Because the main exhibits are likely to elicit strong emotions, these are recommended for kids ages eleven and older. For ages eight and above, visit "Remember the Children: Daniel's Story," an exhibit dedicated to the 1.5 million children who died in the Holocaust. This exhibit, told from a child's point of view and using interactive exhibits, traces Daniel's experience of the Holocaust from a happy childhood to a concentration camp survivor.

Government Buildings

The Capitol, First Street between Independence and Constitution avenues (202–225–6827), sitting majestically atop the mall's gentle rise, lends a commanding presence to the city. Inside, the building reveals a richness of intricate decoration complete with elaborate frescoes, murals, paintings, and mosaic tiles. Tours, which depart every five minutes from 9:00 A.M. to 3:45 P.M., start at the Rotunda.

In the main complex check out **Statuary Hall,** the old meeting chamber of the House of Representatives, which is lined with bronze and marble statues of two of each state's notable personages (some have spilled over into adjacent hallways). Children not only love finding their state's designee but also giggle at discovering the "secret of the whisper." Because of an architectural anomaly, discussions on one side of the room could be overheard across the floor at the spot where John Quincy Adams sat at his desk. Legend has it that Adams owes much of his political acumen to this eavesdropping.

When the House or Senate is not in session, line up before or after your tour for a peek at these august rooms. To view these chambers when elected officials hold sway, *obtain a pass ahead of time from your congressperson or senator.*

In the Jefferson Building, across the street from the Capitol, at First and East Capitol Street, SE (202-707-5458), the **Library of Congress** reigns. Comprising three entire buildings, it is reputed to be the world's largest library, containing more than 90 million items, 30 million of which are books.

Some architectural critics deem the Reading Room, now completely renovated, to be one of the nation's best interior spaces. The reading room, open to any researcher eighteen years and older, is a sweep of mahogany desks set off by cream and red-hued marble pillars and archways, all topped with a grand, decorated dome.

At the **White House,** 1600 Pennsylvania Avenue, NW (202-755-7798), more of the official rooms that dominate the public images of power come into view. As you walk through these carefully decorated spaces, you can imagine the pomp and flourishes of formal Washington. *A VIP pass from your representative* (ask as far in advance as possible) gains you entrance into one of the less crowded and more informative guided tours that depart at 8:00 and 10:00 A.M. Tuesday through Saturday. The regular tours (10:00 A.M. to noon Tuesday through Saturday) take you through the same rooms, although the crowds are continuous and the information from the guides less detailed.

To eliminate the long lines and waits, the National Park Service now operates the White House Visitors Center, located at the U.S. Department of Commerce, 1450 Pennsylvania Avenue, NW; (202) 208-1631. Come here for free, same-day timed tickets to tour the White House. The center also has educational video and gift items. Open 8:00 A.M. to 5:00 P.M. daily; from Memorial Day to Labor Day, extended hours are from 7:00 A.M. to 7:00 P.M.

To stir interest, especially for the kids, and to pick your favorite items to gaze at, purchase *The White House: An Historic Guide* before your

A seventy-second elevator ride will take you and your family to the top of the Washington Monument. (Courtesy of the Washington, D.C., Convention and Visitors Association)

tour. This informative book, published by the White House Historical Association, features color photographs and lots of details about furniture, paintings, and china. (Available at bookstores or by mail from the White House Historical Association, 740 Jackson Place, NW, Washington, D.C. 20506; (202) 737–8292.)

Historic Sites, Monuments, and Memorials

Visit Cedar Hill, 318 A Street, NE; (202) 543–5579, Frederick Douglass's Washington home. This often overlooked National Historic property conveys the personal side of this powerful and important leader. Sit on his front porch and you can literally look out over the capital as he did.

Monuments and memorials adorn the city, part of the nation's homage to its heroes. **The Washington Monument,** Constitution Avenue at Fifteenth Street, NW (202-426-6840), a marble obelisk rising 555 feet and ⅛ inch, dominates the city's skyline. While the panoramic view from the top is among the best in town, the wait to board the elevator can stretch to hours. To beat the crowds, try lining up before 8:00 A.M.

The Jefferson Memorial, just off Fifteenth Street, NW, in West Potomac Park (202-426-6821), adorns the south bank of the Tidal Basin. In spring you may find yourself surrounded by a sea of pink flowers if you are lucky enough to catch the famous cherry trees in blossom. The graceful, domed building reflects the architectural shape Jefferson used in designing Monticello, his Virginia home. Inside the columned rotunda, a 19-foot bronze statue of the statesman captures your attention. Passages from his writings, including quotations from the Declaration of Independence and the Virginia Statute of Religious Freedom, are engraved on the walls.

Like the Jefferson Memorial, the **Lincoln Memorial,** Independence and Constitution avenues, SW (202-426-6895), reminds the visitor of the leader's commitment to liberty. See sculptor Daniel Chester French's masterpiece at night, highlighted by the moon and subtle spotlights surrounding the monument. Seated, pensive, and brooding over the concerns of the Civil War, this Lincoln depicts a man burdened. Carved on the memorial's walls are Lincoln's stirring Gettysburg Address and his second inaugural speech.

The Vietnam Memorial, Twenty-first Street and Constitution Avenue, NW (202-634-1568), is perhaps the most moving monument in the city. As people walk along the path in front of the black granite monument set into the ground, they become quiet and contemplative, moved by the thousands upon thousands of names of that era's dead. Sometimes a mother or a child, or even someone the soldier never knew, leaves flowers, a flag, or a note next to their loved one's name. Few people walk away from this simple monument unmoved. Nearby, the **Vietnam Women's Memorial,** Twenty-first Street and Constitution Avenue, NW (202-426-6841), is located in a grove of trees across from the Vietnam Memorial. This bronze statue depicts three women and one wounded man supported by sandbags.

The 612-acre **Arlington National Cemetery,** in Fort Meyer across the Memorial Bridge in Virginia; (703) 692-0931, honors more than 200,000 of our war dead as well as several national heroes. Sites not to be missed include the changing of the guard every half-hour (every hour from October through March) at the Tomb of the Unknown Soldier, where the remains of soldiers from both world wars, the Korean War, and the Vietnam War are interred; Arlington House, the residence of General Robert E. Lee restored to its Civil War appearance, and the gravesites of John Fitzgerald and Robert F. Kennedy.

The Korean War Veterans Memorial, between Independence Avenue, SW, and the Lincoln Memorial (202) 208–3561), has statues of nineteen soldiers marching toward Old Glory.

Green Spaces, Zoo, and Recreation

Be sure to see Amazonia, an indoor re-creation of a tropical rain forest, at the Smithsonian-affiliated **National Zoological Park,** 3001 Connecticut Avenue, NW; (202) 673–4800 or (202) 673–4717. The elaborate exhibit includes waterfalls, 300 species of plants, and an adjacent gallery with hands-on exhibits for kids who want to learn more about rain forests. Visit with Hsing-Hsing, the male panda (Ling-Ling died); then go over to the renovated Reptile Discovery Center, where you'll see the crocodiles, poison elf frogs, and Komodo dragons and learn about the scent trail of snakes. Kids are fascinated by the interactive exhibits that explain how reptiles get by in daily life. Peek in on the cheetahs at the Cheetah Conservation Center, where experts research these oversized cats and watch primates think at the Think Tank.

A winter visit to the city wouldn't be complete without an ice-skating session on the mall, an often overlooked capital splendor. Glide in tune to your own political promises, with the National Archives as your backdrop, at the **rink on the Mall,** Seventh Street and Constitution Avenue, NW, or at **Pershing Park,** Fourteenth Street and Pennsylvania Avenue, NW, where you can easily escape into the grand Willard Hotel for warmth. And if the weather is cold enough, take to the ice on the Mall's **reflecting pool.** Framed by the Lincoln Memorial and the Washington Monument, this rink exudes a special glory on a starry winter night.

In summer take time to golf at **East Potomac Park Golf Course,** in the East Potomac Park, Ohio Drive at Haines Point, 20011; (202) 863–9007. Near the Jefferson Memorial, this facility has an 18-hole course, a driving range, and a miniature golf course. For information on miniature golf, call (202) 488–8087.

When it's spring in Washington, enjoy the outdoors by foot, by bike, and by boat. Take the time to smell the flowers, literally, at the

U.S. Botanic Garden, First Street, SW, near the Capitol; (202) 225-7099. Enjoy the greenhouses, where kids love the fossil-filled dinosaur garden. Also walk through the greenhouses to the open courtyards that bloom with seasonal delights. Cross the street to the iron **Bartholdi Fountain,** Independence Avenue and First Street, NW (202-224-3121), surrounded by a variety of small gardens, which kids are encouraged to enjoy.

Dumbarton Oaks Park, Dumbarton Oaks, Thirty-first and R streets (202-338-8278), is located in Upper Georgetown and is part of a chain of parks. Donated by the Robert Wilson Bliss Estate to the National Park Service in 1920, Dumbarton Oaks Park has retained its woodsy feel by forgoing formal landscaping. Dumbarton Oaks' beauty attracts many people to its twenty-seven acres of woods.

Take a stroll through one of the largest urban parks in the country, **Rock Creek Park,** a wonderful oasis that encompasses northwest Washington. Contact the Rock Creek Park Office of the Superintendent, 5000 Glover Road, NW; (202) 426-6832. The park's miles of wooded trails and paths for horseback riding and bicycling run from the Potomac River by the Kennedy Center all the way north to the D.C.-Maryland border. On Saturdays and Sundays the long stretch of Beach Drive that hugs the creek from Broad Branch Road to Military Road, NW, is closed to traffic from 7:00 A.M. to 7:00 P.M. Join the locals who roller skate, bike, and stroll along this scenic stretch. Horse lovers can saddle up and take scenic trail rides at the Rock Creek Park Horse Centre 5100 Glover Road, NW, in Rock Creek Park; (202) 362-0117. The one-hour trail rides cost $17. Riders must be twelve years of age.

For those who like to bike, the **C&O Canal** is popular. The C&O Canal and its towpath stretch for 184.5 miles from Georgetown in the District to Cumberland, Maryland. If you don't want to bike, try a mule-drawn barge trip narrated by costumed interpreters. These operate from mid-April to mid-October. The 1½-hour trips originate at Georgetown (202-653-5844), and at the Visitors Center in the park at Great Falls, Maryland (301-299-3613). The falls, not high but powerful, draw crowds, but the biking trails that are farther away from the park's Visitors Center are peaceful. A snack bar offers light fare for the hungry traveler.

Contact the National Park Service's Office of Public Affairs of the National Capitol Region, 1100 Ohio Drive, SW (202-619-7222), for detailed information about the district's many parks. Those who would like to venture to a park outside of D.C., contact the National Park Service at 1849 C Street, NW, Room 1013; (202) 208–4747.

Special Tours

D.C. has two fun options that take the weariness out of walking for small children. Buy a ticket for the Old Town Trolley Tours or the **Tourmobile.** Along its two-hour narrated tour, **The Old Town Trolley,** 5225 Kilmer Place, Hyattsville, Maryland (310–985–3020), makes stops throughout Washington, including at some hotels, a bonus that many parents enjoy. After leaving the trolley, visitors can reboard for another stop along the route. The trolley runs every thirty minutes seven days a week from 9:00 A.M. to 4:00 P.M.

The **Tourmobile,** 1000 Ohio Drive, NW (202–554–7950), offers a year-round narrated tour that stops at eighteen sites, including the White House, Washington Monument, Smithsonian Museums, Arlington National Cemetery, and Mt. Vernon. Riders are allowed to reboard and ride to another stop on their route.

Both **Gray Line Double Decker Tours** (202–289–1995) and **Double Decker Bus Tours W.D.C.** (800–742–1142) employ English double-decker buses for their tours. The Gray Line narrated tour lasts about forty-five minutes. Passengers may get on or off at any of the thirteen stops. Buses run every thirty minutes between 8:00 A.M. and 5:30 P.M. Double Decker Tours, with departures every thirty minutes between 9:00 A.M. and 6:00 P.M., has eighteen stops. This narrated tour lasts about two hours, but passengers may get on and off at any stop.

Scandal Tours of Washington serves up an irreverent look at the sites of D.C.'s past and current scandals, which are especially appreciated by parents and teens. This ninety-minute bus ride presented by a local comedy group, Gross National Product, careens past such infamous sites as the Vista Hotel, where former D.C. mayor Marion Barry was arrested, and the Tidal Basin, where former congressman Wilbur Mills splashed with "exotic dancer" Fanne Fox. On board, the Gross National Product actors bring the satire to life. Tours depart on Saturdays outside the Washington Hilton Hotel, 1919 Connecticut Avenue, NW. Call ahead for reservations; (202) 783–7212.

The Black History National Recreation Trail is a self-guided walking tour that highlights several black history sites throughout Washington, D.C., including the Metropolitan A.M.E. Church, Frederick Douglass's home, Howard University, and more. Informational pamphlets are distributed at each of the trail's sites. For a pamphlet and more information, call the National Park Service at (202) 619-7222.

Athletic families might enjoy a guided bicycle tour along the trails and streets of the nation's capital. DC Bike Tours (202-466-4486) covers approximately 8 miles in a leisurely fashion, with frequent rest and photo stops. Bikes and helmets are provided. Allow about three hours.

Older teens and parents should try dining aboard the *Odyssey III,* operated by Odyssey Cruises; (202) 488-6010. This sleek ship, constructed low enough to pass underneath D.C.'s bridges, serves up the city's monument-filled skyline along with dinner. Cruises depart from the Gangplank Marina at the Southwest Waterfront, Seventh and Water streets, SW.

Theater, Music, and the Arts

The **John F. Kennedy Center for the Performing Arts,** New Hampshire Avenue, NW near D Street (202-416-8341/800-444-1324), offers a schedule of cultural, theatrical, and dance performances. Ticket prices vary per event, and the box office is open from 10:00 A.M. till 9:00 P.M. Monday through Saturday, Sunday noon to 6:00 P.M.

In March and April the Kennedy Center hosts The Imagination Celebration, where the best of children's theaters across the country put on a variety of plays, dances, and inspired puppet shows for preschoolers through preteens.

The Shakespeare Theatre, 450 Seventh Street, NW (202-547-3230), shows Shakespeare's finest. Contact the box office for the latest production at (202) 393-2700. This relatively small theater is the place to introduce your preteen to an English classic. Children under five are not admitted.

Ford's Theatre, 511 Tenth Street, NW (202-638-2941), is a family-oriented theater, featuring plays and musicals most of the year. They are known for their annual Christmas showing of Charles Dickens's *A Christmas Carol.* Shows normally take place every Tuesday through Sunday evening, with Thursday and Sunday matinees.

SPECIAL EVENTS

Festivals

January: Martin Luther King's Birthday. Every four years, enjoy the Inauguration Celebration.

February: Black History Month.

March: Smithsonian's Annual Kite Festival on the grounds of the Washington Monument.

March/April: National Cherry Blossom Festival. Don your Sunday best for the White House Easter Egg Roll, where children ten and under can roll eggs on the White House lawn. Imagination Celebration at the Kennedy Center.

May: Festival of the Building Arts, National Building Museum.

June: The Festival of American Folklife on the Mall.

July: The best, brightest Fourth of July. Celebrate independence with fireworks and the sounds of the National Symphony Orchestra near the Capitol.

August: The Lollipop Concert at the Jefferson Memorial features Navy-sponsored music and favorites from the world of Disney.

September: The International Children's Festival in Vienna, Virginia, with plays, dances, and puppet shows for the kids. Toss a disc around at the National Frisbee Festival.

October: Explore the Rose Garden and the South Lawn of the White House on the Garden Tour.

November: Veteran's Day remembrances at Arlington National Cemetery.

December: The President lights the National Christmas Tree at the Pageant of Peace.

WHERE TO STAY

Washington D.C., offers a wide range of accommodations for a variety of budgets. Visitors can choose from luxury hotels to more moderate accommodations. Some of the District's best lodging buys are weekend hotel packages. These special room rates reduce prices as much as 30 to 50 percent.

Near necessities for a family vacation hotel are a metro stop within walking distance and an indoor pool for cooling off and reenergizing after a day full of walking.

Hotels that frequently run weekend packages include **Hyatt Regency Washington-Capitol Hill,** 400 New Jersey Avenue, NW (800-233-1234 or 202-737-1234); **Loews L'Enfant Plaza,** 480 L'Enfant Plaza, SW (202-484-1000); **Hotel Washington,** Fifteenth Street and Pennsylvania Avenue, NW (202-638-5900), just one block from the White House; **Washington Hilton,** 1919 Connecticut Avenue, NW (800-HILTONS or 202-483-3000); and the **Four Seasons Hotel,** 2800 Pennsylvania Avenue, NW (202-342-0444).

For reduced rates every night of the week, call **Capitol Reservations,** 1201 K Street, NW; (800) VISIT-DC, (800) 847-4832, or in D.C. call (202) 842-4187. This reservation service advertises discounts of approximately 30 percent at 70 area hotels, all in safe neighborhoods.

For all suite properties that offer more space and a kitchenette, consider **Embassy Suites Hotel-Downtown,** 1250 Twenty-second Street, NW (202-857-3388); **Embassy Square Suites,** 2000 North Street, NW (202-659-9000); **Carlyle Suites,** 1731 New Hampshire Avenue, NW (202-234-3200); **Capitol Hill Suites,** 200 C Street, SE (202-543-6000); and **Guest Quarters Suite Hotel** at two locations: 801 New Hampshire Avenue, NW (202-785-2000) and near Georgetown at 2500 Pennsylvania Avenue, NW (202-333-8060).

If you don't mind a bit of a commute (about a half-hour drive in non-rush hour or a fifteen-minute drive to the Vienna Metro subway stop), try **Summerfield Suites Dulles Airport,** 13700 Coppermine Road, Herndon, Virginia (703-713-6800 or 800-833-4353). This lodging chain offers one- or two-bedroom suites with kitchen facilities and a daily continental breakfast plus breakfast buffet. There are also children's videos to rent (the two-bedroom units have three televisions plus a VCR) and a twenty-four-hour convenience store on-site. Ask about special weekend rates.

WHERE TO EAT

Washington hosts a number of good American restaurants located in all sections of town. Union Station, 50 Massachusetts Avenue, NE (202-371-9441), just north of the Capitol, offers a vast food court on the lower level, where even the pickiest eater will be satisfied. The **Old Post Office Pavilion,** Pennsylvania Avenue and Twelfth Street (202-289-4224), features an open-air food court in its renovated central courtyard. Here you combine history and good eats, and there's often live music. Go for lunch or stop in for a homemade ice cream cone at **Scoops Homemade Cones.**

American Cafe (202-682-0937), located in Union Station, Georgetown, and downtown, offers fresh sandwiches and salads. For inexpensive Tex-Mex, check out the **Austin Grill,** 2404 Wisconsin Avenue; (202) 337-8080. Pizza lovers will find a creative twist and a tasty crust at **Pizzeria Paradiso,** 2029 P Street; (202) 223-1245. **Pizzeria Uno,** 3211 M Street, NW (202-695-6333), is another favorite for deep-dish Chicago-style pies as well as burgers and pasta.

Two favorite spots for teens: The **Hard Rock Cafe,** 999 E Street, NW (202-737-7625), features rock memorabilia along with burgers and such; and for film buffs and the star-struck, **Planet Hollywood,** 1101 Pennsylvania Avenue, NW (202-783-7827), serves a similar menu, but the setting features movie memorabilia.

Sequoia, in Georgetown along the Potomac River, 3000 K Street, NW #100 (202-944-4200), has indoor and outdoor dining plus great views of the Washington harbor and the Kennedy Center.

Down by the Mall it gets a bit tricky to find good lunch spot outside of the museum cafes and cafeterias. These are most crowded during the peak lunch hours, so eat early or snack on some popcorn and wait until two o'clock or so. The *Sunday Magazine,* the *Washington Post,* and the *Washingtonian* frequently review restaurants.

DAY TRIPS

Monticello

From D.C. it's easy to visit Thomas Jefferson's Monticello (804-295-8181), 125 miles away and just 3 miles southeast of Charlottesville, Virginia. See for yourself how the house reflects Jefferson's passions, architectural genius, his inventions, and love of gardening. Step outside to the eighteen acres of gardens, re-created from Jefferson's personal records. There are horticultural exhibits and plant sales at the Thomas Jefferson Center for Historic Plants, and on Saturdays in summer, you can take a wildflower walk or a planting workshop for which you must preregister.

Show yourself around Mulberry Row, the workplace of the laborers and the site of woodworking shops, slaughterhouses, and smokeshops.

Mount Vernon

The home of our nation's very first president, George Washington's **Mount Vernon** is just 16 miles outside Washington; (703) 780-2000. The property is accessible by car or by Metrobus; (202) 637-2437. You may even get there by boat in the summertime by calling Spirit of Mount Vernon at (202) 554-8000. Get to know Mr. Washington, the farmer, as you learn of his cultivation of tobacco and wheat. Inside the mansion see Martha's porcelain tea service, the grandiose, two-story-high dining room, and paintings of Washington area landscapes as interpreted by eighteenth-century artists. Meander through the gardens, and enjoy a respite while admiring the trees that George Washington himself so adored.

Old Town Alexandria

With its centuries of history, its legendary tales, and its sophisticated restaurants and shops, Old Town Alexandria makes for an enjoyable outing that is hardly out of the city, merely across the Potomac River. First, stop by the visitor's center at the **Ramsay House,** 221 King Street, and stock up on brochures about Alexandria's boutiques and history.

Wear your sneakers because the best way to explore Old Town is by walking. Stroll along King, Cameron, Queen, and Duke streets, names that harken back to the town's colonial past.

Visit **Gadsby's Tavern,** in the Old City Tavern and Hotel, 138 North Royal Street (703-548-1288), the gentleman's pub often frequented by the Marquis de Lafayette, James Madison, and Thomas Jefferson, and take the tavern museum tour. Drop by **Robert E. Lee**'s boyhood home, 607 Oronoco Street (703-548-8454), a stately Federal house. See one of the gathering places of the merchants, the **Carlyle House,** 121 North Fairfax Street (703-549-2997), a sandstone manor dating to 1753. If you plan on touring many properties, consider purchasing a block ticket.

Also of interest is the **Alexandria Black History Resource Center,** 638 North Alfred Street; (703) 838-4356. Follow their walking brochure to black historic sites, which include streets where the first free blacks lived.

Stop by the waterfront **Torpedo Factory Art Center,** 105 North Union Street (703-838-4565), the 1918 manufacturing site of World War II torpedo shell cases where 160 professional artists not only work at their craft but display their wares.

For a river view board the *Admiral Tilp,* 205 The Strand (703-548-9000), for a forty-minute narrated tour.

Additional day trips worth a stop are **Baltimore, Annapolis** (see Baltimore chapter), and **Philadelphia** (see Philadelphia chapter).

FOR MORE INFORMATION

Contact the **Washington, D.C., Convention and Visitors Association,** 1212 New York Avenue, NW (202-789-7000), which has many pamphlets for tourists that are distributed by the **Visitor Information Center,** 1455 Pennsylvania Avenue, NW, open Monday through Saturday, 9:00 A.M. to 5:00 P.M.; (202) 789–7038.

Several free periodicals serve as good references for current exhibits and special happenings for families. *Potomac Children,* a newspaper published ten times a year, P.O. Box 151544, Chevy Chase, MD 20815 (301-656-2133), has a calendar of events. *Washington Parent* appears six times a year and focuses on happenings around town and informative articles, although much of this information may be more useful to residents than visitors. Contact the Parent Connection, 5606 Knollwood Road, Bethesda, MD 20816; (301) 320-2321.

Emergency Numbers

Ambulance, fire, and police: 911

Children's National Medical Center, 111 Michigan Avenue, NW; (202) 745-5000

George Washington University Medical Center Emergency Room, 901 Twenty-third Street, NW; (202) 994-3211

Metropolitan Police: (202) 727-1010, TDD Users (202) 727-9334

Poison Control Center: (202) 625-3333

Twenty-four-hour pharmacies: CVS Drug at 6-7 Dupont Circle, NW (202-785-1466); CVS Drug at 1121 Vermont Circle, NW (202-628-0720)

MONTREAL

Montreal, an island city on the St. Lawrence River, is exciting and dynamic, with a distinctively Continental flavor. French is the official language, though you'll find English widely spoken, especially in the western half of the city. If your kids have never been to Europe, a visit here will definitely make an impression; they'll certainly notice the cultural differences and may even pick up some French. Indeed, in Montreal there is so much to see and do that your family will pronounce it "magnifique!"

GETTING THERE

Montreal International Airport in Dorval (514–842–2281) services approximately forty major American and Canadian airlines. The airport, twenty-to-thirty minutes from downtown, can be reached by taxi or regular bus lines. Call Autobus Aero Plus (514–934–1222) for information. Car rentals are available at the airport.

Voyageur, which provides bus service from other Canadian cities, has a terminal at 505 boulevard de Maisonneuve East (514–842–2281), situated above Berri/UQAM Metro station. Other bus service: Greyhound from New York and Vermont Transit from Boston.

Train service from the United States is provided by Amtrak (800–426–8725) and from Canadian destinations by VIA Rail (514–871–1331/800–361–5390–Quebec/800–561–8630–Canada). Both arrive and depart from Central Station, 935 de La Gauchetiere Street West (under the Queen Elizabeth Hotel), at Bonaventure Metro station.

The major artery leading to Montreal from Toronto and Ottawa is Highway 401; from Quebec you can take Highway 20 or 40. Most U.S. interstates connect with Highway 10, which runs through the Eastern Townships area.

GETTING AROUND

Montreal has a quiet, clean, and efficient Metro subway—an experience not to be missed. Save money by buying a strip of six tickets or one of three types of day passes. Four color-coded interconnecting lines service sixty-five station stops. In addition, there are more than 150 bus routes. Call (514) 288-6287 for transportation information. The Metro connects a huge underground city network of shops, restaurants, banks, hotels, theaters, and railway and bus terminals.

The city is divided into east-west streets by boulevard St. Laurent (The Main), which runs north-south. Montreal is a compact city and highly walkable. Old Montreal (*Vieux Montréal*), where you'll find the Old Port (*Vieux-Port*), is a great place to stroll. In summer water shuttles operate between the Old Port and the city's two islands, Île Notre-Dame and Île Sainte-Hélène (see Parks section) as well as to Cité du Havre Park, where there are outdoor children's activities, picnic tables, and bicycle paths.

WHAT TO SEE AND DO

Museums

This sophisticated city has a rich assortment of fine museums. Unless your kids are avid museum-goers, however, they may find some too sophisticated or esoteric. Actually, many of the most stimulating exhibits and experiences in Montreal are not in traditional museums. The following are surely worth a visit.

Canadian Railway Museum, 122-A Saint-Pierre Street West, Saint-Constant; (514) 283-4602/4623. If your kids love trains, it's worth going out of your way for this collection of railway, tramway, and steam-locomotive equipment. It's in suburban Monteregie, so you'll have to drive or take the Longueuil or Angrignon metro to a Monette bus (514-632-2020) to the museum. Stop by on Sunday when visitors are treated to a train ride. During the week there are tram rides.

Dow Planetarium, 1,000 Saint-Jacques Street West; (514) 872-4530. A lecturer provides live commentary for original star shows presented under the theater dome. Shows alternate in English and French.

Montreal at a Glance

- A delightfully European city in North America

- Many beautiful parks

- Île Notre-Dame and Île Sainte-Hélène, two man-made islands

- Thousands of insects at the Insectarium

- Professional hockey and baseball teams

- Greater Montreal Convention and Visitors Bureau, (800) 363-7777 or (514) 873-2015

The International Museum of Humour, 2111 St.-Laurent Street (414-845-4000), opened its doors on April Fool's Day 1993. You won't find a museum like this anywhere else. The fun exhibits here exude laughs and treasured memories of days past. Two favorites are the Birth of the Couch Potato, which commemorates the American sitcom, and a replica of a city street from the 1920s, where the audience watches Charlie Chaplin on the big screen as they are served refreshments by Keystone Cops. Stop by the Humour Hall of Fame, where your kids can watch Mickey Mouse cartoons as they relax in huge, cushy chairs.

Montreal Museum of Fine Arts, 1379 and 1380 Sherbrooke Street West; (514) 285-1600. Head to Canada's oldest art museum on Sunday, when family activities, such as films and workshops, are included with the admission. The impressive collections of paintings, furniture, sculpture, and other art may not capture a younger child's interest without some parental guidance.

Redpath Museum, 859 Sherbrooke Street West, (514) 398-4086. Kids are captivated by the old fossils, rocks, crystals, and gems and by the fascinating antiquities of ancient Egypt.

Parks

You'll find superb parks throughout the city. Here are the best for families.

MacDonald Campus of McGill University, 21-111 Lakeshore Road, Sainte-Anne-de Bellevue (Route 40). Located on Montreal's southwest tip, this vast area features three attractions with family appeal. **The Morgan Arboretum** (514-398-7812) has nature and wooded trails and cross-country skiing. **The Ecomuseum** (514-457-9449), devoted to the St. Lawrence Valley, features sixteen exhibits in outdoor settings that include turtles, bears, and a walk through a waterfowl aviary. **The Farm** (514-398-7701) welcomes families to view its animals and use the picnic and play area.

Mont Royal Park, the lush green stretch of land that sweeps up the highest peak of Mont Royal (from which the city took its name), is the finest in town. The 83-foot cross at the top of the mountain, lit at night and visible for miles, was installed in 1924 and paid for mostly with children's donations. It commemorates the cross that Maisonneuve, founder of Montreal, carried to the mountaintop in 1643 after the colony was spared from a flood.

Approach this must-see park from Camillien-Houde Parkway from the east or from Remembrance Road from the west. Frederick Olmsted, who also planned New York's Central Park, designed this oasis. Picnic, stroll, bike, jog, and enjoy spectacular vistas of downtown and the Appalachian Mountains from Mountain Chalet and Parkway lookouts. Winters bring cross-country skiing, skating, and sledding.

The Centre de la Montagne (514-844-4928), a nature appreciation center, offers interpretive programs and information. The kids will enjoy seeing the only Mounted Police in Montreal patrolling the park. Their horse stables are open to visitors from 9:00 A.M. to 5:00 P.M.

The Metro or water shuttle will get you to **Île Notre-Dame** and **Île Sainte-Hélène,** both man-made islands constructed for Expo '67; (514) 872-4537.

Île Notre-Dame now serves as a recreational haven with a beach, boat rentals, winter ice skating, a lovely floral park, and a world-class casino.

Island attractions on **Île Sainte-Hélène** include swimming pools, picnic tables, and in the winter, skiing and snowshoeing. Families usually head straight to **La Ronde,** an amusement park that has the highest wooden double-track railroad in the world. A simulation volcano, The Cobra, and more than thirty-four rides, including ten kiddie rides, and an Animation Circus round out the fun. There is also water skiing, the Nintendo Mega Dome and the Biosphere. The **Old American Pavilion** of Expo '67 is now a learning and observation center on water and the St. Lawrence River/Great Lakes ecosystem, housing four interactive exhibition halls; (514) 283-5000.

If you can, stop by the **Stewart Museum** (also known as the Old Fort or Le Vieux Fort). Its unique collections of old maps, documents, firearms, and other displays (mostly military) of colonial Canada make it a journey through four centuries. The real attractions in summer are the medieval village, fireworks, and outdoor demonstrations of eighteenth-century military drills. Call (514) 861-6701 for information. The island, site of the spectacular annual fireworks competition (see Special Events), has two restaurants and a theater for concerts and shows.

Lafontaine Park is centrally located (bordered by Sherbrooke, Rachel, Papineau, and Park Lafontaine streets). Stroll through this park and see a slice of Montreal life, including street musicians and, on weekends, families out to have fun. There are wading pools, pedal boats, tennis courts, and a puppet theater. In winter cross-country skiing and illuminated skating rinks make this a popular retreat. Call (514) 872-6211 for information.

More Attractions

The Old Port, 333 de la Commune Street West, between McGill and Berri streets; (514) 496-7678. This lively developed riverfront area in Old Montreal offers families the chance to watch street performers, rent a bicycle (or quadricycle), have a picnic (or eat at a restaurant), and stop by noteworthy attractions.

Expotec, IMAX Cinema, Saint Laurent Boulevard and de la Commune Street; (514) 496-4629. An interactive scientific exhibit and game for all ages, the theme display changes yearly. **The Lockkeepers Hut** (514-496-7678), at the entrance to the Lachine Canal, is a tourist information and interpretation center dispensing facts on the Canal locks. **S.O.S. Labyrinthe,** King Edward Pier; (514) 496-7678. Here visitors wander through twisting paths and conquer challenges such as a net ladder, secret passage, and tunnel. Guides assist those who need it, and the course changes weekly. **Images du Futur,** 1505 St-Paul Street West; (514) 849-1612. This fascinating multimedia exhibition changes its theme every year. Whenever you visit, you'll be treated to a huge panorama showing how technology is applied to art and communications. Laser images, holographic pictures and sculptures, computer-drawn pictures and videos, and electronic music combine to create a fascinating exhibit that includes interactive participation. **IMAX Cinema** (514-496-4629) shows breathtaking films on a seven-story-high screen.

Olympic Park, 4141 Pierre-de-Coubertin Avenue; (514) 252-8687. There's much to do around this site of the 1976 Summer Olympic Games. Start with a tram ride up the world's tallest inclined tower for great views of the surrounding city. The stadium (the site of Expo baseball) is open to the public, as are the complex's swimming pools. Summer shuttles connect the park to the not-to-be-missed **Botanical Gardens *(Jardin Botanique),*** the second largest in the world, after Kew Gardens. This indoor/outdoor treat for the senses delights all with the largest Chinese garden outside Asia, a huge bonsai collection, serene Japanese garden, spectacular displays of orchids and chrysanthemums, and more. There are frequent shows and special events. Call (514) 872-1400 for information.

Admission includes entry into a real kid-pleaser—the *Insectarium,* with thousands of living and mounted insects. Watch butterflies flutter about in their own aviary while bees buzz around a working hive. Hands-on games and activities help kids learn about the variety, function—and, yes (sometimes) beauty—of these little creatures. For more information call (514) 872-1400.

The Biodome, at 4777 Pierre-de-Coubertin, is an environmental museum located in the former Olympic Velodrome. It's not a zoo, though four complete reconstructed ecosystems are inhabited by birds, mammals, and fish. The Polar World, Tropical Forest, Laurentian Forest, and Saint-Laurent ecosystems include waterfalls, towering trees, and an interactive discovery room that kids will like. Call (514) 868-3000 for special program information.

Steeped in history, the Old Port section of Montreal offers an exciting array of cultural, historic, and scientific attractions. (Courtesy Greater Montreal Convention and Tourism Bureau)

Special Tours

Call **Lachine Rapid Tours** and shoot the only rapids on the St. Lawrence River in a jet boat. It's definitely not for kids under six or the faint of heart: You wear slickers and get wet. The trip lasts about ninety minutes. Call (514) 284-9607. More sedate river tours include the glass-roofed **River Boat** *(Bâteau Mouche),* which leaves from the Old Port for the restored section of the Canal, then heads into the Port of Montreal, around Île Sainte-Hélène and Île Notre-Dame. Call (514) 849-9952.

Shopping

Because of Montreal's extreme temperatures—frigid winters and hot summers—many of the city's shops and services are part of a vast **Underground City** network. It's connected throughout by the Metro, so you can enter from any stop or from the **Place Bonaventure,** which houses delightfully diverse shops.

Performing Arts

Montreal offers a wide variety of cultural activities, including some of special interest to kids. The **Théâtre Biscuit** (514-845-7306) is the only permanent puppet theater in the city, and has weekend performances. All of the plays at **Maison-Théâtre** (Salle Tritorium) are geared to children; call (514) 288-7211. If you're in town when the **Cirque du Soleil** is performing at the Old Port, run—do not walk—to see this incredibly original theatrical performance. This is not a conventional circus (there are no animals), but it is a truly unique experience. Performances are generally from late April to June. Call (514) 522-2324.

SPECIAL EVENTS

Montreal's **Expos** play eighty-one home games during baseball season (April to October) at the stadium in Olympic Park. For more information call (514) 253-3434/3595/(800) 361-6807. **Montreal Canadien Hockey Club** plays forty home games at the Montreal Forum from October to March. Tickets frequently sell out early, so call (514) 932-2582.

Admission Network (514-522-1245/800-361-4595) sells tickets for sporting events, concerts, and a number of seasonal festivals, including the popular fireworks festival listed next.

Fairs and Festivals

They don't call Montreal "Festival City" for nothing. It seems that no matter when you come, there's something special—and fun—going on. The Greater Montreal Convention and Tourism Bureau (GMCTB) has a complete calendar of events.

June–July: Benson & Hedges International Fireworks Competition, weekends.

July: International Jazz Festival features more than ninety indoor and 200 outdoor shows and events. Just For Laughs, the world's largest comedy festival, includes outdoor performances. Player's International Tennis Tournament.

August–early September: World Film Festival.

WHERE TO STAY

The Tourist Guide from the GMCTB has listings that classify some (but not all) lodgings by type and quality and include details on accessibility for persons with reduced mobility: **Reservation Center** provides a free service for all major hotels of Greater Montreal, including special packages; Hospitalité Canada: (514) 393-9049/(800) 665-1528. There are also several bed and breakfast services; contact the GMCTB for more information, at (800) 363-7777.

There are so many hotels in Montreal in so many price ranges that deciding on one can be an arduous task. You'll find many familiar, reliable names such as Best Western, Holiday Inn, Hilton, Le Meridien, Intercontinental, Journey's End, and Ritz Carlton Travel Lodge. This small selection—all conveniently located downtown—indicates the variety available for families:

Delta Montreal, 450 Sherbrooke Street, offers both rooms and suites, two pools, and a game room. The supervised Children's Creative and Activity Center is open weekends year-round for ages two to twelve (small fee) who may stay for up to three hours. Call (800) 877-1133/(800) 268-3777—Canada/(800) 877-1133—United States.

Hotel Novotel, 1180 Rue de la Montagne, lets kids up to sixteen stay free and enjoy a free breakfast when sharing with parents (maximum 2 kids). There's indoor parking. Call (514) 861-6000/(800) 221-4542.

Le Quatre Saisons, 1050 Sherbrooke Street West, lives up to the Four Seasons standard of luxury, with 300 rooms with sitting areas, twenty-six suites, an indoor pool, and elegant restaurant. Call (514) 284-1110/(800) 268-6282—Canada or (800) 332-3442.

WHERE TO EAT

The *Montreal Restaurant Guide* from the GMCTB contains tips on a number of fine dining experiences, including elegant restaurants for special nights out. But, honestly, you don't have to spend a fortune to eat well in this city. In summer, residents and tourists take to the streets to eat at outdoor cafes and bistros. Your kids will want to try *poutine,* a mixture of cheese, gravy, and *frites* (French fries) served at establishments around town, including McDonalds. Do give Montreal's ethnic restaurants a try. The Jewish area north of downtown, for instance, has superb bakeries and great delis. Montreal's bagels are said to rival, even surpass, New York's—taste for yourself. Those from the brick oven at **La Maison de Original Fairmount Bagel,** 74 West Fairmount Street (514-272-0667), are reputedly the best in town.

DAY TRIPS

Where do Montreal families go for a nearby getaway? The **Laurentian Mountains** and **Eastern Townships** are each about two hour's drive from the city and present a wealth of recreational opportunities, from skiing and skating in winter to summer activities. A one-hour drive east on Highway 3 is the **Granby Zoo,** where the kids can take an elephant ride and delight in seeing more than 750 animals, including wildlife species from all continents. Call (514) 372-0113 for information. South of the city in Hemmingford, **Safari Park** combines a drive-through animal reserve, petting area, deer trail, water play area, and amusement park. For information call (514) 247-2727/(800) 465- 8724—Ontario and Quebec. Quebec City, the provincial capital, is about two-and-one-half hours east, whereas two hours to the west lie the pleasures of Ottawa.

Gray Rocks, P.O. Box 1000, St. Jovite, Quebec, JOT 2HO (819-425-2771/800-567-6767), about 75 miles northwest of Montreal, is sprawled on 2,000 acres in Mont Tremblant. Before or after a city tour, this mid-price resort offers a friendly respite for families. In winter Gray Rocks features ski programs for kids along with other outdoor activities. In summer there are supervised children's programs for ages three to twelve. Warm-weather fun includes boating on the lake plus perfecting your tennis game at the intensive camp.

Near Gray Rocks is **Tremblant,** 3005 Principal, Mont-Tremblant, Quebec; (800) 461-8711. Tremblat, a major eastern ski area, is a great place for families. The bustling pedestrian village, just part of the ski area's $350 million renovations, adds charm, an off-the-slopes focus, and a variety of restaurants and eateries. The lack of cars makes this area particularly family friendly. The kids' ski and snowboard programs are good and there's child care for non-skiing tots. Teens have Bizztrado, a supervised juice bar for teens to hang out and meet each other. Slopeside hotel rooms and condominiums are available for rent.

FOR MORE INFORMATION

To request Montreal information by mail, write to Greater Montreal Convention and Tourism Bureau, *Les Cours Mont-Royal,* 1555 Pell Street, Suite 600, Montreal H3A 1X6, or call (514) 873-2015/(800) 363-7777. In person visit INFOTOURISTE, 1001 Square-Dorchester, for tourist information, services, and brochures on Montreal and Quebec province. They have branches at Place Jacques-Cartier in Old Montreal and at Montreal International Airport. Tourism Quebec also operates several seasonal bureaus at major highways throughout the province.

Montreal has several associations and referral centers for the handicapped, including *Association régionale pour le loisir des personnes handicapées de l'Île de Montréal* (514-933-2739), which offers ways for both residents and nonresidents to participate in recreational activities. Canadian National Institute for the Blind (514-284-2040) supplies volunteer escorts, if needed. Reserve in advance. Keroul (514-252-3104) gives assistance and pertinent information to those with impaired mobility.

Emergency Numbers

Ambulance, fire, and police: 911

Sainte-Justine Hospital, 3175 Côte-Sainte-Catherine Road; (514) 345–4931

Montreal Children's Hospital, 2300 Tupper Street; (514) 934–4400

Poison Hotline: (800) 463–5060

Twenty-four-hour pharmacy: Pharmaphix at 901 Sainte-Catherine Street East (514–842–4915) and 5122 Côte-des-Neiges Road (514–738–8464)

NEW BRUNSWICK

New Brunswick, an Atlantic province, shares a common border with Maine, but once you enter the area you know you're not in New England any more. Of the approximately 34,000 Loyal Americans who fled the Thirteen Colonies for Nova Scotia at the end of the American Revolution, more than 14,000 settled in present-day New Brunswick. This Loyalist fervor is alive and well in some quarters, although American tourists are graciously welcomed (bygones are indeed bygones). There's a French influence as well in the eastern and northern sections, where descendants of the Acadians, French settlers, still reside.

New Brunswick is a beautiful province, bordered on the east by the Gulf of St. Lawrence and on the south by the Bay of Fundy. It offers rocky coasts, lush green countryside, and several interesting cities. The Fundy Coast and the St. John River Valley are of special interest because of their proximity to the United States and their many offerings for families. If you have time to explore more, however, we urge you to sample all of New Brunswick's delightfully diverse districts.

GETTING THERE

The main commercial airports, in Fredericton, Moncton, and Saint John, are served by major Canadian airlines and Northwest Airlines, which operate to and from Boston.

VIA Rail serves much of this area. For information and reservations, call (506) 642–2916.

SMT Eastern Limited is a regional bus service that has links to bus routes in other provinces and in the United States. Call (506) 648–3500.

Coastal Transport Limited ferry to Grand Manan leaves from Blacks Harbour, just off Route 1. Call (506) 662–3606. Marine Atlantic's ferry to Digby, Nova Scotia, leaves from Saint John. For general information call (506) 636-3606; for central reservations call (902) 794-5700.

New Brunswick can be reached from Maine via I-95, which turns into the Trans-Canada Highway, Route 1, in New Brunswick.

GETTING AROUND

Public buses are available in the larger cities. Fredericton issues tourist parking passes for all visitors, permitting free parking at all municipal parking meters and parking lots for three days. Obtain them from the Information Centre at City Hall or during the summer at the Legislative Assembly and the highway information center.

WHAT TO SEE AND DO

Fundy Coastal Drive

This beautiful stretch of coast boasts the highest tides in the world, due to the shape and dimensions of the bay. Approximately every twelve hours and thirty minutes, one hundred billion tons of ocean pour in from the open Atlantic, a quiet-but-steady swirl. **Note:** Bay waters are cool, so be prepared for a brisk dip. East of Moncton the waters are warmer.

If you're entering the area from Maine, the coastal city of **St. Stephen** will be your first stop. Downtown traffic is usually bumper to bumper, but stop at the Information Center for maps, literature, and advice. Next, head to the **Ganong Chocolatier Shop,** 73 Milltown Boulevard; (506) 466-6437. There you can watch chocolate-dipping demonstrations and see the world's tallest jelly bean display. The world's first candy bar was supposedly created at the Ganong candy factory in 1910. You can tour the factory, on the outskirts of town, during the annual Chocolate Festival in August. Nearby, Oak Bay is one of the province's seven supervised saltwater beaches.

Your next stop, **St. Andrews-by-the-Sea,** is where you will want to stay awhile. At the tourist information center on the way into town, get maps and walking-tour brochures. Many of the gracious homes date to the 1880s, and some to the 1700s. Some Loyalist settlers who came here during the American Revolution dismantled their homes and brought

New Brunswick at a Glance

- Rocky coasts, lush countrysides, and an eclectic cultural mix

- Drive the Fundy coast and the River Valley

- See the famous reversing falls

- Visit a 300-acre historical Loyalist community at King's Landing Historical Settlement

- Explore the nearby sea caves of St. Martin's

- Information Centres, (506) 458-8331, (506) 458-8332, and (506) 452-9500

them over in barges to reassemble here. In this charming town on the shores of Passamaquoddy Bay, whale-watching tours leave from the town wharf. Some additional local sights your family will like follow.

Atlantic Salmon Information Center, Route 127; (506) 529-4581. True, it doesn't sound fascinating, but you'll be surprised how much you and the kids will learn. Walk along the nature trail by the stream that shows the fish in their natural environment. A coloring book detailing the salmon's life cycle is for sale.

Huntsman Marine Science Centre and Aquarium, Branch Cove; (506) 529-4285. This aquarium is a must-see, with a "Please Touch" Tank, harbor seals, and interpretive displays.

Nearby, high over the bay in a lovely setting, sits the historic **Blockhouse,** once used to keep watch in case of invasion by sea. You can go inside to have a look around; a guide will answer questions.

Heading east, you arrive at **Saint John,** on the Bay of Fundy at the mouth of the Saint John River. This is Canada's oldest city and New Brunswick's largest. If you're driving here in the morning, watch out for the thick fog that is a trademark of this area. Saint John (it's not abbreviated in order to avoid confusion with St. John's, Newfoundland) is full of surprises and family pleasures. An industrial city and international seaport, Saint John has undergone major restoration in recent years. Today the **Market Square Waterfront** complex, with its hundred-year-old brick facade, is a charming area of shops, boutiques, and restaurants. Historic walking tours are guided by costumed leaders daily in July and August. Tours leave from Barbour's General Store, Market Slip, restored and stocked with goods from the years 1840 to 1940.

Another family-friendly highlight is **Saint John City Market,** 47 Charlotte Street; it is believed to be the oldest building of its kind in use in Canada. Stop at a cafe or buy snacks of fresh cheese, baked goods, produce, maple syrup, and other goodies. Often Indians sell hand-woven baskets here.

Let your kids try dulse, the local sea-vegetable specialty gathered from rocks along the Bay of Fundy and dried in the sun. While an acquired taste, the locals love it, and some prefer it to popcorn. The Market is closed Sundays.

Reversing Falls is a natural phenomenon occurring where the Saint John River empties into the Bay of Fundy. The falls are really below the water: Explain this to the kids first, or else they might be disappointed. During low tide, tidal waters drop 14½ feet below river levels, causing the full force of the 450-mile river to crash through a narrow gorge into the harbor. As the tides rise in the bay, the river waters gradually calm and actually reverse in direction as the bay waters rise above them. To get the most out of this sight, try to observe the falls twice on the same day: at or near high and low tides. For a short interpretive film explaining, but not actually showing, the phenomenon, go to the rooftop theater at the Reversing Falls Tourist Information Center; (506) 658–2937. It's at the west end of the Route 100 bridge that crosses the river.

Rockwood Park, in the middle of the city, covers 2,200 acres, so plan to spend some time here. The freshwater lakes offer supervised swimming, canoeing, and paddle boating. Visit the zoo and children's petting farm, enjoy the hiking and jogging trails, and try the bumper boats and miniature golf. The park also has camping and trailer facilities.

Canada Games Aquatic Centre, 50 Union Street, just across from Market Square, is a find. This modern facility features two huge warm-water, shallow leisure pools, separated by an island with a double looping water slide. There's also a competition pool and two exercise rooms. Visitors pay a small fee. Call (506) 634-7946.

Aitken Bicentennial Exhibition Center (ABEC), 20 Hazen Avenue, is a colorful and lively arts-and-sciences museum. It features ScienceScape, a permanent children's gallery. Call (506) 633-4870.

Fort Howe Lookout, Main Street (North End), is a blockhouse that formerly protected the harbor. Though you can't go inside, the grounds offer a great view of the city and port.

River Valley Scenic Drive

Northwest of Saint John is **Fredericton,** the provincial capital. Called the "City of Stately Elms," it is situated along the picturesque Saint John River. Fredericton is small, very walkable, and a pleasant place to spend some time before or after you visit the Fundy Coast. At one time an important military center, much of its historic past remains. The *Fredericton Guide* has a suggested walking tour, and some sites may pique your kids' interest. Your best bet: Take the walking tours led by historically costumed guides who offer dramatic commentary. Call City Hall information at (506) 452-9500. Another option, especially with younger children, is to take a Victorian-style horse-and-carriage tour of downtown. Even if they don't absorb the history, kids love the ride. Call (506) 444-1044 for prices and reservations.

A riverfront pathway ideal for strolling stretches along the green, starting at the Sheraton Inn and extending to the Princess Margaret Bridge. Stop in at the **Fredericton Lighthouse Museum.** As you walk to the top level, a variety of interactive exhibits describe the history of the region. The view is lovely on a clear day. Call (506) 459-2515 for information.

Fredericton has lots of inviting, green spaces, including **Odell Park,** where landscaped paths lead to geese, ducks, and deer, and a lovely arboretum. **The Mactaquac Provincial Park,** just outside town on Route 105, is the largest recreation park in the province, with more than 1,400 acres of open land and forest. The two supervised beaches are a draw for families, as are the self-guided nature trails, an eighteen-hole golf course, camping facilities, and a restaurant. In winter the park is popular for its skating, sledding, snowmobiling, cross-country skiing, and horse-drawn sleigh rides. Call (506) 363-1011 for information.

Your kids will enjoy the **Changing of the Guard,** which takes place July and August in Officers' Square and at City Hall, Tuesday through Saturday. The Sentry changes every hour on the hour. The Guard was formed in 1793. Call City Hall information for details. **The Guard House,** Carleton Street, appears as it was in 1866, when the Fifteenth Regiment was in residence. In summer guards wearing the regiment's red-coated uniforms give tours.

The Legislative Assembly Building, Queen Street, is very British and quite majestic. Even young kids will say "wow!" when they see the throne (Speaker's Chair), set on a dais in the Assembly Chamber under a canopy bearing a carved Royal Coat of Arms. You can visit the Chamber while the Legislature is in session, although chances are your kids will appreciate it more when it's empty. Call (506) 453-2527 for information.

On Saturday mornings visit the **Boyce Farmers Market,** just behind the Old York County Jail, between Regent and Saint John Street. Farmers and their wares, artisans, and craftspeople make this a colorful place to linger, browse, and buy; (506) 451-1815.

Don't miss **King's Landing Historical Settlement,** 23 miles west of Fredericton, off the Trans-Canada Highway (Route 2) at exit 259; (506) 363-5805/(800) 561-0123. A visit to this nearly 300-acre re-created Loyalist settlement circa 1790–1870 will be a high point of your family's stay in the area. The setting, high above the Saint John River, is stunning: green and lush, with winding dirt roads, open expanses of farmland, and woods. You can—and should—hitch a ride aboard a horse-drawn wagon: there's much to cover here and lots of walking. The village buildings, which were brought from nearby, include houses varying from plain and simple to utterly grand, a church, a one-room schoolhouse, a general store, a tavern and inn, blacksmith shop, and a bakery. The smell of baking, the sights of men tilling the fields and women weaving, the sounds of children playing are all part of this wonderful experience. Costumed interpreters include children age nine and older who take part in a five-day live-in Visiting Cousins program, which transforms them into children of the 1800s. After a visit your kids may want to come back and participate. Special theme weekends, such as the Scottish and Harvest festivals and the agricultural fair, add zest to this well-done settlement. There's a self-service restaurant as well as the full-service King's Head Inn.

Combine this with a visit to nearby **Woolastook Park,** 15 miles west of Fredericton on Route 2, the Trans-Canada Highway. Your kids will like the giant water slides, wading pool, beach, minigolf, and nature trails along which animals ranging from raccoons to bobcats are housed. Call (506) 363-5410.

Performing Arts

Fredericton Outdoor Summer Theater, downtown on the lawn of Officers' Square, features theater-in-the-square seven days a week from July 1 to September 6. The Square is also the setting for the July and August Summer Music Concerts, held weekly at 7:30 P.M. Call (506) 452-9500 for information on both programs. In Saint John, the **Classical Music Summer Sounds Concerts** at Centenary Queen Square, United Church, Princess Street, are held Tuesdays at 8:00 P.M. Call (506) 634-8123. The city also has free **Outdoor Concerts,** mid-June to late July, at King's Square, featuring a variety of performers; (506) 658-2893.

Shopping

New Brunswick is well known for its crafts—from folk art to dolls to pottery and metal. The Department of Economic Development and Tourism publishes a *New Brunswick Craft Directory* that lists studios, boutiques, and outlets. Fredericton, with the highest concentration of craftspeople, is known as the pewter-smithing capital of Canada.

SPECIAL EVENTS

Fairs and Festivals

Contact the individual tourist associations for information on the following festivities.

Late June–early July: Festival International de la Francophonie offers music, art, dances, literature, and food indigenous to the francophone culture; (506) 395-9746.

The Salmon Festival, in conjunction with Canada Day celebrations, features children's activities, picnics, a circus, giant bingo, a beer garden, and of course, a salmon dinner; (506) 789-2700.

July: Loyalist City Festival reenacts the 1783 Loyalist Landing.

There is an authentic eighteenth-century military encampment, pageants, parades, and fireworks; (506) 634–8123.

August: Celebrate Acadian culture at the Festival Acadien with a variety of activities such as concerts, exhibitions, and the Blessing of the Fleet; (506) 727–6515.

The Chocolate Festival allows everybody to be a kid again, with pudding-eating contests, candy treasure hunts, a cookie-decorating contest, and chocolate Olympic games; (506) 465–5616.

September: During the Atlantic Balloon Festival, watch twenty balloons take flight twice daily. The merriment also includes helicopter rides, parachute demonstrations, the Maritime Craft fair, and an antique car show; (506) 432–9444.

Harvest Jazz and Blues Festival brings you great music performed in a variety of exciting and different venues, both indoors and out; (506) 454–2583.

WHERE TO STAY

New Brunswick has a free, in-province reservation system, Dial-A-Nite, available at provincial tourist information centers (shown at major entry points on the New Brunswick Highway map). The system enables travelers to make advance reservations directly with hotels, motels, inns, outfitters, farm vacations, and many privately owned campgrounds. Here are some picks for families.

Fredericton

Lord Beaverbrook Hotel, 659 Queen Street, is conveniently located. It has been here for years and is still perfectly comfortable. There's a nice family restaurant, and the kids will like the indoor pool. Call (506) 455–3371.

Sheraton Inn Fredericton, 225 Woodstock Road, is the city's newest. Located on the banks of the Saint John River, the hotel has 223 rooms, with fourteen suites. Indoor and outdoor pools, tennis courts, a family restaurant, and free parking are some of the offerings. Call (506) 457–7000/(800) 325–3535.

Near King's Landing, in Prince William, the **Chickadee Lodge** is a cozy log bed and breakfast by the river, set back from the Trans-Canada

Highway. You have to share a bath, but the rooms are clean and comfortable. This is a good place to stay if you're en route or spending the day at King's Landing: otherwise, you're basically in the middle of nowhere. Call (506) 363-2759.

The Carriage House Bed and Breakfast, a three-story Victorian home in downtown, welcomes children even though it is decorated with antiques. Call (506) 452-9924.

St. Andrews-by-the-Sea

The Algonquin, 184 Adolphus, is a large and luxurious Canadian Pacific resort with a pool, golf, tennis, biking, and more. In July and August there's a supervised program for a fee for ages five to twelve from 10:00 A.M. to 4:00 P.M. Call (506) 529-8823/(800) 268-9411—Canada/(800) 828-7447—United States.

The **Walker Estate,** built in the grand style of 1912, has been restored to its original elegance. The former home of the Hiram Walker distillery family is situated on eleven acres in the heart of town. Friendly, efficient service, combined with elegant grandeur, will make your visit truly memorable. All rooms have private baths. Call (506) 529-4210.

Saint John

Delta Brunswick, 39 King Street, has a great downtown location, indoor pool, and family restaurant with a kid's menu. An unsupervised Children's Creative Centre is open from 6:00 A.M. to 11:00 P.M. with games, movies, and toys. Call (506) 648-1981/(800) 268-1133.

Shadow Lawn Inn is located in the quaint town of Rothesay, 13 kilometers from Saint John and ten minutes from the airport. This understated elegant Victorian inn offers nine luxurious rooms, beautifully furnished with antiques; private baths. Call (506) 847-7539.

WHERE TO EAT

In Fredericton stop by the Tourist Information Centres to look through their menu binders. In-the-know locals in Saint John congregate at **Reggie's Restaurant,** 26 Germain Street, famous for its bagels and smoked meat from Montreal, hearty breakfasts, and inexpensive lunches that include clam and fish chowders, lobster rolls, and bagel burgers; (506) 657-6270. Indeed, lobster is everywhere: in summer even McDonald's serves McLobster sandwiches, although this isn't the best way to sample this seafood delight. **Keystone Kelly's,** in Saint John's Market Square Complex, has a menu to please all, with Italian, Mexican, and Canadian cuisine. Call (506) 634-0616.

DAY TRIPS

There's lots to explore east of Saint John. On your way to **Moncton,** detour on Route 111 to **St. Martin's** and explore the long stretch of beach and sea caves (but note the tide schedules first). There are twin covered bridges at the harbor and a tourist information center. As you drive east, you're entering the Southern Shores District, home of **Fundy National Park,** on Highway 114 between Saint John and Moncton. Hike, fish, boat, beachcomb, or take part in nature interpretation programs. Kiosks in the park have information about special activities for kids age six to twelve, campfire programs, and entertainment, which takes place at a natural amphitheater. Salt water is piped in from the Bay of Fundy and heated for the swimming pool. Lodging is available in the park's hostel or in nearby Alma. Call (506) 887-2000.

The lively city of **Moncton** has great family appeal. At **Magnetic Hill,** Mountain Road, just off the Trans-Canada Highway on the northwest outskirts of town, cars appear to coast uphill and water seems to flow upwards. Set your car in neutral and feel it coast uphill backwards; trained staff is there to help you experience this optical illusion.

Magnetic Hill's Wharf Village has enough attractions to encourage families to stay the day: **Mountain Magic Water Park** (open mid-May to mid-October), **Magnetic Hill Zoo,** an outdoor concert center, mini-steam engine rides that transport visitors around the complex, crafts and souvenir shops, and **Wharf Village Family Restaurant.** Across from the complex, the **boardwalk** has go-carts, miniature golf, batting cages, fishing, and other attractions. For information on Magnetic Hill attractions, call (506) 853-3516.

In downtown Moncton's **Bore Park,** just off Main Street, twice daily, the Bay of Fundy tides rise up to 30 feet in little over an hour, creating a wave known as the Tidal Bore. The town of **Dieppe,** which

The sea caves at St. Martin's, a short drive from New Brunswick, are great places to explore.
(Courtesy New Brunswick Department of Tourism)

adjoins Moncton's eastern borders, boasts the **Crystal Palace,** 499 rue Paul, a huge indoor amusement park with roller coaster, carousel, playground areas, games of skill, a science center with twenty-nine interactive exhibits, and lots more. The complex also includes four cinemas, a food court, McGinnis Landing Restaurant, and a Best Western hotel (506-858-8584 or 800-528-1234). Call (506) 859- 4FUN for Crystal Palace Information. For complete information on the area, contact the Convention and Visitor Services, 774 Main Street, Moncton, NB E1C 1E8; (506) 853-4352.

FOR MORE INFORMATION

Fredericton has two Tourist Information Centres: Trans-Canada Highway near Hanwell Road, exit 289 (506-458-8331/8332), and City Hall, corner of Queen and York (506-452-9500). Saint John has several Tourist Information Centres around town. For information contact their Visitor and Convention Bureau, P.O. Box 1971, Saint John E2L

4L1; (506) 658-2990. Tourism New Brunswick can be reached at (800) 561-0123. The province maintains Tourist Information Centres at major entry points.

Emergency Numbers

Ambulance, fire, police, and poison control in Fredericton: 911. Police, fire, and rescue squad in Saint John: 911

Poison control in Saint John: (506) 648-7111. Elsewhere, consult the front of the phone book.

Twenty-four-hour emergency room in Fredericton: Dr. Everett Chalmers Hospital, Priestman Street; (506) 452-5400

Twenty-four-hour emergency room in Saint John: Saint John Regional Hospital, Tucker Road; (506) 648-6366

Shopper's Drug Mart is a provincewide chain of pharmacies open late and on Sundays. In Saint John the store at 57 Landsdowne Place is open from 8:00 A.M. to midnight, seven days a week.

NOVA SCOTIA

Nova Scotia's beautiful, diverse landscape, which consists of the Atlantic coastal region and the interior woodlands, has long attracted tourists. This peninsula province is 350 miles from end to end, with a coastline that stretches for 4,625 miles. Visitors are never far from rugged shores dotted with sandy beaches, picturesque fishing villages, and scenic coves. **Greater Halifax,** the capital, sits about midway along the Atlantic coast, making these areas an ideal base from which to explore the province. Perhaps your family will eventually wend its way east to Cape Breton Island to the spectacular Cabot Trail that winds around Cape Breton Highlands National Park. Or you may choose to follow one of the province's other ten scenic trailways that reflect its rich ethnic and geographic diversity. But don't rush off from Halifax: The area has some pleasures in store for families who linger.

GETTING THERE

Air Canada has daily flights to Nova Scotia, from New York, Boston, Toronto, Montreal, and St. John's, Newfoundland; other carriers include Canadian Airlines, Northwest, and American. An affiliate offers connections within Atlantic Canada. Limousine service and car and motor-home rentals are available at Halifax International, Sydney, and Yarmouth airports; call (800) 565-0000 for information. Halifax Airport, Highway 102, is 24 miles from downtown. Airbus shuttle buses (902-468-4342) travel to major downtown hotels. Share-A-Cab (902-429-4444) services the airport from any part of Halifax, but the service suggests a three-hour notice.

Acadian Lines (902-454-9321) operates buses throughout the province. Greyhound from New York and Maine, and Voyageur from Quebec City and Montreal, connect in New Brunswick with SMT Bus Lines, which in turn connects with Acadian Lines. The Halifax bus terminal is at 6040 Almon Street; (902) 454-9321.

VIA Rail travels throughout Canada. Amtrak passengers from Montreal or Toronto can connect with VIA Rail to reach the Halifax station, 1161 Hollis Street, in the south end; (902-429-8421).

Car ferry service to Yarmouth, Nova Scotia, about 328 miles from Halifax, is a comfortable transportation option. Reserve the following in advance: Bluenose from Bar Harbor, Maine (902-794-5700); Scotia Queen from Portland, Maine (800-341-7540—United States/ 800-482-0955—Maine/800-565-7900—Nova Scotia, New Brunswick, or Prince Edward Island). Other ferry service includes Newfoundland to North Sydney, Nova Scotia; Prince Edward Island to Caribou, Nova Scotia; and Saint John, New Brunswick, to Digby, Nova Scotia. Cruise ships dock at ocean terminals in the south end of Halifax.

Highways from all points in the United States and Canada join the Trans-Canada Highway from New Brunswick into Nova Scotia.

GETTING AROUND

Halifax is a compact city. You can walk to most of the major sights (though it is hilly walking from the harbor to the Citadel). Barrington is the city's main street. Metro Transit (902-421-6600) has buses that run regularly throughout the city and also offers the shopping trolley. For 25 cents this gets you a ride to or from downtown's two shopping districts. Maps are available at any information center. Yarmouth-Halifax ferry operates daily from the foot of George Street, Halifax, to the harbor side of Dartmouth's City Hall. The inexpensive fifteen-minute trip offers a good view of the harbor.

WHAT TO SEE AND DO

Museums and Historic Sites

Combine museum visits with sight-seeing tours of different areas of Halifax. First, head to the **harborfront,** a lively place where your family can stroll through the shops of the nineteenth-century waterfront **Historic Properties** buildings, grab a bite to eat, see (or sail on) the *Bluenose II* schooner, and board the HMCS *Sackville,* a World War II convoy escort, now a Naval memorial with an interpretive center and

Nova Scotia at a Glance

- A unique mix of rugged Atlantic coastline and interior woodlands

- Explore the Halifax waterfront area

- Visit the Maritime Museum of the Atlantic

- A formal English garden right in the middle of Halifax

- Kids will love the Fortress of Louisburg

- Nova Scotia information, (902) 424-4247

multimedia presentation. The **Halcyon Playground,** near the Ferry Terminal, is designed like a tugboat and appeals to younger kids. There are miles of boardwalks, too.

Maritime Museum of the Atlantic, Lower Water Street; (902) 424-7490/7491. This pleasant, airy museum houses some interesting objects, including relics from the *Titanic* (a number of the dead were brought to Halifax, where they were buried), and other vintage Cunard steamship memorabilia. Downstairs is a permanent exhibit of photos and memorabilia devoted to the Halifax Explosion, which older school-age children and teens should find absorbing. Sit down to watch the short video that describes the 1917 disaster, which occurred when two ships—one carrying explosives—collided. The result was the biggest man-made explosion before the nuclear age. More than 1,900 people were killed immediately; 9,000 were injured, and almost the entire north end of Halifax was destroyed.

The museum also has a number of small boats, including one that belonged to Queen Victoria, and a full-size replica of a coastal schooner. The CSS *Academia,* Canada's first hydrographic vessel, is permanently moored outside the museum.

Next door, at the small **Halifax Touch Tank Aquarium,** roll up your sleeves and carefully handle the marine animals in the pool. Young kids love this.

The next day, visit the star-shaped **Citadel Hill National Historic Park** (902–426–5080), which has dominated the city since 1759. This is Canada's most visited national historic park. At the foot of Citadel Hill, the Old Town Clock, a city landmark, was given to the city as a gift in 1803 by Prince Edward. Though the fort was never attacked by the French (or anyone else), it was considered the bastion of the British defense of North America. You can go inside the fortress, actually the fourth built on the site by British soldiers, and have a look around the barracks. Walk along the fortress walls for good views of the city and harbor.

A fifty-minute *Tides of History* audiovisual presentation on Halifax and its defenses may be a trifle too long for some kids, but their attention will be riveted by the college students who, playing members of the 78th Highlanders and Royal Artillery, reenact life within the fort. Activities (summer only) include artillery and infantry drills and firing the noonday cannon. Guided tours and food service are available.

Just behind the hill is **Nova Scotia Museum of Natural History,** 1747 Summer Street; (902) 424-7453. This facility, headquarters of the provincial museum system, presents the human and natural history of the province in an appealing way. Kids will especially enjoy the huge whale, which they can help measure; the stuffed black bear and moose; and—everyone's favorites—lifelike dinosaurs. Artifacts belonging to the province's original inhabitants, the Micmac Indians, are on display, including a 121-pound beaded Indian costume. Changing exhibits frequently reveal the history and contributions of a particular ethnic group: A recent display, for instance, highlighted the Jewish heritage of Canada. Call ahead to find out about regularly scheduled activities.

The Discovery Centre, corner of Barrington and Sackville streets (902–492–4422), offers changing interactive exhibits. Call to ask about their Science Workshops.

Parks and Beaches

Halifax is called "the city of trees." How many cities can boast a formal English garden right in the middle of downtown? **Halifax Public**

Gardens, across from the Citadel, is a wonderful place for a family stroll. Enjoy seventeen acres of formal Victorian gardens—the oldest in North America—including colorful and fragrant roses, hibiscus, magnolias, and formal floral displays. Sundays are especially festive, with afternoon musical performances on the bandstand. If you haven't brought a picnic, bring some bread crumbs to feed the ducks and pigeons.

Halifax Commons, just outside the city center, is Canada's oldest park. It boasts a large playground where your kids are sure to find lots of open spaces and playmates.

Point Pleasant Park, Point Pleasant Drive, at the south end of Halifax, has 186 acres with walking paths that lead along the Atlantic coast (where you can watch ships come in) and through forests. Motor vehicles are prohibited; park in the lots at the entrances. (A city bus comes here from Barrington Street.) The western entrance, at Tower Road and Point Pleasant Drive, features a large map indicating walkways and interesting points, including the remains of several fortresses. Besides picnic facilities, this park features supervised saltwater bathing at Black Rock Beach, which also has canteen facilities. Because of the frequent "red tide," this beach is not always swimmable. (See Day Trips for nearby beaches.) Kids can play in the sand, however, and there are playgrounds nearby.

The heather at the southern tip of the park was brought to Halifax when the Scottish Highland Regiment shook out their mattresses and bedrolls after landing here—and heather seeds came falling out.

Have a look at the **Prince of Wales Martello Tower,** built in the late 1790s by Queen Victoria's father. This round, thick-walled structure, intended as protection against a French attack, was the first in North America of what was later known as a Martello tower. Exhibits portray the tower's history, and staff is on hand to answer questions.

Shopping

Many shops at **Historic Properties** and **Granville Mall** feature locally made products such as hand-knit blankets and sweaters, Nova Scotia tartan kilts, and pewter. Downtown **Barrington Street** has the more conventional shopping complexes of **Scotia Square, Barrington Place,** and **Maritime Mall.** At **Spring Garden Road,** another popular shopping area, **Clearwater Lobster** packs this local specialty for travel (at the airport, Atlantic Seafoods does this, too). **Jennifer's of Nova Scotia** features local crafts and maple syrup recipe books. The **Rose Bowl** deli across the street sells the maple products, including syrup, butter, cream, and sugar. Don't miss the Farmer's Market on Saturdays at the historic **Brewery Center,** where arts, crafts, and foods are sold. An antiques, flea, and produce market takes place on Sundays at **Halifax Forum.**

Performing Arts

Unfortunately for tourists the **Neptune Theater,** the city's leading professional company, and the **Symphony Nova Scotia** don't perform in summer. It's possible, however, that **Halifax Metro Centre** may host a musical performance during your visit. Call their recording: (902) 451-2602. The **Grafton Street Dinner Theatre** features music, comedy, drama, food—and fun for all. Call (902) 425-1961 to see what's on the entertainment menu. Summer theater is available in the town of Chester (see Day Trips).

SPECIAL EVENTS

Contact provincial or Halifax tourist information for more details on these exciting events.

Late June–early July: Nova Scotia International Tattoo, Halifax; military bands from around the world, gymnasts, dancers, choirs, and more.

July: Festival of Light, Halifax and Dartmouth waterfronts and harbors, includes fireworks and other festivities.

July–August: Tea with the Mayor, weekdays from 3:30 to 4:30 P.M. Casual tea, cookies, and chat with Halifax's mayor.

August: BuskerFest features street performers from around the world who converge on downtown Halifax to juggle, clown, and ride unicycles.

September: Shearwater Air Show, Dartmouth, features daring stunts by air force planes.

WHERE TO STAY

Check In Nova Scotia, the province's free reservation system, has a minireservation center in Halifax, but it's best to reserve as far ahead as possible. Their phone numbers are the same as the provincial travel information numbers listed under For More Information. *The Greater Halifax Visitor's Guide* features a comprehensive chart of area lodgings. Here are a few choices for families.

Château Halifax, 1990 Barrington Street, is one of the luxurious Canadian Pacific hotels. You can't miss with their convenient location, indoor pool and parking, and lovely rooms and suites. Call (902) 425-6700/(800) 268-9411/(800) 828-7447—United States.

Delta Barrington, 1875 Barrington Street, is also in a terrific location, only a block from the waterfront. Tastefully decorated rooms include triples and suites. A supervised Creative Children's Centre for ages two to twelve is open weekends. There's a pool and health club, and the hotel is connected to two shopping malls. Call (902) 420-6524/(800) 268-1133—Canada/(800) 877-1133—United States.

Keddy's Halifax Hotel, on Chocolate Lake, St. Margaret's Bay Road, has 135 rooms, including suites, a recreation pool area, and lake swimming. At the family restaurant kids eat for less than $1.00. Call (902) 477-5611/(800) 561-7666.

WHERE TO EAT

The Greater Halifax Visitor's Guide has a listing of restaurants, categorized by type of food. Here are some of the entries for families.

How could you resist a restaurant called **Alfredo, Weinstein and Ho**? Make everyone happy with inexpensive Italian, Jewish, or Chinese food at this delightfully named Grafton Avenue restaurant; (902) 421-1977. Or dine aboard a historic ferry at **Lobsters Ahoy,** anchored next to the Halifax Ferry Terminal; (902) 422-CLAW. There's a kid's menu, open-air and enclosed dining, and a selection that includes lobster, steak, chicken, and mussels.

Summer brings BuskerFest to Halifax, where street performers from all over the world converge here to demonstrate their skills. (Courtesy Nova Scotia Department of Tourism and Culture)

DAY TRIPS

Head southwest along the shore toward Yarmouth, following **The Lighthouse Route.** Some of the lighthouses along the way are still working and accessible by roads; others can only be reached by boats. Although it's 328 miles to Yarmouth, you need not venture that far. The charming fishing village of **Peggy's Cove** is about thirty minutes away. Set atop spectacular granite rocks, it's one of the most photographed spots in Canada. In summer a post office opens in the town's lighthouse. (Be prepared for summer crowds.) Another must-see: a colossal monument to Canadian fishermen, carved into a 100-foot rock face over a ten-year period.

Continue south to **Queensland,** where there are three stretches of sandy beaches. Though it's not large, the Queensland Beach Provincial Park is one of the South Shore's most popular. Arrive early to find a parking space. Farther on, the popular summer retreat of **Chester** sits on a peninsula at the head of Mahone Bay, overlooking some of the bay's 365 islands. A passenger ferry runs to the island of **Big Tanook,** where you can sample a local specialty—sauerkraut. August brings Chester's large sailing regatta and professional Theatre Festival, which starts in mid-July. Cafes and restaurants are plentiful. Stroll to the old railway station, where local artists exhibit their work.

The **Fortress of Louisburg,** P.O. Box 1995, Louisburg (800-565-9464), founded in 1720 by Louis XV of France, is a children's paradise. Open May to October, with summer celebrations from fireworks to parades and concerts, this historical reconstruction is nonstop fun. Visit the Tall Ships, or stroll through the old villages. Nearby, Cape Breton Highlands National Park has more than twenty-seven great hiking trails, and the shores of Cheticamp are a whale-watchers delight.

In addition to the Lighthouse Route and Cabot Trail, Nova Scotia tourism information can provide information about other distinctively different scenic provincial trailways to explore after leaving Halifax. These include Evangeline Trail, the land settled by the French in 1605; Glooscap Trail, with high Bay of Fundy tides, ancient fossils, and cliffs studded with semiprecious stones; and the Sunrise Trail area, where the Scottish influence is strong. This coastal trail skirts the Northumberland Strait, boasting the warmest waters north of the Carolinas and about one dozen beach parks.

FOR MORE INFORMATION

For information on Nova Scotia, including the reservation service, call (902) 424-4247/(800) 565-0000—Canada/(800) 341-6096—United States/(800) 492-0643—Maine. Ask about the Nova Scotia Host program, where your family can meet a compatible local family. Provincial Information Centres are located at Halifax Airport arrival area (902-426-1223) and in Red Store building, Historic Properties, Lower Water Street, Box 130, Halifax B3J 2M7 (902-424-4247). Tourism Halifax is in City Hall, corner of Duke and Barrington streets; (902) 421-8736.

The *Greater Halifax Visitor's Guide* lists wheelchair accessibility for lodgings and restaurants. **Lewis Lake,** a provincial park 12 miles west of Halifax, offers disabled persons outdoor recreation, including wheelchair-accessible nature trails and lookouts, and two specially designed fishing piers.

Emergency Numbers

Ambulance and medical emergencies: Izaak Walton Killam Hospital for Children, 5830 University Avenue; (902) 428–8050

Fire: 4103

Poison Control Centre: (902) 428–8161

Police: 4105

Shopper's Drug Mart, Fenwick Medical Center, 5595 Fenwick Street, is open Monday through Saturday from 7:00 A.M. to 11:00 P.M.; Sunday and holidays from 9:00 A.M. to 11:00 P.M.

OTTAWA

When Queen Victoria selected Ottawa as Canada's capital in 1857, she made a shrewd—albeit unlikely—choice. Although it was then a small wilderness community called Bytown, Ottawa had a central location and was politically acceptable to both upper and lower Canada. Ottawa has come a long way since then. An attractive, down-to-earth, accessible city, it has great museums, natural beauty, and bountiful year-round recreation—much of it centering on the Rideau Canal, which divides the city in two. What's more, Ottawa is the only capital city in the world with an operating farm within its downtown! No matter what time of year your family comes, you'll find a variety of activities to keep everybody happy. Some are in Hull, just over the bridge, which is in the province of Quebec (and has a different area code). **Note:** In Ottawa, where there's a 40 percent French population, everyone is bilingual, although English is the predominant language.

GETTING THERE

The MacDonald-Cartier International Airport, a twenty-minute ride south of the city (613–998-3151), is served by major carriers. Taxi and shuttle-bus services are available. Car rentals are at the airport and in town.

VIA Rail, Canada's national railway, runs several daily trains from Montreal and Toronto to Ottawa's VIA Rail Station, 200 Tremblay Road; (613) 244-8289. Connections with Amtrak (800–USA–RAIL) can be made in Montreal or Toronto.

Voyageur Bus, 265 Catherine Street (613-238-5900), has service throughout Canada. Connections to the United States can be made via Montreal or Toronto through Greyhound.

Cars enter Ottawa by following the red maple leaf signs from Highway 417 and by highways 16 and 31.

Ottawa at a Glance

- Great museums, natural beauty, and a wide range of year-round recreation

- Hands-on fun at the Canadian Museum of Civilization and the National Museum of Science and Technology

- The changing of the guard at the Parliament building

- Agriculture and more at the Central Experimental Farm

- Hiking and cross-country ski trails

- Ottawa Tourism and Convention Authority, (613) 237-5158

U.S. citizens and legal residents don't need passports or visas to enter Canada, though they are preferred. Native-born U.S. citizens should have a birth certificate or voter's registration that shows citizenship, plus a picture I.D. Naturalized citizens need naturalization certificates or other proof of citizenship. Permanent residents who are not citizens need alien registration receipts.

GETTING AROUND

OC Transpo is the city's excellent bus system. Call (613) 741-4390 for route information. All downtown routes meet at the Rideau Centre (Rideau Street between Nicholas and Sussex and the Mackenzie King Bridge). You may purchase tickets at OC Transpo offices, 112 Kent Street or 320 Queen Street (the Place de Ville building fronts on two streets); (613) 523-8880. Two shopping centers, St. Laurent and Place d'Orleans, also have information on outlets on Saturdays.

You'll be able to drive to a number of attractions not in the downtown area, where there's restricted street parking. Along the **Rideau Canal,** which divides the city, are 150 kilometers of recreational pathways for cyclists, pedestrians, and rollerbladers. In the winter you'll see people skating to work on the Canal, which is considered the world's longest skating rink.

Recreational boaters arrive via the Rideau Canal or the Ottawa River.

On summer Sunday mornings, take advantage of the roads closed to vehicular traffic. The more than 25 kilometers of parkways along the Rideau Canal and the Ottawa River are great places for biking, strolling, and rollerblading.

An easy way to get around to major attractions is via **Capital Trolley Tours** (613-729-6888/800-823-6147), sight-seeing buses that allow you to get on and off at any of twenty sites, including Parliament Hill, Canadian Museum of Civilization, Aviation Museum, National Gallery of Canada, and Rideau Falls, plus several hotels.

WHAT TO SEE AND DO

Ottawa has a surprising number of museums. Though we've selected only those of special interest to families, see the complete museum listing in the *Visitor Guide* from Ottawa Tourism and Convention Authority.

Museums

Canadian Museum of Civilization, 100 Laurier Street, Hull; (819) 776-7000. While the name may not sound exciting, don't miss a visit to this architecturally splendid, large, and interesting attraction. Your kids will love this place as soon as they enter the Grand Hall and see the towering totem poles and six longhouses, tributes to Canada's Northwest Coast. At the stage area here, regularly scheduled performances by a variety of colorful entertainers are often geared to kids. The adjoining Canada Hall presents Canada's past through life-size reconstructions, such as a sixteenth-century sailing vessel, that include simulated sounds. Kids will love this experience. The Children's Museum area is extremely popular with visitors as well as school groups. Though it's geared for toddlers to about age eight, changing, hands-on exhibits may pique the interest of an older child. Inside, younger kids play at the circular post office where they can rubber stamp and "mail" letters, try on clothes, and play in an outdoor area. An adjoining room full of art supplies is the site of various projects and programs. Get a schedule when you enter.

The CINEPLUS theater (admission extra) projects either IMAX or OMNIMAX films, so plan to spend the day. Call (819) 776-7010 for show times.

Canadian Museum of Nature, McLeod Street at Metcalfe; (613) 996-3102. The "castle" that houses this museum was briefly the governmental seat after the Parliament buildings burned down in 1916. On display are all the things that school-age kids like: huge dinosaurs, gems and minerals, birds, mammals, plants, and assorted creatures, plus a Discovery Den, with nature-related kid's activities and exhibits.

National Gallery of Canada, 380 Sussex Drive; (613) 990-1985. Yes, this museum houses the world's most comprehensive collection of Canadian art and European, Asian, and American works; chances are that won't impress the kids. What will is the physical appearance of this contemporary glass and granite building, which, as the museum puts it, "rises like a giant candelabrum." Inside, in the Great Hall, enjoy sweeping views of the city. No, there's nothing "just for kids," but if yours haven't been to a strictly-art museum before, this is the place to start.

Most will find something of interest in the Contemporary galleries, flooded with light from the skylights overhead. There are two restaurants, on-site parking, and an excellent bookstore with kids' books. For a visual treat, drive or walk by at night, when this illuminated glass treasure house is a sight to behold.

National Aviation Museum, Rockcliffe Airport (follow biplane signs on Rockcliffe Parkway); (613) 993-2010. True, non-Canadians might not find this collection of Canadian aircraft quite as fascinating as Canadians do. Still, if your kids are turned on by vintage aircraft, they'll love it here. The collection is one of the world's largest. It spans aeronautical history and includes a reproduction of the *Silver Dart* (which Alexander Graham Bell helped to design) and the vintage Stearman biplane, which "passengers" are allowed to board. Family Sundays are held monthly; frequent weekday activities are designed for various ages.

National Museum of Science and Technology, 18678 St. Laurent Boulevard; (613) 991-3044. This informal museum, while not as sophisticated as some big-city counterparts, prides itself on being user

The Canadian Museum of Civilization, in Ottawa, is host to an assortment of kid-oriented exhibits and special programs. (Courtesy Ottawa Tourism and Convention Bureau)

friendly. A push of a button, turn of a dial, or pull of a lever activates such exhibits as printing presses and water pumps. And, take a lop-sided walk through the Crazy Kitchen where nothing is as it seems. Bring a picnic or get something from the cafeteria to eat in the shady adjacent parkland, where there's a real lighthouse, steam train, obser-vatory, and rocket ship. When weather permits, evening astronomy programs are held at the museum and the Helen Sawyer Hogg Obser-vatory; reservations are required. While you're there, discover the nat-ural earth at "The Living Earth" exhibit, where kids can wiggle into a damp cave and stretch their necks as they wander through a rain forest and get showered by the spray of a tall waterfall.

Historical Sites

Parliament Hill's Centre Block is home to the Senate and the House of Commons, where Canada's laws are created. When Parlia-ment is in session, you can get tickets to sit in the public galleries and listen to debates in either of the two chambers. Older kids may find this interesting. Call (613) 992–4793 for information about the days and times.

On **Parliament Hill,** free **sound-and-light** shows (separate English and French performances) take place daily from early June to early September and four nights a week in May. Kids will like the carillon concerts held year-round on most weekdays from 12:30 to 12:45 P.M. On Tuesday and Thursday summer evenings, one-hour concerts are played on the bells in the Peace Tower, with special concerts on other occasions. Call (613) 992–4793 for information.

Changing the Guard is the best show in town—and it's free! It takes place daily at 10:00 A.M. from late June to late August (weather permitting) on the Hill. The Guard is made up of two regiments: the Governor General's Foot Guards (with the red plumes) and Canadian Grenadier Guards (white plumes). The parade forms at Cartier Square Drill Hall (at Laurier Avenue, by the canal) at 9:30 A.M. and marches up Elgin Street to reach the Hill at 10:00 A.M. Don't miss it!

Same-day reservations for free Parliament Hill Tours must be made in the Infotent, east of the Centre Block on Parliament Hill, from mid-May to early September. Tours, however, are available year-round.

Parks and Farms

Central Experimental Farm, Queen Elizabeth Driveway; (613) 995–5222. Located on the edge of downtown Ottawa, this beautiful 1,200-acre working farm makes for a delightful family excursion. Set up by the government in 1886 to improve techniques and offer farmers technical help, the complex attracts some half million visitors a year. Start with a free, fifteen-minute wagon ride, drawn by two Clydesdales (weekdays; just east of the Agriculture Museum). The dairy barn (where the museum and vintage farm machinery display is located) houses fifty cows of various breeds. The kids won't want to miss the calves in the southeast wing. Nearby are sheep, lambs, and piglets. Pack a picnic: There are lots of green spaces, including an arboretum along the canal with panoramic vistas. Take in a tropical plant show in the main greenhouse on Maple Drive or stop by the old observatory, which, though no longer in use, has a rotunda displaying instruments used to measure earthquakes and tides. The Ottawa Tourism and Convention Authority has a map of the farm that includes a self-guided walking tour.

Dows Lake, Queen Elizabeth Driveway; (613) 239-5000. There's lots going on in and around this man-made lake no matter when you visit. In the summer, rent pedal boats and canoes, cycle, stroll, or just relax. In May, come to see the colorful tulips—the pride and joy of this area. During the February Winterlude festival, centered on the Rideau Canal, skaters come to Dows Lake Pavilion (where skate rentals are available) to warm up, use the bathrooms, or to have a bite to eat at one of three restaurants.

Gatineau Park, only minutes north of downtown Ottawa, is a huge recreational paradise. The Gatineau Park Visitor Center, Meech Lake Road, Old Chelsea (819-827-2020), has maps and information year-round. Lac Philippe (Highway 5 then Highway 366 west), forty-five minutes from Ottawa, is the most popular summer area. It offers two beaches with lifeguards (fee), camping sites, picnic facilities, hiking trails, and boat rentals. There's a snack bar and a swimming pier for visitors of impaired mobility. The Lac Philippe Visitor Center is open weekends in the summer.

In all, the Park has 115 miles of hiking and cross-country skiing trails, rolling hills, and scenic lookouts. If you have time, visit the 568-acre Mackenzie King Estate, summer retreat of Canada's tenth prime minister. Take a stroll through the restored cottages and along walking trails and formal gardens that feature interesting ruins collected by King.

Special Tours

Paul's Boat Lines offers seventy-five-minute cruises of Ottawa's attractions on the Rideau Canal from the Conference Center. Call their office at (613) 225-6781, or summer dock at (613) 235-8409.

The **Ottawa River Cruises** (613-562-4888) features one-and-a-half-hour sight-seeing cruises on the Ottawa River. Come aboard the **Hull-Chelsea-Wakefield** steam train (819-77-TRAIN) for a half-day trip (36-mile round trip) ride to Wakefield. The train stops here for a two-hour lunch break (bring a picnic).

Performing Arts

National Arts Centre, 51 Elgin Street, showcases a variety of performing arts from pop to classical music, theater, dance, and other entertainment. Call the box office at (613) 996-5051, or TicketMaster at (613) 755–1111. For specific entertainment information, check the *Ottawa Citizen,* the official daily tourism newspaper, *WHERE Ottawa-Hull* magazine's monthly events listing, and the *Ottawa Sun* English-language newspaper, Sunday through Friday.

Landsdowne Park, Bank Street at the Rideau Canal, hosts programs throughout the year that include stage shows, concerts, craft exhibitions, and other family fare. It's also the home to several sports teams. (See Special Events.) *The Capital Calendar,* available from the Ottawa Tourism and Convention Bureau, has listings, or call (613) 564–1485.

Shopping

The street stalls of the **By Ward Market,** Lower Town, have been selling seasonal produce, ranging from maple syrup to flowers to honey, since 1840. This lively market successfully blends the old with the new: specialty food shops (some more than a hundred years old), art galleries, cafes, restaurants, and, in the old Market building, arts-and-crafts stalls. For more conventional shopping, the downtown **Rideau Centre** is the city's main shopping mall.

SPECIAL EVENTS

Sports

Landsowne Park is home to professional football and National Hockey League teams. For tickets to the Ottawa Football Club Rough Riders' game, call (613) 563–4551; Ottawa Senators play hockey in their new stadium the Palladium (613–599–0100). The farm team for the Montreal Expos, the Ottawa Lynx Baseball team (613–749–9947), plays at the Ottawa Stadium, 300 Coventry Road, from April to September.

Fairs and Festivals

Be sure to get a calendar of events from the Ottawa Tourism and Convention Authority; there's lots going on. Here are some highlights.

February: Winterlude: Watch the family celebration at various sites on the Rideau Canal; includes shows, skating, ice sculptures, kids' snow playground, entertainers, food, fireworks, and more.

May: Canadian Tulip Festival, with entertainment, crafts, food.

Late June: National Capital Air Show.

July: Canada Day (July 1) celebrates the country's birth. Ottawa International Jazz Festival includes Children's Day.

August: The Central Canada Exhibition features midway and exhibits. Hull's International Cycling Festival with family events.

Labor Day Weekend: Gatineau Hot Air Balloon Festival.

November: Chrysanthemum Show, Central Experiment Farm in the main greenhouse.

December: Christmas Lights Across Canada.

WHERE TO STAY

Ottawa has a wide choice of accommodations in every price range. The Visitor Information Center, 65 Elgin Street, offers a free summer booking service with participating hotels, motels, or bed and breakfast inns. Call (613) 233-3035. Their visitor guide has a handy grid chart of hotels and bed and breakfasts that include locations and features. Yes, you can save money by staying on the outskirts of town. But the following lodgings in Central Ottawa frequently have summer packages for families, so check with them first.

Chateau Laurier, 1 Rideau Street, is in a convenient location, overlooking the Canal and next to Parliament Hill. This elegant grande dame has hosted an endless assortment of notables, including Queen Elizabeth. Their vintage indoor pool is delightful. Though the rates can be on the steep side, summer family packages, which include Children's Play Centre activities, can make this an affordable option. Call (613) 232-6411/(800) 268-9411.

Delta Ottawa, 361 Queen, part of the family-friendly Delta hotel chain has a large indoor pool and children's play area. Kids under six eat free. Call (613) 238-6000/(800) 268-1133.

Minto Place Suite Hotel, 433 Laurier Avenue, West, offers various-size suites with fully equipped kitchens. Located close to Parliament, the high-rise hotel has an indoor pool, restaurants, shops, and indoor parking. For the past few summers, they've had a summer Kids' Club, with supervised activities and outings for ages four to fourteen; ask if it's in operation when you call: (613) 782-2350/(800) 267-3377—Ontario and Quebec/(800) 267-3377.

WHERE TO EAT

The *Visitor Guide* groups restaurants by specialty and includes price ranges and other features. For a special treat, take your tykes to **The Tea Party,** 119 York Street, near Byward Market, for English afternoon tea, complete with scones and cream. The atmosphere is charming, and the shelves of teapots and collectibles are all for sale; (613) 562-0352. **Boko Bakery,** in the By Ward Market, is popular with locals for its tasty breakfasts and light lunches; (613) 230-1417.

DAY TRIPS

Following the Ottawa River west of the capital region, you'll find scenic farm country, nature trails, beaches, and riverside parks. At **Pinto Valley Ranch,** near Fitzroy Harbour, there's horseback riding or wagon rides, nature trails, pony rides, and a petting zoo; (613) 623-3439. In Lanark County, **Fulton's Pancake House and Sugarbush,** near Pakenham, has cross-country skiing, sleigh rides, maple sugaring, a playground, nature trails, and guided tours; it's open winter weekends and daily in the spring; (613) 256-3867. **Storyland,** 50 miles west of Ottawa, just west of Renfrew, is a theme park, with minigolf, pedal boats, nature trails, and more; (613) 432-5275. Or head to **Logos Land Resort,** farther west near Cobden, an amusement park with water slides, horseback riding, minigolf, and pedal boats. Call (613) 646-2313/(800) 267-5885—Canada. In the winter, skiers head to Mont Cascades, twenty minutes north of town.

FOR MORE INFORMATION

Ottawa Tourism and Convention Authority, Visitor Information Centre, National Arts Centre, 65 Elgin Street, offers visitors free half-hour underground parking. Call (613) 237-5158; automated line: (613) 692-7000. Canada's Capital Information Centre is opposite the Parliament Buildings at 14 Metcalfe Street. Call (613) 239-5000/ (800) 465-1867—Canada/United States. For information on the entire province of Ontario, call 800-ONTARIO.

Special Needs

Door-to-door wheelchair accessible service is available to qualified disabled visitors in Ottawa-Carleton. Call Para Transpo at (613) 244-4636 before arrival. All national museums and attractions in Ottawa and Hull are universally accessible. Wheelchair accessible codes are listed in the *Visitor Guide*.

Emergency Numbers

Ambulance, fire, and police: 911

Ontario Provincial Police: (800) 267-2677

Poison Control: (613) 737-1100

Twenty-four-hour emergency service: Children's Hospital, 401 Smyth Road (located between Ottawa General Hospital and National Defense Medical Center); (613) 737-7600

Twenty-four-hour pharmacy: Shoppers Drug Mart, 1460 Merivale Road: (613) 224-7270. A list of pharmacies open until midnight appears in the Sunday edition of the *Ottawa Citizen*.

QUEBEC CITY

Quebec City offers families a distinctly different vacation experience. Perched atop the rocky Cap Diamant (Cape Diamond) and overlooking the St. Lawrence River, this provincial capital is the only fortified city in North America. Indeed, from the seventeenth through the nineteenth centuries, Quebec was vital in the ultimate defense of all of northeastern America. The historic district, Old Quebec *(Vieux Québec)*, has been proclaimed a "world heritage treasure" by UNESCO. Wherever you venture in this district, you'll be immersed in history. The French influence dominates in culture, cuisine, and language: at least 95 percent of the population is French-speaking. It helps to speak the language, though it's possible to get by without it. Just minutes from the city, your family will find unlimited outdoor activities in stunning natural settings.

GETTING THERE

Quebec City Airport in Sainte-Foy, 10 miles outside town, is served by Air Canada and affiliates and by Northwest Airlink. Daily shuttles from the airport to major city hotels are run by Maple Leaf Sightseeing Tours; (418) 649-9226. Car rentals are available at the airport.

VIA Rail Canada arrives and departs from *Gare du Palais* and Sainte-Foy station. For information and reservations call (418) 692-3940. It's possible to connect with Amtrak trains in Montreal or Toronto.

Orleans Express bus lines, whose main station is at Gare du Palais, 320, Abraham-Martin (418-525-3000), serves this area. You can make connections with Greyhound in Montreal. A number of highways connect to Quebec City, which is approximately six hours from Boston and eight-and-one-quarter hours from New York City.

GETTING AROUND

CTCUQ *(Commission de transport de la Communauté Urbaine de Québec)* buses run regularly. Call (418) 627-2511 for routes and schedules. During ski season the daily Skibus leaves from seven downtown hotels to Mont Sainte-Anne and Stoneham and also offers sight-seeing tours from all hotels. Call (418) 653-9722.

A ferry leaves opposite Place Royale to Lévis on the south shore. The scenic ten- to fifteen-minute ride affords panoramic views of Old Quebec from the St. Lawrence River. Call (418) 644-3704.

WHAT TO SEE AND DO

Museums and Historical Sites

Wherever you go in and outside the walls of Old Quebec, you'll be near a monument, museum, or historical site. If your kids are school age, prepare them with a brief historical summary; it will make their visit much more meaningful. The city's history in a nutshell: Quebec served as the base for early French explorers and missionaries in North America. In 1608 Samuel de Champlain built its first dwelling; the town ultimately grew into a fortified city. In 1759 British troops defeated the French, and, in 1763, Canada was ceded to Great Britain. The British, in turn, threatened by the patriot army during the American Revolution, rebuilt many of the French fortifications and constructed structures of their own. The last battle was fought in Quebec City in 1776, when the British repulsed an American patriot army invasion led by Benedict Arnold.

There's lots to see in Old Quebec, but be selective. Balance museum and historical sites with parks and cafe stops. You can take a tour of Old Quebec, but it's more fun to explore it yourself. Make sure you have a good map (available from the Convention and Visitors Bureau), cluster the sights you want to see, and take your time. Here are some highlights.

The Citadel and Parc des Champs-de-Bataille

At the Promenade des Gouverneurs, a stairway and scenic boardwalk with river views lead uphill to the star-shaped **Citadel,** dramatically set atop Cap Diamant, the eastern flank of Quebec's fortifications.

Quebec City at a Glance

- A unique vacation destination in the only fortified city in North America

- Numerous museums and historical sites in Old Quebec

- Thirty-six green spaces within the city

- A big Ferris wheel and an IMAX theater at Centre recreatif des Galeries de la Capitale

- A six-month ski season

- Quebec information, (800) 363-7777

The entrance is on rue St. Louis, (418) 694-2815. The facility comprises twenty-five buildings, including the officers' mess and Governor General's residence. Guided tours are available. Some kids may enjoy the **Royal 22e Regiment Museum,** an old military prison, with a collection of uniforms, documents, firearms, and other memorabilia from the seventeenth century to the present. The regiment still guards the citadel. A must-see: the Changing of the Guard, held at 10:00 A.M. daily from mid-June to Labor Day (weather permitting); it lasts forty minutes. The noon and 9:30 P.M. cannon is another military tradition, as is the Beating of Retreat, four nights a week in July and August.

Next to the citadel is the **Parc des Champs-de-Bataille** (Battlefields Park), located between Grande Allée and Champlain Boulevard. The park is the site of the Plains of Abraham, where the 1759 battle between British and French forces took place. Besides viewing the numerous military artifacts and monuments, come here for the 250 acres of gardens and woodlands. Picnic and hike, or, in winter, cross-country ski and skate.

A summer shuttle takes passengers to a number of the park's main sites including the *Musée du Québec* (418-643-2150), which spans generations of Quebec art. Two museums that will be of more interest to kids, however, are listed in the following section.

Museums and Parliament

Take the Promenade des Gouverneurs downhill to Terrasse Dufferin promenade. At the bottom of this popular promenade rises the huge, baroque **Château Frontenac** (418-692-3861), built in 1893 by Canadian Pacific Company and now a luxury hotel. If you're not staying here, stop in for a peek at its grand hall. Nearby, the Place d'Armes has fountains and horse-drawn buggies *(calèches)*. While not inexpensive, the rides provide a picturesque mode of transportation.

Next to the Place d'Armes, you may want to stop in for a look at the interior of the ornately decorated **Notre Dame Basilica,** 16 rue Buade; (418) 692-2533. Nearby are two museums of interest to families.

Musée du fort, 10 rue Sainte-Anne; (418) 692-2175. This is a good way to introduce the kids to the city's history. There's a model of the city as it looked in 1750. A sound-and-light show reenacts the six sieges fought to control Quebec.

Musèe historique de cire-Grivin (wax museum), 22 rue Sainte-Anne; (418) 692-2289. Kids (and adults) may not recognize many of the eighty figures represented here, such as Montcalm and Réné Levesque, but most kids like wax museums. Christopher Columbus and his shipmates are included.

Many sidewalk cafes and restaurants line rue Sainte-Anne, where these museums are located. In summer musicians and street entertainers make this a lively place to linger.

From here it would be convenient to walk east down the *casse cou* (breakneck) stairways—not really that bad—or to the funicular, to go down to the Lower City, the oldest part of Quebec.

If you're interested in seeing **Parliament Hill,** however, head southwest to avenue Dufferin and the tree-lined Grand Armée Est, considered the Champs Elysées of Quebec. Stop for a bite at one of the many restaurants along the way. You can take a guided tour of Parliament, including the National Assembly Chamber, where Quebec's elected representatives meet, although the experience may be lost on the very young. Call (418) 643-7239.

Lower City

In Place Royale, one of the oldest districts on the continent, stroll through narrow streets, past historic homes, boutiques, and workshops. The parks of Place Royale host a number of events with family appeal, including plays and variety shows. Stop by the Information Centre, 215 rue du Marché-Finlay, for schedules of activities. In the Quartier du Petit Champlain, at times, the quaint, narrow streets sport musicians, clowns, and jugglers. **Explore,** 63 rue Dalhousie (418-692-2175), is a sound-and-light show that retells the discovery of America and the voyages of early French explorers up the St. Lawrence River. The lively Old Port includes a farmer's produce market and a cinema.

Parks

In addition to thirty-six green spaces within the city, The Greater Quebec Area, with its St. Lawrence River location, has a number of parks and wildlife reserves where families can enjoy the great outdoors. Going east along the Côte de Beaupré, you'll find these attractions.

Cap-Tourmente National Wildlife Area, Saint-Joachim; (418) 827-4591 from April to October and (418) 837-3776 from November to April. About thirty-five minutes east of Quebec, this striking preserve on the St. Lawrence River's north shore was created especially to protect the natural habitat of the Greater Snow Goose. During migration periods the area attracts some 300,000 geese. The preserve is made up of four separate environments: marsh, plain, cliff, and mountain. Footpaths reveal a wide variety of plants, trees, nesting and migratory birds, and mammals. Some trails lead to the summit of Cap Tourmente, or you can opt for the views from an observation tower. The welcome and interpretation centers have exhibitions and films. In season, naturalists offer activities and guided tours.

North of the city: Parc de la Jacques-Cartier, Route 175 north; (418) 848-3169 during the summer, 622-5151 the rest of the year. Summer canoeing, rock climbing, mountain biking, and hiking are the big attractions at this beautiful provincial park on the Jacques-Cartier River. You can rent equipment. During mid-May to October, activities include canoe excursions, outings, and a moose and wolf observation safari in September and October.

West of the city: **Lac-Saint-Joseph,** in Sainte-Catherine-de-la-Jacques-Cartier, has a beach that is popular with local families. It adjoins the *Station forestière de Duchesnay* (Forest Educational Centre), which is open to the public for nature walks. Call (418) 334-2900.

Attractions

Aquarium du Québec, 1675 avenue des Hôtels, Sainte-Foy (Quebec); (418) 659-5264. Located in a wooded area southwest of Old Quebec, with nice views of the St. Lawrence River, the aquarium is home to some 2,000 sea creatures. The ever-popular seals perform twice daily. You might combine a trip here with another Sainte-Foy attraction: **Musée de géologie,** Pavillon Adrien-Pouillot (fourth floor), avenue de la Médecine; (418) 656-2131, ext. 8127. Most kids like fossils and minerals, and you'll find hundreds of them here from all around the world.

Centre récréatif des Galeries de la Capitale, 5401 boulevard des Galeries; (418) 627-5800. This enormous recreation center, part of a shopping mall, sports a Ferris wheel and roller coaster among its rides, and, for more fun, there's a skating rink and minigolf, also the IMAX Maison de l'image (418-627-IMAX).

Jardin Zoologique du Québec, 9141 avenue du Zoo, Charlesbourg (Quebec); (418) 622-0312. Along with the usual bears, chimps, and wild cats, kids enjoy the sea-lion show and the farm. A river linked by waterfalls crosses through the zoo, and, in winter, the surrounding trails are open for cross-country skiing and snowshoeing.

Village des Sports, 1860 boulevard Valcartier, Saint-Gabriel-de-Valcartier (Quebec); (418) 844-3725—Canada. Bring your bathing suits: This place boasts a huge wave pool, water games, water slides, and acrobatic diving shows. When you dry off, choose from roller-skating trails, Maxi-Golf, and a racing-car circuit. Winters, this enormous recreation center north of the city has sledding on inner tubes or carpets, skating paths with music, and cross-country skiing.

Ski Areas

The ski season can last almost six months in Greater Quebec. Two of the province's best downhill-ski areas are within a half-hour's drive of the city. **Parc du Mont-Sainte-Anne,** Route 360, Beaupré; (418) 827-4561. This enormous park, thirty minutes east of downtown

If you visit Quebec during February, be sure to participate in the Winter Festival happenings. (Courtesy of Quebec Tourism)

Quebec, includes Mont-Sainte-Anne, a popular winter downhill-ski area, the largest in Quebec. Day care and a kinderski program are available for ages two to six. In summer the park becomes a recreational mecca, with golf, mountain biking, picnicking, and cable-car rides to the mountain summit of Mont Sainte-Anne. Ski area reservations: (418) 827–4561.

Stoneham, 1429 avenue du Hibou, Stoneham (Quebec); (418) 848–2411/(800) 463–6888—Canada. Twenty-five minutes north of town, Stoneham offers a network of twenty-five runs on four mountains. The nursery takes kids two years and up, and teens meet at the Coketail Bar. Lodging includes 600 hotel or condo rooms, either slopeside or at the mountain base.

Special Tours

Try a scenic boat ride with **Quebec City Cruises,** Quai Chouinard at 10 rue Dalhousie. From mid-June through Labor Day, choose from one-hour harbor tours, ninety-minute excursions to **Île d'Orléans** (418) 692–1159. (See Day Trips.)

Performing Arts

Among the city's cultural attractions are the **Quebec Symphony Orchestra,** which performs at the Grand Théâtre de Québec, the **Trident** theater troupe; the **Danse-Partout Dance** company; and the **Quebec Opera,** with spring and fall productions. In addition, the Greater Quebec area has excellent summer theater performances. Listings of area cultural events are published every Wednesday in English in the Quebec *Chronicle Telegraph.*

Shopping

In Quebec's Lower City stroll and browse along rue Saint-Paul's antiques shops, boutiques, and art galleries. Across from the Château Frontenac, sketches and watercolors are sold on the narrow rue du Tresor. At **La Cabane,** 94, Petit Champlain in Old Quebec, sample (and buy) maple sugar products: (418) 692-1543.

On your way back into the United States, you might want to do some shopping at the duty-free shops at **BHTE,** at junction 55 and 91, Rock Island (819-876-5249), or **IGL,** at junction 15 and 87, Saint-Bernard de Lacolle (514-246-2496).

SPECIAL EVENTS

Fairs and Festivals

The Greater Quebec area abounds in year-round fairs and festivals. *The Greater Quebec Area Tourist Guide* has an exhaustive listing of events. Some highlights include the following.

February: Winter Carnival, the world's largest, features seventeen days of parades, ice-sculpture contests, and numerous other activities and events.

July: Quebec International Summer Festival, French-speaking cultural events held in the streets and parks of Old Quebec.

August: Expo Quebec, Parc de l'Exposition, is a huge agricultural exhibition with a fair, rides, and entertainment.

September: Festival of Colors includes sports, outdoor activities, and cultural events to herald the start of the fall and winter season, Parc du Mont Sainte-Anne.

WHERE TO STAY

The Greater Quebec Area Tourist Guide features listings of hotels. If you're on a budget, consider one of the convenient lodgings outside the city. In Parc du Mont-Sainte-Anne area, call (800) 463–1568. Here's a family-friendly selection that includes a variety of locations and price ranges.

Downtown

Hotel Classique, 640 St.-Jean Street, offers large rooms with kitchenettes, indoor pool, and parking. Call (418) 529-0227/(800) 463–5753—Canada.

Hotel La Citadelle, 410, rue Sherbrooke Ouest (514-844-8851), has redecorated their rooms, and offers junior suites with kitchenettes. Amenities include television, minibar, and hair dryer. The hotel features a health club with a pool and sauna.

Old City (outside walls)

Ramada Quebec, 395 rue de la Coutonne, is within walking distance of Old Quebec's walled city. The eighteen-story high rise features 232 rooms, with seven suites. The kids will love the pool—the largest in town. Call (418) 647-2611/(800) 267-2002.

Old City (inside walls)

L'Hôtel du Vieux Québec, 1190 rue Saint-Jean, is housed in a historic building. Twenty-seven comfortable rooms feature kitchenettes; (418) 692-1850.

Côte-de-Beaupré

Chalets Montmorency et Motels, 1768 avenue Royale, Saint-Ferreol-les-Neiges. In a quiet setting near Mont-Sainte-Anne, this Swiss-style apartment lodge features spacious one- to four-bedroom suites, an indoor pool, and golf packages. Call (418) 826-2600/(800) 463-2612.

WHERE TO EAT

A dining guide is available from the Tourism and Convention Bureau. The local cuisine has lots for kids to like: try *croque monsieur,* an open ham sandwich covered with melted cheese, and *crêpes.* Depending on the filling this serves as either a main course or a dessert. For inexpensive *crêpes* try **Casse Crêpe Breton,** 1136 rue St. Jean, where you can also get sandwiches, salads, soups, and a hearty breakfast; (418) 692-0438.

Fondue is fun: dip right in at **Au Café Suisse,** 32 rue Sainte-Anne (418-694-1320), where seafood, steaks, and *raclette* are also on the menu. Two-hour free parking at city hall is included. The location is good, too, right near the Musée du fort and the Musée historique de cire-Grivin.

Kids love the pink pig statue outside of **Le Cochon Dingue,** 46, boulevard Champlain, across from the Lévis ferry. The house specialty: steaks and fries. Call (418) 523-2013. For a big-splurge meal with a twist, head to **L'Astral,** at Loews Le Concorde, 1225 Place Montcalm. The restaurant slowly revolves to reveal fabulous vistas below; (418) 647-2222.

DAY TRIPS

Île d'Orléans, about 6 miles downstream from downtown and accessible by car, is a pleasant excursion for those who like simple charms. This sparsely populated island (about 7,000 people) offers historic homes, churches, mills, and chapels. In season, roadside stands have fresh produce, and some producers allow the public to pick their own strawberries, apples, and corn. Call (418) 828-9411 for information. In the village of Saint-Laurent, where shipbuilding was once the largest industry, there's a maritime museum and riverfront views. An arts-and-crafts center sells handmade traditional handicrafts, such as pottery, wood carvings, knitted garments, and porcelain jewelry. During July and August weekends, local artists offer demonstrations.

From the Île d'Orléans head east to Route 138 to the lower section or **Chute Montmorency,** in Beauport-Boischatel (bus 50 or 53). The upper section is accessible via Route 360. This is a breathtaking waterfall, one-and-one-half times as high as Niagara Falls. The site, divided into upper and lower sections, features lookout points, trails, picnic tables, and a tourist information center, which is open from mid-May

to late October. Upstream, Manor Montmorency, now a hotel surrounded by lovely gardens, offers a terrific lookout. In winter an
unusual phenomenon occurs. The crystallized water vapor forms an
enormous ice cone that locals call *pain de sucre,* or sugar loaf.

Continue east about 13 miles to **Sainte-Anne-de-Beaupré Basilica.** It's long been believed that Sainte-Anne, mother of the Virgin
Mary, has saved shipwreck victims off Cap Tourmente. Many still
believe she works miracles. Every year, more than 1,500,000 pilgrims
come to pray to this saint.

Farther east, near **Parc du Mont-Sainte-Anne,** the Grand Canyon
des chutes Sainte-Anne is a waterfall with breathtaking chasms and
streams. Shuttle service in open sight-seeing cars is included in the
admission fee (open May to October). There's also a cafeteria and picnic area. Call (418) 827-4057.

FOR MORE INFORMATION

For booklets and maps of the area: Maison du Tourisme de Québec,
12 rue Sainte-Anne (across from Château Frontenac), is open seven days
a week; or write to Tourisme Quebec, Case postale 20,000, Quebec,
Canada G1K 7X2. In the summer in Old Quebec's historic area, motor-
ized tourist information agents ride green mopeds with a "?" sign.
Information on Quebec's nineteen tourist regions is available by calling
(800) 363-7777 from Quebec, Canada, and the United States.

Emergency Numbers

Fire and police in Quebec: (418) 691-6911

Pharmacie Brunet, Les Galeries Charlesbourg, 4266, 1ère (Pre-
mière) Avenue, Charlesbourg, is open until midnight seven
days a week, opening at 8:00 A.M. Monday through Saturday
and 10:00 A.M. on Sunday: (418) 623-1571.

Poison Control: (418) 656-8090 or (800) 463-5060

Twenty-four-hour emergency room: L'Hôtel Dieu, 11, Côte du
Palais, Old Quebec, (418) 691-5151. A hospital specializing in
children's health: CHUL (Laval University Hospital Center), 2705
boulevard Laurier, Sainte-Foy (a western suburb); (418) 656-4141

TORONTO

If you shy away from city vacations because of the hassles associated with large metropolitan areas, take a trip to Toronto, Ontario, Canada's largest city and top visitor destination. This spanking-clean city offers families everything a major metropolitan area should—without the hassles. Your family will find all the things you might expect: interesting sights, kid-friendly museums, arts and entertainment, shopping, great restaurants, and a wide selection of accommodations. You'll also find some things you might not expect: a sparkling, lively waterfront; safe, clean streets; and a friendly, ethnically diverse population that adds much to Toronto's character and charm.

GETTING THERE

U.S. citizens and legal residents don't need passports or visas to enter Canada, though they are preferred. Native-born U.S. citizens should have a birth certificate or voter's registration card that shows citizenship, plus a picture I.D. Naturalized citizens need naturalization certificates or other proof of citizenship. Permanent residents who are not citizens need alien registration receipts.

Metropolitan Toronto is a major transportation center. Some thirty-five major airlines offer regular service through three terminals at Pearson International Airport (416-612-5100), in the northwest corner of metropolitan Toronto. Car rentals are available at the airport. Only taxis with TIA on their license plates are authorized to pick up passengers. Toronto Island Airport (416-868-6942) services a number of commuter airlines, including flights originating in the United States. The airport can be accessed via a brief public ferry ride that leaves from the foot of Bathurst Street.

Amtrak (800-USA-RAIL) runs trains from New York and Chicago to Toronto, where passengers can link up to the VIA Rail Canada, Inc.

Toronto at a Glance

- A clean, exciting, friendly, and ethnically diverse city

- Innovative museums, including a shoe museum and SPORT

- Several harbor cruises to choose from

- Black Creek Pioneer Village, a nineteenth-century living-history community

- Sky Dome, home of the Toronto Blue Jays

- Performing arts year round

- Metropolitan Toronto Convention and Visitors Association, (800) 363-1990 or (416) 203-2500

(416-868-7277), which provides rail service throughout Canada. Union Station is downtown on Front Street, directly on Toronto's subway line.

Greyhound, Voyageur, and regional bus lines serve Metro Toronto, arriving and departing from the bus terminal at 610 Bay Street. Fares and schedules for all bus companies may be obtained by calling (416) 393-7911.

Those coming by car can reach Toronto by one of several major routes that parallel Lake Ontario's shores: Highway 401 and Highway 2 from the west and east; Queen Elizabeth Way from the west only; and Highway 400, which connects with Highway 401, from the north.

Note: While you're at Pearson airport, check out the boutique complex at the new terminal, where there's the only Harrod's in North America.

GETTING AROUND

Metro Toronto is made up of six municipalities: the City of Toronto, the Borough of East York, and the Cities of York, North York,

Scarborough, and Etobicoke. Shared transit service via Toronto Transit Commission (TTC) includes 818 miles of subway, bus, trolley and streetcar, and ferry routes. Riders must have exact change or purchase TTC tickets and tokens at subway stations or from stores displaying the EXACT FARE sign. For information about routes, schedules, and fares, call (416) 393-4636 or pick up a *Ride Guide* at subway entrances.

Toronto has so many diverse, decentralized neighborhoods that you may sometimes prefer your car to public transportation. The Metropolitan Toronto Convention and Visitors Association (MTCVA) has free maps that include area highways. Avoid heavy rush-hour traffic. Street parking, when you can find it, is usually limited to one hour, although you may park overnight until 7:00 A.M. Day parking is also free at outlying subway stations. The city streets are arranged in a grid pattern, running north–south and east–west.

Ferries operated by the Metro Parks Department (416-392-8193) leave from the foot of Bay Street to the three Toronto Islands on a regular schedule. Gray Coach Lines (416-594-0338) has scheduled service every twenty minutes between most major downtown hotels and the airport. Taxis cruise throughout the city.

WHAT TO SEE AND DO

Museums

Toronto's museums are inspired and innovative places where even the fussiest kid will find something to tickle his or her fancy.

Bata Shoe Museum, 327 Bloor Street West (416-979-SHOE), proves that museums can be fun. Although the kids may be skeptical at first ("We're going to a shoe museum?"), this fascinating collection soon wins them over. Astronaut Buzz Aldrin's moon boot, tiny 2-inch slippers worn by Chinese women with bound feet, Elton John's sandals are here along with much else. Tours by appointment.

Ontario Science Center, 770 Don Mills Road, Toronto; (416) 696-3127. Plan on spending the better part of the day here; you'll enjoy it as much as your kids. Located in a pleasant setting about a half hour from downtown, the museum is famous throughout North America for its innovative exhibits. There are more than 800 exhibits, including The Space Hall, popular with older school-age children, teens, and adults. Interactive options include experiencing weightlessness by riding in a rocket chair and the Challenger Learning Centre, a hands-on space shuttle mission.

SPORT started as a temporary exhibit but was so well received it's now permanent. The hands-on, bodies-on exhibit includes a radar-clocked baseball pitch, climbing rock wall, bobsled video run, and the chance to judge sports performances, comparing scores with a replay of reactions from real experts.

Although especially relevant for high school students, even younger kids will be fascinated by some of the exhibits at the Chemistry Hall, called Matter, Energy, Change. Inside the Hall an ultraviolet light makes visitors' clothes glow. Kids can leave their shadow behind "trapped" by a strobe light on a phosphorescent vinyl wall and witness the melting and reforming of crystals on a large screen.

Inquire about OSCOTT weekend and vacation discovery classes for ages three to thirteen. There's a fee for parking and special family admission.

Royal Ontario Museum (ROM), 100 Queen's Park, Bloor Street at Avenue Road (416-586-5551), is Canada's largest museum and a real gem. The dinosaur exhibit is the biggest attraction for the younger set; the armor display and the Ancient Egypt gallery, especially the mummies, score with kids of school age and older. There are also artifacts from other civilizations—such as a complete Ming tomb—that everyone will find fascinating. The life sciences exhibit, complete with stuffed animals and live insects, is educational and fun. Be sure to inquire about Family Sundays, workshops for adults and kids. The McLaughlin Planetarium at the museum features star shows on astronomy and laser concerts. Both are closed on Monday.

Historical Attractions

These next two sites are fun ways for all ages to learn more about this area's fascinating past.

Fort York, Garrison Road off Fleet Street; (416) 392-6907. *Toronto,* a Huron Indian word for "meeting place," was established as a French fur trading post in 1750 and colonized by the British in 1793 on this site. This is also where the Battle of York was fought in the War of 1812. The American raid of York, resulting in the burning of the parliament building, led to retribution by the British, who invaded

"Please Touch" is the policy at the Ontario Science Center, which features more than 800 hair-raising exhibits. (Courtesy Metropolitan Toronto Convention and Visitors Association)

Washington and tried to burn down the president's residence. Although the building wasn't destroyed, the scorched walls outside had to be whitewashed, resulting in what was thereafter known as The White House. All has been forgiven, of course, and today costumed soldiers and their wives give tours and are delighted to answer any questions you and the kids have.

Black Creek Pioneer Village, 1000 Murray Ross Parkway, Downsview, northwest Toronto (416-736-1733), is an authentic mid-nineteenth-century village that re-creates life of that period in a most interesting way. Costumed interpreters are here to answer questions and demonstrate crafts of the day, such as broom making, weaving, baking, and tinsmithing. More than forty restored homes and shops plus a cafeteria and restaurant are on the premises. Be sure to ask about their special weekends throughout the year, which include an apple-pie baking contest (where visitors can buy what's left after the judging) and fall fair. Open mid-March–December 31.

Parks and Zoos

High Park, west of downtown, south of Bloor Street and north of Queensway, is accessible by streetcar or subway. It's a good place to toss a Frisbee or take a stroll. Considered Toronto's "Central Park," there's a menagerie, hiking trails, sports fields, pond, and restaurant on the premises.

Kortright Centre for Conservation is south of Major MacKenzie on Pine Valley Drive in suburban Kleinburg, about a thirty-minute drive (416-661-6600). Here kids and adults can commune with nature. Daily 1:00 P.M. programs vary according to the season, weather, and specialty of the naturalist leader; reserve in advance. The scenic hiking trails are popular with families, and there's a marsh habitat on the premises. Ask about special seasonal events: the fall honey festival (there's a beehouse here) for instance, or the popular maple syrup demonstrations in spring.

Metro Toronto Zoo, in Scarborough on Highway 401 at Meadowvale Road (416-392-5900), is rated as one of the world's best. There are more than 4,000 animals, eight tropical pavilions, and Monorail and Zoomobile rides for viewing outdoor exhibits. Look for a schedule of the daily demonstrations and zookeeper talks. This is the only zoo to match prospective mates of endangered species by computer. You can see the result of a successful match: the first Great Indian rhinoceros ever born in Canada. In 1998, the zoo adds African Savannah, a $17-million reconstruction of a national park.

Attractions

CN Tower, 301 Front Street West (416-360-8500) the tallest free-standing structure in the world, has a glass elevator that leads to three observation decks, with spectacular views of the city, Toronto Islands, and Lake Ontario. There's a revolving restaurant on top. But the most fun for kids won't be the view. Ecodeck intrigues children with its interactive computers designed to teach kids about environmental issues such as clean air, water, and land conservation. Q-ZAR employs high-tech just for fun in a futuristic game of laser-tag. MindWarp is high-flying fun—almost literally—combining full-motion flight simulation with surround-sound films; (416) 363-TOUR.

SkyDome is adjacent to the Tower (416-341-3663). The stadium has a fully retractable roof and is home to the Toronto Blue Jays,

Toronto Argonauts, and other events (see Special Events). Even if there's nothing going on, sports nuts will enjoy the guided tour.

Canada's Wonderland, Rutherford Road exit from Highway 400 (905-832-7000), a thirty-minute drive north of Toronto, is a full-service amusement park. This enormous attraction is divided into seven theme areas, including Hanna Barbera Land, Smurf Forest, and White Water Canyon. The fifty-four rides include eight roller coasters. While your teen might want to try Vortex, Canada's only suspended coaster, lead younger kids to their own ride area. A theme water park, strolling entertainers, dolphin shows, cliff divers, restaurants, shops, free summer concerts, and more make this an all-day commitment. Arrive early.

Centreville, on Toronto's Centre Island, is accessible via a five-minute city ferry; (416) 363-1112. This theme park is composed of a scaled-down version of a nineteenth-century Ontario village. School-age kids and younger tots will have a blast: There's a fire hall, with red fire engines to ride, model 1890s steam-engine rides, paddleboats shaped like swans, minigolf, a cable car, and a farm with cows, geese, and pigs. Don't forget the Centre Island attractions: a public beach, park, picnic areas, maze, gardens, roller blade and bike rentals, and more. A free tram transports passengers around the island.

Harbourfront Centre, on the south side of Queens Quay West, including York, John, and Maple Leaf Quays (416-973-3000), is a non-profit cultural organization that produces events year-round, many of them free. The HarbourKid programs vary from month to month and might include free family concerts and family workshops. Call to ask if there's a Day Camp in session. Ages five to sixteen (divided into age groups) can register for one day or more. In winter there's free ice skating at York Quay, the world's largest artificial skating rink.

The **Hockey Hall of Fame,** inside BCE Palace at Front and Yonge streets (416-360-7735), opened in spring of 1993. Inside the $25-million, 51,000-square-foot building, you will find museum-style exhibits, theaters that show hockey's best plays, trivia games, and a plastic ice rink that the aspiring player can glide across. Walk through a re-creation of the Montreal Canadiens' dressing room and feel the spirit that surges through Canadian hockey fans. The Hall of Fame's Bell Great Hall is expected to become the home of the precious Stanley

Cup and is dedicated to Canadian hockey greats including Woody Dumart, Lanny McDonald, and Marcel Dionne.

Ontario Place, 955 Lake Shore Boulevard West (416-314-9811), stretches out over three man-made islands into Lake Ontario. This is the place to be in summer (open mid-May to Labor Day), particularly when the sun is shining and the lake seems to sparkle. Here you'll find strolling mimes and musicians, minigolf, and a water-play area with water slide, bumper boats, pedal boats, and Wilderness Adventure ride. The Children's Village is terrific, with a LEGO creative play center, award-winning playground, and more. Evenings are lively, with IMAX movies shown in the Six-Storey Cinesphere and frequent concerts, bands, and fireworks. In addition to an admission charge, you'll pay extra for some things (such as bumper boats). There are lots of cafes, pubs, and restaurants.

Performing Arts

No matter when you visit, you're sure to find something exciting going on in the performing arts. Get the monthly events calendar, *About Town,* and the *Where Toronto* publication put out by the MTCVA, available at most hotels. Toronto has three daily papers with listings of events, including the "What's On" section in Thursday's *Toronto Star.*

The Toronto Symphony frequently performs young people's and special family concerts at Roy Thomson Hall; (416) 593-4828. The Canadian Opera Company and National Ballet of Canada performances take place at O'Keefe Center; (416) 393-7474. In summer the **Canadian Stage Company** stars in the outdoor Shakespearean festival "The Dream in High Park," which older kids may enjoy, particularly because of the setting. Call (416) 367-8243 for schedules.

Toronto has a large theater industry, with plays being performed in forty-odd theaters. These include the **Pantages Theater,** where the long-running *Phantom of the Opera* was playing at press time, and the **Elgin and Winter Garden** complex, with theatrical, musical, and dance performances. If you don't mind standing in line (arrive before the noon opening), Five Star Tickets (416-596-8211) sells half-price tickets to all arts events on the day of performance from their booth in front of the Eaton Centre on Dundas and Yonge streets.

SPECIAL EVENTS

Sporting Events

The Toronto Maple Leafs, in the National Hockey League, play in Maple Leaf Gardens, Carlton and Church streets; (416) 977-1641. The big summer attraction is the Toronto Blue Jays, in the American League, winners of the 1992 World Series, who play in the SkyDome. Although games sometimes sell out, you can often get tickets at the box office (416-341-1000). The Toronto Argonauts football team also plays in the SkyDome; call (416) 872-5000 for tickets. Get tickets for the Player's International Tennis Tournament, held in late July, by calling (416) 665-9777 or from TicketMaster (416-870-8000), which also can provide tickets to some (but not all) sporting, theatrical, and other events.

Fairs, Festivals, and Special Events

Call the Convention and Visitors Association for more information on the following events.

June: Benson & Hedges Symphony of Fire, fireworks competition at Ontario Place. Dragon Boat Race Festival on Toronto Islands, with traditional Chinese dragon-shaped boats and concession stands.

August: Player's International Tennis Championship; Canadian National Exhibition, the world's largest annual fair. See Canadian arts, agriculture, architecture, and more at the Canadian National Exhibition.

Labor Day: Canadian National Air Show, over the harbor, can be watched from Ontario Place, Harbourfront, or Toronto Islands.

WHERE TO STAY

Toronto has two free reservations services: Accommodation Toronto (416-629-3800) is operated by the Hotel Association of Metropolitan Toronto and features more than one hundred luxury, moderate, and economy properties; Econo-Lodging Services (416-494-0541) offers hotels in all price ranges as well as short-term furnished apartments. There are also a number of bed and breakfast reservation services listed in the *Metropolitan Toronto* publication, free from the

MTCVA, which sponsors seasonal package deals. Here are some choices for families.

Downtown

The Delta Chelsea Inn, 33 Gerrard Street West; (416) 243-5732/(800) CHELSEA—Canada, New York, Ohio, Pennsylvania, or Michigan/(800) CHELSEA—elsewhere in the United States. Family area with pool, separate adult pool, whirlpool, and games rooms, plus Children's Creative Centre with supervised activities, make this inn special. It houses 1,600 rooms and several restaurants.

Royal York Hotel, 100 Front Street West; (416) 368-2511/(800) 441-1414—Canada/(800) 828-7447—United States. Newly renovated, with 1,408 rooms, this hotel has a health club with pool and whirlpool plus a wading pool. The ten restaurants here include a coffee shop.

The Cambridge Suites Hotel, 15 Richmond St. East, (416-368-1990; 800-463-1990) works well for families. The suites have a dining/work area and separate bedrooms, plus microwave and refrigerator.

Midtown

The Best Western Roehampton Hotel, 808 Mt. Pleasant Road (416-487-5101/800-387-8899), has moderate rates that include a free continental breakfast. Pricey, but posh, are the **Four Seasons Hotel Toronto,** 21 Avenue Road (416-964-0411/800-268-6282), and the **Hotel InterContinental Toronto,** 220 Bloor Street West (416-960-5200/800-327-0200), which also pleases children with its lap pool.

East/Parklands

Four Seasons Inn on the Park, 1100 Eglinton Avenue East; (905) 444-2561/(800) 268-6282—Canada/(800) 332-3442—United States. Though not in the thick of things, this hotel is close to attractions, such as the zoo and Science Centre, and across from 600 acres of parkland where you can picnic, stroll, or jog. Inn Kids, an activity program for ages five to twelve, takes place seven days a week during summer and weekends year-round (free, except for lunch charge). Other features: indoor/outdoor pool, health club, squash and tennis, free parking, weekend packages, and dining room.

Scarborough

University of Toronto, Scarborough Campus, 1265 Military Trail; (416) 287-7369. Families on a budget love these eighty-one furnished town houses located in a beautiful, parklike Student Village, thirty minutes from downtown Toronto. Available from mid-May through the third week in August, units have equipped kitchens and sleep four to six in rooms with one or two twin beds (minimum stay two nights). There's a recreation center, free parking, and dining hall—but no TV, air conditioning, or room phones.

WHERE TO EAT

Toronto is packed with 5,000 restaurants, many reflecting the city's diverse ethnic population, including Greek, Italian, and Chinese. If you're exploring some of the various ethnic neighborhoods on foot, watch and ask where the locals eat. (While these explorations can be fascinating for adults who enjoy local color, kids might be bored since there's not much "action" in these neighborhoods, some of them thirty to forty minutes from downtown.)

The MTCVA has several guides listing restaurants, including *Toronto Day and Night,* which lists both eateries and shopping by neighborhood and category. Downtown has its share of fine dining spots, including these with family appeal: **Hard Rock Cafe-SkyDome,** 300 Brenner Boulevard, has great burgers and Canada's largest rock 'n' roll collection; (416) 341-2388. Eat in style and watch your favorite team play at **Cafe on the Green,** SkyDome Hotel, 45 Peter Street South, where the sports-theme dining room provides a great view of the SkyDome playing field; (416) 341-5045. **The Old Spaghetti Factory,** 54 The Esplanade, is economical, casual, and fun—and there's a children's menu; (416) 864-9761. **Mr. Greenjeans Galleria** has an entertainment theme that kids love and menus bigger than your table. It's located in the downtown Eaton Centre, an enormous shopping mall; (416) 979-1212. (Cross the street to show the kids the World's Biggest Bookstore, on Eaton Street.) Make a "knight" of it at the Medieval Times Dinner and Tournament, Arts, Crafts, and Hobbies Building, Exhibition Place (416-260-1170) where you can dine and watch jousting knights astride Andalusian stallions (Thursday through Monday).

DAY TRIPS

Niagara Falls, 90 miles from Toronto, is one of the great natural wonders of the world. En route, stop by **Royal Botanical Gardens,** Hamilton (30 minutes from downtown Toronto), to stroll among vibrant flowers. If you're headed to Montreal, stop in **Whitby,** a forty-minute drive from downtown, where **Cullen Gardens and Miniature Village** features flowers (there's a tulip festival every April), 140 miniature buildings (built to $\frac{1}{12}$ scale), puppet shows, and more. About an hour west of Toronto, near the town of Cambridge, is **African Lion Safari** (open until early October), where you can drive through game reserves in your own car or take a guided bus tour. Call (519) 623-2620.

FOR MORE INFORMATION

Metropolitan Toronto Convention and Visitors Association has multilingual information counselors and helpful publications. Call (416) 203-2500/(800) 363-1990, or write to MTCVA, Queen's Quay Terminal at Harbourfront Centre, 207 Queens Quay West, Box 126, Toronto, Ontario, Canada M51 1A7. You may visit their office in the Queen's Quay Terminal on weekdays from 9:30 A.M. to 5:30 P.M. Call about additional kiosk locations during summer. On Highway 401, at Winston Churchill Boulevard exit 333 off the eastbound lanes, stop by the Shell Info Centre, which has year-round, twenty-four-hour interactive computer facilities and a video on the area.

For visitor's information on the Province of Ontario, visit the Ontario Ministry of Tourism and Recreation's Travel Centre in the Eaton Centre, 220 Yonge Street, or call (416) 965-4008/(800) 268-3736.

Kid's Toronto, free at many locations, is an excellent monthly source for family-oriented events. Single issues are mailed for $2.50. Call (416) 481-5696, or write to them at 540 Mt. Pleasant Road, Suite 201, Toronto, Ontario M4S 2M6. Community Information Centre of Metro Toronto (416-392-0505) offers complete information on services for the disabled, twenty-four hours a day.

Emergency Numbers

Ambulance, fire, and police: 911

Poison Information Center: (416) 598-5900

Twenty-four-hour emergency service: Hospital for Sick Children, 555 University Avenue; (416) 597-1500

Twenty-four-hour pharmacy: Shopper's Drug Mart, 700 Bay Street at Gerard (downtown); (416) 979-2424

INDEX